iDo

Planning Your Wedding
with Nothing but 'Net

Christa Terry

Simon Spotlight Entertainment
New York   London   Toronto   Sydney

Simon Spotlight Entertainment
A Division of Simon & Schuster, Inc.
1230 Avenue of the Americas
New York, NY 10020

First Simon Spotlight Entertainment trade paperback edition June 2008

SIMON SPOTLIGHT ENTERTAINMENT and colophon
are trademarks of Simon & Schuster, Inc.

For information about special discounts for bulk purchases,
please contact Simon & Schuster Special Sales at
1-800-456-6798 or business@simonandschuster.com.

Book design and chapter illustrations by Kate Susanna Moll

Manufactured in the United States America

10 9 8 7 6 5 4 3 2 1

Library of Congress Cataloging-in-Publication Data
Terry, Christa.
iDo / Christa Terry.
1. Wedding—United States—Planning. 2. Weddings—United States—
Costs. 3. Teleshopping—United States. I. Title. II. Title: I do.
HQ745.T47 2008   2007049615
395.2'2—dc22

ISBN-13:978-1-4165-7854-3
ISBN-10:   1-4165-7854-4

For my family and friends,
who in my mind are one and the same.

Acknowledgments

This book would not even exist were it not for The Manolo, who somehow knew the whole thing was hiding in my brain waiting to be written. Once I actually sat down to write, my number one cheering squad consisted of Tedd Terry, Xena Ugrinsky, and Kathleen McLane.

When there were more blank pages ahead of me than there were finished pages behind me, legions of Webers and Ugrinskys reminded me that the best things in life are worth the struggle.

Many thanks to "A. J." Kane, Jeanette Murray, and Leah Woods, who put up with the tight deadlines I threw at them with patience and grace. Their weddings were an inspiration, and their happy marriages are a joy to behold.

My wonderful agent, Michael Psaltis, and my fabulous editor, Abby Zidle, deserve a world of gratitude for the help and encouragement they gave me along the way. Together, they made an intimidating and confusing process much easier and more fun than it otherwise might have been.

Thank you all a million times over.

Contents

Chapter 1
Lunch Hour Wedding Planning

Congratulations! You're engaged! And it's no secret that engagements are a stressful period in the lives of couples. After saying, "I will," but before saying, "I do," every newly engaged couple experiences one single moment of sudden and perfect clarity of mind. During this revelatory period, they realize that in the few seconds it took to slip a ring on a finger, they inadvertently agreed to plan a hugely elaborate party for 150 or so relatives, friends, acquaintances, and, in some cases, strangers. No, wait, make that 200—Mom has demanded that her flock of high school girlfriends be invited, and Dad says everyone should be allowed to bring a date.

No wonder so many future husbands and wives contemplate running off to Vegas.

In the not-so-distant past, newly engaged women and their parents were responsible for planning the entirety of the future wedding. This meant they had to do a nasty thing called "legwork." To gather dress, tux, floral, favor, cake, and catering ideas, they were forced to first phone for catalogs and then wait until they arrived via mail.

After browsing these thick tomes of nuptial niceties, mothers and daughters (and, less frequently, fiancés and fathers) had to hoof it from vendor to vendor, often with a gaggle of female relatives in tow. In extreme cases, brides-to-be guilty of nothing more than indecision were subject to endless, boring sales pitches, usually given by salespeople more interested in profits than true love.

Now, some future brides still do have endless hours at their disposal to stroll leisurely from boutique to boutique. And some future grooms think nothing of whiling away hours inspecting ceremony sites and interviewing reception hall managers. But no doubt these people exist in tax brackets so high they can't even see the rest of us. Lucky them.

Here's a quick reality check: The majority of modern brides- and grooms-to-be spend their days working and, in their off hours, have plenty of errands and obligations to fill their agendas. They're getting married in towns and cities hundreds or thousands of miles from where they actually live. And their best pals, moms, and siblings reside nowhere near either of those places, making it almost impossible for anyone involved to casually jet off to meet with bakers, caterers, or DJs. That's why more and more engaged couples faced with the prospect of sneaking wedding planning into the gaps between work and play and food and sleep are turning to the one friend they know will never let them down: the Internet.

Let's face it. Most of us are pretty adept at navigating the virtual world. We socialize, schmooze, and share our journals online. We shop without ever changing out of our pajamas.

Yet while more than three quarters of all engaged couples fire up their web browsers when planning their weddings, only a little more than 10 percent ever buy or reserve headpieces, cakes, shoes, centerpieces, or other wedding gear on the net. Why? Maybe people don't feel comfortable putting their matrimonial happiness in the hands of the postal service. They may also crave the security of knowing who they're dealing with when dropping mad cash on stuff they'll only ever use once. But a friendly face is no guarantee of quality. And since online sellers who deal in cake toppers, freeze-dried rose petals, and other nuptial knickknacks are in it to make a buck just like a brick-and-mortar retailer, they have as much riding on a customer's happiness.

So why research and buy on the Internet? Because being able to plan your wedding during your lunch hour is awesome. More time online means less time spent wandering the streets of your town trying to track down elusive bakeries, less time wasted trying to make bridal salon employees understand that, yes, you really want black bridesmaid dresses, and less time avoiding the puppy-dog stares of bad eighties hair bands desperately looking for work.

That means more time to snuggle with your honey, more time to nurture those new familial relationships, more time to relax, and more time to simply enjoy being someone's future spouse.

Saying "I Do" with iDo

This book serves two purposes. Its pages are filled with easy-to-use matrimonial info that will introduce you to the wide (and wacky) world of weddings, and it also contains tons of tips and tricks that will show you how easily you can plan a wedding using the Internet as your primary—or only—tool. Impossible, you say? Get real. Just about everything you need to orchestrate picture-perfect nuptials can be found online.

With a little forethought, you, too, can use the Internet to take the stress out of wedding planning. Seriously. There is no reason whatsoever that getting engaged should sentence otherwise rational people to months or even years of pounding the pavement in search of products and services that are right there on the net for all to see. Being engaged should be fun! You should be able to look back on this period of your life without gritting your teeth.

. . . .

Leah, A. J., and Jeanette—three wired brides who share their experiences in sidebars scattered throughout this book—wanted no part of the prenuptial hassle so many people assume is unavoidable. Instead of stressing out, they and their geeky grooms typed in a few keywords and were good to go. All right, maybe it wasn't quite *that* easy. But by turning to their computers first instead of immediately running full speed into the offices of their local wedding retailers, they saved some cash and found almost everything they needed with a minimum of fuss.

Leah, a graphic designer from North Carolina, met Will, a programmer from Massachusetts, at a party populated by people who previously knew each other only through the collaborative writing site Everything2.com. Once she and her web-savvy beau were engaged, Leah fired up her browser and started collecting wedding ideas: "Since I could check out things online in a few seconds at work, I could take care of tasks like looking up the wording for my invitations or finding the perfect shoes incrementally over the course of a few days, as opposed to spending hours on the phone."

Without the Internet, Leah maintains, the wedding planning process would have felt like a full-time job. Because she and Will were responsible for coordinating the comings and goings of a large number of out-of-town relatives, guests, and attendants, they needed some way of ensuring that all the essential information was easy for everyone to access.

"Both our parents—mine in Alabama, his in Massachusetts—and our entire wedding party lived far away, so getting a consensus on some wedding plans required us to be able to contact them all at the same time with our questions and concerns. E-mail and our wedding website were invaluable in this regard."

Leah's main regret? That she couldn't find a web-based retailer selling her perfect gown.

While A. J. and her husband Matt didn't meet through online acquaintances, the Internet did play a big role in their courtship.

They planned their first date over AOL Instant Messenger and kept love alive via e-mail when Matt spent an extended period of time in France. In fact, before he proposed, A. J. was already scouring online jewelry stores looking for the perfect ring. And when Matt popped the question, A. J. put her own spin on the wedding planning process by turning to the web for ideas and then taking those ideas to brick-and-mortar vendors.

"I found my reception venue online, as well as my dress and bridesmaid dresses. I decided on my color and theme ideas after coming across pictures of stuff I liked that was similar to what I already had in mind. But I mainly used the web to do price comparisons, because I am more comfortable with person-to-person contact. Still, I spent a lot of time researching flowers, decorations, and hairstyles online."

Throughout the planning process, A. J. and Matt used Yahoo! Notepad to keep track of wedding-related purchases, ideas, and vendor information.

Jeanette and Chris's romance got its start in an online chat room, which was fortuitous, considering that they lived more than two thousand miles away from one another. A long engagement meant that they spent quite a few years avoiding the wedding planning process altogether. When they finally buckled down and got started, the Internet was the first resource Jeanette turned to.

"Unlike most little girls, I didn't have my wedding planned from the moment I turned five. I didn't have *any* ideas. And I needed to get some, fast. As for bridal magazines, the more I looked, the more I found that most of them were focused on what is 'in fashion.' But I wasn't interested in the latest trends. Part of my problem was that I was planning a wedding that didn't follow the traditional patterns of events. I needed to figure out what I had to do, what I wanted to do, and what I could skip without offending anyone."

Jeanette believes that her wedding would never have gotten off the ground without the Internet. Being able to search and shop and plan online allowed her to devote bits and pieces of time to her wedding searches, as opposed to whole days or weekends.

"The thing I valued the most about having Internet resources available to me during my lunch hour or at four in the morning or whenever was that I didn't have to make my wedding my whole life. I could continue to work and relax and have fun, because I knew that when I needed to, I could get a whole lot done in just a few hours."

Using This Book

Right now you're probably freakin' excited. You may even be turning on your laptop as you read this sentence. But there are some things you should know before you get started. First, this book doesn't acknowledge the existence of the mythical beasts known as bridezillas and groomzillas. Planning a wedding is usually stressful and can set even the most saintly person's teeth on edge. It's perfectly natural to feel a little frenetic when you're dealing with an industry that thinks a six-month lead time constitutes serious lag. When you feel as if your wedding is driving you out of your mind, take a break and remember that, with luck, you'll never have to do this again.

Secondly, wedding planning is, or at least should be, at two-person procedure. Matrimony itself is the joining of a man and a woman (or two men or two women, depending on your preferences), so there really should be two people shouldering the prep work. Men and women may not always possess the same aptitudes, but very few aspects of the wedding planning process are firmly gender specific. You'll see the words "bride" and "groom" a lot in this book, but feel free to gender-bend as necessary.

Finally, family members can be an invaluable gift to those harried individuals navigating the often tricky road from engagement to happily wedded life. The stereotype of the meddling future mother-in-law (or the envious sister or bitter brother) is only as real as you allow it to be. A little understanding (coupled with a lot of forgiveness and just a touch of strategic apathy) can go a long way toward keeping family harmony intact.

In conclusion, this book doesn't contain any bride bashing, groom bashing, family bashing, or any other kind of bashing. It does not make grooms-to-be look like twits or categorize all mothers-in-law as screeching harpies. Yes, there are pushy parents and angry siblings and jealous best friends, but that's no reason to make assumptions. Vendor bashing? Well, there's going to be some of that . . . the WIC is huge and sharklike, after all.

›What's the WIC? Get familiar with the initialisms below before you read on, and refer back to this chapter as necessary

SO	Significant other	MIL	Mother-in-law
MOB/G	Mother of the bride/groom	FIL	Father-in-law
FOB/G	Father of the bride/groom	SIL	Sister-in-law
BM	Best man or bridesmaid	BIL	Brother-in-law
MOH	Maid of honor	FMIL	Future mother-in-law (also FFIL, FSIL, and FBIL)
GM	Groomsman	DIY	Do it yourself
FG	Flower girl	WIC	Wedding Industrial Complex
RB	Ring bearer	STD	Save the date (What did you think STD cards were, anyway?)

At the end of each chapter, you'll find all the recommended URLs for its topic organized into a simple list. Ready to start clicking? All right, let's plan your wedding!

Chapter 2

At the Foot
of the Aisle

Engaged couples, still starry eyed and optimistic, tend to assume that the references to wedding stress they come across are nothing more than a tool devised by the WIC to keep brides- and grooms-to-be in line. While this is partly the case—modify any word with the adjective "wedding" and retailers will automatically pump up the price—there is a grain of truth hiding beneath all the tulle and lace. Throwing together a big bash for friends and family on the fly? Easy, when your home is your venue and you know you can fall back on old culinary staples because it just so happens your favorite aunt loves to cook. Orchestrating a wedding that features huge buffets, complicated cakes, unification rites, live flowers, DJs, and everything else people associate with matrimony can be a lot more problematic.

Right now you may be thinking that you don't want to buy into all of the hype. The wedding you envision may involve none of the elements mentioned above, but even if you're dreaming of funky DIY centerpieces and plugging your MP3 player into your reception site's sound system, the established standards have likely been

Christa Terry

Why Jeanette Hit Up the Big Sites

"I think there are upsides and downsides to the big conglomerate sites. For what it's worth, I spent a hell of a lot of time on Weddingchannel.com and got a lot out of its tools. I even spent some time browsing the hair and dress ideas, though I didn't wind up finding anything like what I was looking for.

"When I first started planning, I went to Theknot.com a couple of times, but it didn't seem very user friendly. My preference for Weddingchannel.com was more of an accident than anything else. We signed up for a Macy's registry, and Macy's is affiliated with Weddingchannel .com, so I was automatically signed up for an account.

"I liked the all-inclusive sites because I'm lazy and they're fairly well organized. On the other hand, I didn't have a lot of free time to devote to planning my wedding, and it was kind of a no-frills affair, so I didn't need all of the local information that everyone seems to want to provide. Incidentally, the local listings were mostly crap anyway, because half the time they'd turn out to be nowhere near local!

"The one time I did go looking for nearby hair salons on the big sites, it took me two hours to find one. The town I got married in was small, so there weren't any listings that were actually close by. It would really have been nice to have had a resource besides Yahoo! Yellow Pages."

lurking in your subconscious for many a decade. At some point, you may wonder if you should buy favors or meet with a priest or buy dyeable shoes.

So why is wedding planning this complicated? Step back into history a few centuries and you may be surprised to discover that unless you were an aristocrat, your wedding likely consisted of little more than a trip to the chapel and a postmatrimonial meal. In some cases, getting married was a simple matter of kissing your family good-bye and going to live with a new family. Or your parents might have made a suitable match for you while you were still in diapers, and being that there were no provisions for divorce, you had to make do with what you got. In some cultures, two people declaring themselves married was all it took to solidify the bonds of matrimony. And if you *were* a part of the aristocracy, your match made in heaven was more than likely a match made in practicality. There's no better way to sanctify an alliance than bartering for a bride price.

It's interesting to note that the rites and rituals of matrimony most of us view as being traditional are seldom as ancient as we imagine them to be. Take white gowns, for instance. A few hundred years ago, those not lucky enough to be a part of the gentry wore their Sunday best to their weddings. Some colors were considered luckier than others, but you wore either what you had on hand or what could be worn again for thrift's sake. The whole white-wedding tradition was likely inspired by the opulent gown Queen Victoria wore at her wedding to Prince Albert in 1840. If you're curious (or proving to insistent relatives that you don't *have* to wear white) you can see how dress styles have evolved at Members.aol.com/waltz tyme/brides.html, Vintagewedding.com, and Fashion-era.com/ Weddings.

While ancient brides from many cultures wore veils before, during, and after their weddings for a wide variety of reasons, veils only really gained popularity in the United States in the 1700s, after a certain Miss Nelly Curtis donned one at her wedding to Major Lawrence Lewis, one of George Washington's nephews. Gals who like the look of veils but hate their potentially patriarchal connotations can always tell anyone who asks that they're following in Miss Nelly's footsteps.

The cake served at weddings pays homage to the bread that played a ritualistic role in weddings held thousands of years ago, but the multitiered confections so common today originated in the court of King Charles II in the 1600s. A French baker, tired of the same stacked pile of pedestrian sweets, created the lavish iced tower of cake with which we're so familiar. The trend swept upward into the British isles, and the rest is, as they say, history. What did they serve before that? Find out in chapter 12.

And the big ceremony followed by an even bigger reception? As sweet as it is to be able to gather family and friends in one place to enjoy an overblown matrimonial celebration, it's nice to know that brides- and grooms-to-be who want understated weddings aren't bucking tradition. As late as the early to mid-1900s, weddings were hosted in homes or church fellowship halls. If the guest list was limited, a sit-down breakfast or dinner might be served. For larger parties, simple buffet refreshments were the order of the day. A sample menu from a wedding taking place in 1905 might offer chicken croquettes, lettuce salad, bread-and-butter sandwiches, fruit and sherbet, angel food cake, and coffee. That's it—no appetizers circulating on silver trays, no choice of beef or fish, and no dessert buffet.

The modern traditional wedding really is a mishmash of customs and conventions hijacked from cultures both ancient and contemporary, and even these change as one decade passes into another. Whether the brides and grooms of days past adhered to tradition often had a lot to do with whether or not their parents could afford to. While you and your intended will likely be told over and over again that you need to execute your nuptials in a certain way because that is simply how things have been done for thousands upon thousands of years, you can smile politely, nod, and then go off and do whatever it is you feel like doing without fearing the wrath of the wedding gods. There is no right or wrong way to plan what should be one of the happiest days of your life. When you're feeling the pressure to conform, Google up some wedding history (like Hudsonvalleyweddings.com/guide/customs.htm) and remind opinionated people how far removed from those ancient traditions we really are.

It's About Time
(and Money and Etiquette and Organization)

Whatever your wedding vision, it's important that you recognize that planning a ceremony and reception (or some combo of the two) is a race against the clock. That's not to say that you need to put your life on hold while you search for the perfect first-dance tune or a mixed lot of glass bubble bowls—the fact that you're reading this book is a good indication that you're not willing to drop everything to achieve matrimonial bliss. Gone are the days when it was essential to spend whole weekends walking around the nearest urban center looking for bridal salons and print shops. If you've got a few lunch hours and evenings to spare between now and your wedding day, everything will work out beautifully.

But good vendors and venues book up fast, and the calendars of great vendors and venues are sometimes full a year or more in advance. Likewise, when you're shopping for wedding goods online, you're going to find that certain retailers and designers are going to expect you to give them a lot more lead time than you might anticipate. This is where prioritization becomes vital. For example, if photos aren't your thing, don't knock yourself out trying to find a photographer the day after you get engaged. But if the thought of living out the rest of your life without a screenworthy wedding video makes you shudder, the right time to start looking for a videographer is now. Almost anything that is custom-designed for you, whether it is something as intricate as a piece of jewelry or as simple as a monogrammed napkin, will take six weeks or more to arrive on your doorstep. And if you plan to buy a gown or bridesmaids' dresses online, you need to be sure you have plenty of time to deal with any problems that arise and have all of the necessary alterations done.

The easiest way to avoid all of the wedding stress invented by the WIC is to stay on top of the details you really care about and to get everything else done within a reasonable time frame. What's a reasonable time frame? Enter the ubiquitous matrimonial checklist. Every wedding-related site worth its web space is going to have one, and they all cover what amounts to the same tasks in the same twelve months. Some timelines are longer and cover more ground (the extremely comprehensive checklist at Weddingsgalore.com/wedding_checklist.html suggests that brides buy their wedding footwear a whopping ten months before the wedding), but almost any checklist will give you a basic wedding planning guide to work with.

Jeanette Was Ahead of the Game

"Because I did a lot of things ahead of time, I'd forget to put a check mark next to whatever I'd done. And then there were so many things I couldn't do early, like pay my caterer, so it wasn't worth my time to scan through the checklist over and over again. But I did get a fairly complete picture of what I had to do after downloading a few different checklists, which meant I didn't accidentally leave anything until the last minute."

There may not be twelve months between now and the big day. You may not need to worry about uncomfortable shoes because you're planning a barefoot beach shindig. If you're planning a booze-free reception, there is no need to research liquor options. Heck, half of the items on your chosen checklist may not apply to the wedding taking shape in your brain. No problem—just get rid of the superfluous tasks and add your own.

Here's a sampling of duties you can add to the common checklist to usher it into the modern age:

Twelve to Nine Months Before

- Find out the average cost of a wedding in your locale at Costofwedding.com.

- Browse wedding blogs like Manolobrides.com for inspiration.

- E-mail your preferred vendors to discuss availability.

- Research the standard prices and shipping times for matrimonial goods online.

- Send out engagement announcements via Sendomatic.com.

Six to Nine Months Before

- Build a budget spreadsheet at Numsum.com.
- Create a bookmark filing system using your browser.

- Order wedding gown and bridesmaids' dresses from an online bridal shop.
- Create your wedding website at Weddingwindow.com.

Four to Six Months Before

- Shop for one-of-a-kind favors, decor, and other accessory items at a site like Etsy.com.
- Order your invitations and other personalized stationery online.
- Design and ship STD (i.e., save-the-date) cards using Premium postcard.com.
- Make postwedding travel arrangements on Expedia.com.

Two to Four Months Before

- Start compiling and organizing your wedding playlist in iTunes.
- Familiarize yourself with online map tools like Weddingmapper .com.
- Find dance tutorials on Youtube.com and practice.

Four to Eight Weeks Before

- Order gifts for your attendants and parents from Amazon .com.
- E-mail your wedding announcement to your local newspaper.
- Finalize your reception seating plan with Simpleseating.com.
- Set up an online RSVP system on your website prior to mailing invitations.

- Look up the marriage license laws in your state at Marriagelaws.info.

One Week Before

- E-mail your vendors and your officiant to confirm dates, times, and locations.

- E-mail last-minute details to your attendants.

- Change your mailing address at Moversguide.usps.com.

These are, of course, only suggestions. Checklists you can download and edit using spreadsheet programs like Excel (e.g., Rbytes.net/software/wedding-checklist-for-excel-review) are best because you can add and subtract tasks with impunity. The one drawback to predesigned customizable checklists is that they tend to cost money. If you'd rather not pay for something you can get for free, you can always print out an HTML checklist and attack it with a Sharpie.

No One Is Born Knowing How to Plan a Wedding

Unless you're already a professional wedding planner or one of those wedding junkies who peruses *Modern Bride* in the checkout lane for no good reason, your knowledge of matrimonial accoutrements is probably incomplete. Don't sweat it. Weddings are a huge business, which means that from the moment you hit up Google, you're going to find yourself inundated with information. Some of it will be super-useful, and some will be utterly useless. Probability states that Theknot.com, Weddingchannel.com, and Brides.com will be

"Why Pay?" Asks A. J.

"The checklists I came across were helpful, but you can find the same information in magazines and on tons of websites. I used the lists that allowed me to delete the tasks I didn't need and add my own, but I sure wouldn't pay for them. If I had a second to spare at work, I was looking at bouquets or dresses or favors online. I created a free account at Theknot.com so I could check out flowers, hair design, and invitations. The more I looked around, the more I saw that the ideas and products on the big sites were exactly the same. Then I found out that Theknot .com actually owns Weddingchannel.com."

some of the first search results you encounter, and they are great jumping-off points. At Brides.com, you can browse thousands of pictures of dresses, cakes, table decor, invitations, and just about everything else related to weddings. The best part? No registration necessary to take a peek.

There's also plenty of solid content at Theknot.com, but anything that isn't textual requires registration. Register for free with your real info if you don't mind the resultant spam, or create a catchall e-mail account and a fake snail mail address to avoid receiving pitches for products that don't interest you. Weddingchannel .com also requires that you share your demographic with the site before you can partake of its visual content and customizable tools. You're going to get a good idea of what you can buy and a taste of accepted wedding etiquette at these, the big dogs of the online wedding world, but you're going to have to put up with their advertising for the privilege. Theknot.com is particularly insidious in this area, with some featured content that reads more like an advertorial for the products it carries in its store.

Big doesn't necessarily mean bad. Use the advice and the tools on the three largest sites freely, but don't believe them when they say any one item is absolutely 100 percent essential. If you love a product, rest assured that you'll be able to find it or something very similar to it somewhere else on the web at a better price. And if you're not sure you really need a particular item, the answer is probably that you don't. In fact, take everything on the major matrimonial sites with a grain of salt. The writers who craft the editorial content for these sites are on a mission to convince you that you need multiple showers, an engagement soiree, a bachelorette party with faux penis props, hand-painted invitations, and sequined undies that have "The Future Mrs. So-and-So" emblazoned across them. If you like this stuff, great. If you think it's all too, too corny, don't buy the hype.

The main exceptions to the WIC rule are sites like Gayweddings .com, Gayrites.net, and Idotaketwo.com, all of which break away from the typical wedding paradigm and carry some items and advice you won't easily find anywhere else. Even so, be prepared to see the same old toasting flutes and cake knives alongside dual groom engagement announcements, butch-femme cake toppers, and blended family medallions. Sure, these sites do push some WIC products, but they shine when it comes to the information they offer. Don't automatically assume that information doesn't apply to you. After all, you don't have to be gay to want to use gay-friendly vendors, and you don't have to be an encore bride to want to include your family in your nuptials.

Let's say you're the kind of person who spends all morning scrolling through the posts on your personalized RSS feed. You've probably already perused the archives of five or six or twenty wedding blogs. Some people, however, think blogs are the result of a flood of mediocre writers desperate to have their say. Yes, the word "blog" is stupid, and there are thousands of absolutely awful blogs out there. Add to that the link-farm blogs that exist solely to support an eye-numbing amount of Google AdSense adverts, and the blogosphere (another horrible word) can seem like an immense black hole of know-it-alls with chips on their shoulders. But some of those know-it-alls really do know it all—they love weddings, they've taken the time to learn all they can about etiquette and design, and they take pride in knowing about obscure products and services that you won't find in the pages of your average bridal rag.

Being Able to Share Was Important to Leah

"Weddingchannel.com's scrapbook lets you browse through products on its site and bookmark them to a page that you could access from anywhere when you were logged in. It was also incredibly useful in that you could give different users access to your account—such as the groom and MOB. It was just so much easier to tell my mom to look at my scrapbook than to e-mail her twenty-five links to things I liked.

"And the site had a great breakdown of what you should be doing and when you should be doing it. It would automatically e-mail you at the beginning of the month with the different benchmarks that you should be meeting. It was definitely very useful as we got closer to the wedding, because it was so easy to forget about things like making the rehearsal dinner reservations."

The banter on these blogs is edgy, fun, sappy, and practical. Sometimes it's even irreverent, angry, or bitchy in a good way. Unlike articles and editorials penned by paid writers who have to adhere to the standards laid out by a stodgy editorial team that is at its very core a slave to advertisers, bloggers can write whatever they want to. That means you get to read about sweet dress deals, kooky registry ideas, chic DIY projects, and all of the trials and tribulations of planning a wedding from people for whom composing matrimonial missives is a labor of love. Yes, you will see advertising—if you're not already using an app like the one at Adblockplus.org for Firefox, that is—but most bloggers have the luxury of picking and choosing their ads carefully. Their blogs are their babies, and they're not going to post anything that will sully their reputation as independent sources of all things trendy, beautiful, and unique. The one downside to the whole labor-of-love shtick? The blogs you like best may be updated only sporadically.

When your eyes aren't being bombarded with ads, you can make up your own mind about what is and what isn't important to you. If no one is telling you how important it is that you have monogrammed napkins, it's a lot easier to resist the temptation to blow your budget on pricey paper that will be wadded up and greasy by the end of the night. And when you have a firm goal in mind—

let's say, inexpensive tea favors or wedding shoes that cost less than $100—you're better prepared to make sound decisions. Sometimes the best wedding gear is for sale on sites that have nothing at all to do with weddings, but that doesn't mean you can't boost your nuptial knowledge on sites selling both nuptial know-how and all of the relevant accessories. Just remember to be cautious about any advice that's paired with targeted advertising.

Can We Talk?

Bridal meltdowns are all too common, thanks to the overblown expectations outlined by the WIC. In between researching the traditional meanings of individual in-season blooms and rushing to that third gown fitting, many brides-to-be begin to ask themselves why they should waste so much energy on dresses that will be worn once and cake that will be devoured, then forgotten. Faced with relatives eager to see their progeny all dressed in white, they wonder how to tactfully tell Grandma that they're planning to wear red. It's easy to feel utterly alone when you're the only person you know planning a wedding and the only feedback you're getting is criticism. Thankfully, it's just as easy and way more fun to take your frustrations to all of the wedding message boards out there.

Misery does indeed love company, but you're more likely to be bombarded with sympathy than schadenfreude when you sign up for one of the many online forums designed to give brides-to-be somewhere to vent. In posts and replies, you can connect with people who are going through exactly what you are. The same people who will cheer you on when you angrily rant and rave about your second cousin twice removed who invited herself to your wedding will then applaud your decision to take the high road. It's nice to know that everyone hiding behind an anonymous profile is a bride- or groom-to-be who's willing to share their horror stories with you, giving you definitive proof that your circumstances are not so terribly unusual.

A thick skin is a blessing when you're an active member of a message board community, but you'll find that most board members are tactful and respectful. Read a handful of posts by people eager to share photos of their dress, ceremony site, hairstyle, or cake, and it becomes obvious that the majority of the replies are of the "OMG gorgeous!" and "Sooooo pretty!" variety. Every now and again you'll come across a dissenting opinion from someone who is either honest to a fault or just plain contrary, but don't expect to see a lot of real feedback on pics. The real meat of a forum can be found in the aforementioned rants and raves, the cries for etiquette help, the exchange of ideas, and the camaraderie.

Ready for some more initialisms? In addition to the ones mentioned in the previous chapter, you're going to encounter a bunch more as you cruise the nuptial forums. FI occasionally stands in for fiancé, and DH, DW, DD, DS, and DC, respectively, refer to "dear husbands," "dear wives," "dear daughters," "dear sons," and "dear children." When discussing grandparents, posters may refer to them as GPs, as in "The GPs are hesitant to attend the RD" (RD means "rehearsal dinner"). It's considered polite to mark posts unrelated to weddings as NWR, or "not wedding related." As these boards exist so that brides (and a handful of grooms) can share their stories, it's unlikely that you'll see many posts tagged WR, or "wedding related," as almost all will be just that. Lesser-used initialisms include DW (destination wedding), HM (honeymoon), and OOTG (out-of-town-guests). If you don't know what something means, just ask.

Kvetch.indiebride.com is one of the best and most active message boards. A ton of new posts and replies go up every day, and the participants tend not to take themselves (or the WIC) too seriously. Registration is required, but it's more than worth it if you're fuming about some trivial detail that has become way more complicated than necessary and you need some help moving on. This is the place to read up on wedding anxiety, multiple views on monogamy, the relationship between marriage and feminism, gown alternatives, and crazy breaches of etiquette. And it's one of the best places to go when you're feeling confused, irritated, or less than confident, because someone on the boards is going to understand exactly what you're going through and know just what to say to cheer you up.

There may be times when a companionable "I know how you feel" just doesn't cut it. The forums at Topweddingquestions.com are a little different in that all members can post questions, but only experts can weigh in with answers. There are discussion threads for every conceivable matrimonial subject, from bad bridesmaids to tipping etiquette to second weddings. There are literally thousands of threads, so you may be able to find an answer to your question without even registering for an account.

Of course, the answers you need might be right in your very own brain. What so many wedding sites (be they info clearinghouses, blogs, forums, or retail hubs) fail to mention is that you can have the wedding you want without going all bridezilla on your friends and family. The hundreds of Q&As involving brides-to-be asking "Is it okay if I . . ." are not a good primer for the real world.

Whether you want the fairy-tale princess butterfly wedding that you first conceived of when you were five years old or the flashy, crazy, so-weird-it's-practically-sinful wedding you conceived of last year, the answer to the old "Is it okay if I . . ." question is usually going to be yes. As long as what you want to do is legal and won't piss too many people off, go for it.

Jeanette Wanted Actual Help

"I joined a couple of communities, but they were pretty much worthless to me because I was going to do the things I was going to do whether or not I got some stranger's approval. Plus, I can't stand listening to people bitch when their problems have solutions. Whenever I felt like complaining, I tended to do it around people who could actually fix my problems in real time. I think it's more important to find someone who can help you or cheer you up than someone who's going to gush over your choices."

Begin Your Journey

- Brides.com

- Gayweddings.com

- Howtoremarry.com

- Idotaketwo.com

- Marthastewart.com/weddings

- Theknot.com

- Weddingchannel.com

- Weddings.about.com

Consult a Checklist

- Blissweddings.com/library/checklists.asp

- Evahforsyth.com/bridechecklist.ivnu

- Keepandshare.com/htm/free_wedding_planning.php

- Weddingsgalore.com/wedding_checklist.html

- www.Bridesclub.com/bridesclub-wedding-planner.cfm

Read a Blog

- Alwaysabridesmaid.typepad.com

- Blog.thehandcraftedwedding.com

- Bridezilla.com

- Diybride.com

- Etsywedding.blogspot.com

- Herecomestheblog.com

- Junebugweddings.com/blogs/what_junebug_loves

- Kenziekate.blogspot.com

- Manolobrides.com

- Offbeatbride.com

- Ohjoy.blogs.com/my_weblog/here_comes_the_bride

- Stylemepretty.com

- Thepreppywedding.blogspot.com

- Weddingbee.com

- Zzilch.com/thrynandgabe/blog

Make a Connection

- Boards.weddingbee.com

- Bunchobrides.com

- Ethicalweddings.com/forum

- Kvetch.indiebride.com

- Pashweddings.com/weddingforums

- Topweddingquestions.com

- Weddingannouncer.com/forum

- Weddingwire.com

Chapter 3
Your Virtual Assistants

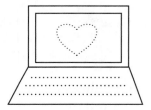

In the not-so-distant past, frenzied brides-to-be and their busy moms and dads fielded phone calls from relatives and friends wanting to know where the engaged couple was registered, how to get to the reception site, and where they could find a list of the area's accommodations. While these ever-patient souls no doubt still spend a great deal of time sharing information with elderly uncles and technophobic grannies, there's no reason anyone intimately participating in or attending a wedding should have to live with their cell phone strapped to their ear for fear of missing some piece of crucial info. The same clever STD cards that will inform people you're getting hitched can guide them toward your wedding website. That's right, the wedding site you're about to create. If you and your intended just happen to be seriously into web design, you've probably already set up a totally sophisticated portal into your matrimonial world.

Your more voyeuristic and nosy guests may already be thanking you for your thoughtfulness. But paranoid guests are likely won-

Christa Terry

For Leah, DIY Meant Coding

"Will and I created a wedding website for our guests to use because it's something we like doing. We've built and maintain a number of sites, so for us it was just a matter of making one more. Our site let our guests know where and when the wedding was taking place, which hotels to use, and how to get in touch with us. We even built a basic RSVP application into the website so people could respond online—though if we ever had to do that part again, we'd make a better form.

"Overall, I liked that we didn't have one of the generic wedding sites you end up with when you use the template services, but that's because working with websites is something we do both professionally and for fun. I think it would have reflected badly on us if we hadn't designed our own wedding website! One of the coolest things we did was to add photos to the site using Flickr.com, which has all of these tools that let you use your pictures in clever ways. I made a new set with twenty or so photos of me and Will, and small versions of those images appeared in a rotation on our website. Being able to do that just made me really happy."

dering what the hell you're thinking, putting all your precious information where everyone and their mothers can access it. Ignore the detractors—as long as you haven't shared your Social Security numbers, full mailing addresses, work hours, or online banking passwords, you should be just fine. If you're nervous, password-protect the whole thing for safety's sake . . . just be sure to give guests the password in your STDs or invitations.

When you're not particularly HTML savvy, the notion of putting together a working website that doesn't look like a late-nineties AOL reject can seem daunting. After all, with everything else you have on your plate right now, do you really want to spend even more time gazing into your monitor? Luckily, with a relatively small outlay of money comes the middle ground. At some point in the past decade, enterprising computer-literate entrepreneurs saw a gap dividing recently engaged web designers and recently engaged everyone else. They created companies with no other purpose than to host the wedding sites they help brides- and grooms-to-be put together.

Websites are a great way to get your nuptial info out into the open without crowding all of the images off your STDs in favor of massive amounts of text. When composing your STDs, put your site's URL under your names, the date of your nuptials, and the approximate location where the event will be taking place, and you can be sure that everyone outside of the most technophobic invitees will have no trouble staying well informed. What should you put on the site itself? If guests are coming from out of town, they'll probably be interested in an area map, links to nearby airports and hotels, driving directions, restaurants, and the area's attractions. They might also be interested in your attendants . . . namely, who they are, what they look like, and what their relationship to you is. Plus, almost everyone you know will want to take a quick peek at photos of you and your spouse-to-be and read your "how we met" story before adding their own two cents in your guestbook. There is almost nothing people like more than being given permission to comment on someone else's personal life!

While including registry information in your engagement announcements or invitation envelopes is (and probably always will be) totally tacky, websites that link to wedding registries still haven't caught the eye of the established etiquette mavens. But before you create an entire page comprised of link after link to your favorite online retailers in a mad grab for swag, consider the culture of your social circle. Will your loved ones appreciate knowing precisely what you and your future spouse want most? Or bring up what they regard as a massive faux pas at the next gathering of the group? You know your family, friends, and acquaintances best, so don't feel the need to be bound by old conventions in this fairly new area of etiquette.

If you're having one of those marathon weddings that lasts all weekend and involves preplanned events in multiple locations, your website can stand in for the activities coordinator you either can't afford or just don't feel like hiring. Your relatives will thank you when they realize how many questions and calls they would otherwise have had to field as eager guests make their way to a variety of destinations safely and without incident. All you need is a list of activities, times, and locations. Your guests will do the rest.

Your site (like your STD cards, invitations, and just about everything else you share with people before the main event) will help your guests anticipate the tone and formality level of your wedding. That doesn't mean that you can't have a little fun in the process of disseminating information! If you like to write, try improving upon the tale of your courtship using proven literary techniques like exaggeration, thickly veiled metaphors, and outright lies. Attendant bios aren't exactly the best medium for a roast, but a gentle ribbing can add interest to an otherwise yawn-worthy website. Can't think of anything witty to say? Pretend you work in advertising—if you actually work in advertising this should be exceptionally easy to do—and really sell yourself and your intended to your audience. This is your chance to get creative.

But not too creative. Ally yourself with a website hosting service with almost unlimited space like Wedshare.com, and you may just be tempted to fill that space with music, videos, and photos you associate with your blossoming relationship. The problem is that the companies that own the rights to that media associate those same files with lawsuits, not love. Post as many snapshots of you, your intended, and your favorite places to your website as you like, but don't use images you suspect are copyrighted. The same goes for clips of TV shows or movies and music not currently in the public domain. You can't be too careful with all of the intellectual property lawsuits being thrown around.

As an aside, exercise the same degree of caution if you decide to

Leah and Her List

"I built an e-mail list that included our parents and the members of the wedding party. I'd send out updates when something changed or we updated our website. The list also provided our attendants with a no-fail method of asking me or Will questions about how things were progressing. It ended up being a really convenient way for us to communicate with everyone on a mass scale, and the people on the receiving end of our e-mails could refer back to them if they forgot something."

augment your site with a group blog. Blogs (or online journals, or whatever else you want to call them) let you stay connected to your attendants and family members without having to create an e-mail list that will clog inboxes for months to come because one of your bridesmaids is incapable of hitting "reply" instead of "reply all." Of course, you might just be too busy to moderate a group blog using Blogger.com (create your blog, go to Settings, go to Permissions, go to Invite Blog Authors) or ask everyone involved in your wedding to sign up at Livejournal.com so you can create a private community, in which case a simple e-mail list can start to look pretty good.

Share Without Shelling Out

When you're not fully sold on the wedding website idea, you're probably not going to want to drop dough on one. No problem. Keep your debit card in your pocket for now—websites are one of those rare things that only cost money sometimes. The upside of free site hosting is that you won't feel like you've been tossing money into a virtual pit if no one is able to find your site because the URL reads like something from 1997. You can play around with templates and color schemes until you have an idea of what you like and dislike, trashing the whole thing over and over until you're satisfied. The downside is that "free" typically translates to limited functionality, an even more limited range of choices, and a site address that looks like this: Ourweddingdaysite.net/sites/rej5466/peterand petunia/index.html.

To get the most out of a free site, look past your first few search results, because the biggest players in the wedding world tend to be the biggest losers in this particular area. Theknot.com's websites are really just individual web pages that flow on and on and on in your browser window, depending on how much information you decide to enter. After you've signed your demographic info away to

Christa Terry

No Action for A. J.

"I set up a free wedding website using Theknot.com, but I had very few visitors. Our site just had a little background info on my sweetie and me, directions to the wedding and reception, and links to our registries. I had friends help me track registry gifts as they came in, but overall, our site didn't get a lot of traffic."

Theknot.com, you get a single left-justified page with a single photo oriented just under the site's nav bar. In terms of content, resign yourself to big blocks of plain text. You can play around with your site's colors and background graphics, but that's about it.

Weddingchannel.com's free site builder is surprisingly useful, with attractive templates, photo albums and guestbooks, and on-line RSVP capability. But the end result isn't so wonderful, because whatever cute template design you pick out is eaten up by the big ol' Weddingchannel.com banner splashed across the top of the page. And if visitors to your site aren't careful when signing the aforementioned guestbook, they'll end up receiving "occasional updates and special offers" from Weddingchannel.com . . . possibly for life.

As you browse the free wedding site builders, you'll notice that many of them exist in tandem with not-so-free services offered by the same company. Ewedding.com will provide you with a free site, but that site won't do nearly as much as its subscription sites, and the company takes great pains to remind you of that in its sidebars. You may not initially feel like paying for something as silly as the polls and quizzes supported by its premium packages, but the site is banking on the chance you'll reach for your wallet as soon as you're told you've reached your limit for photo uploads.

Two of the best freebies out there are Momentville.com and Weddingannouncer.com. Build your site with the former and it will last forever instead of going dead six months or a year after your nuptials like a lot of other sites, both free and for pay. Your site will also be carbon neutral (i.e., technically nonpolluting) because

{30}

Momentville.com has bought up a big batch of carbon offset credits in the form of planted trees that suck up carbon dioxide from Tick green.com. Build your site with the latter and you'll get almost all of the same functionality you get with paid site services, though you do sacrifice the ability to use HTML.

Don't think you have to go all-out girly when you're creating your site. A search for free wedding websites is going to net you services with templates that are pink or Tiffany blue and adorned with calla lilies because brides-to-be as a group have shown a marked preference for these things. If that doesn't sound like something you'd like at all, nix the word "wedding" and look for free websites that won't force you to put a wedding countdown clock or registry page on your site. At Members.freewebs.com, you can choose from more than three hundred templates and add all sorts of multimedia content, plus the page editor and file managers are easy to use. Should you decide you really, really, really want one of those countdown clocks, you can still snag one for free at Whenismywedding .com.

The bottom line is this: A good free wedding website service should include site hosting, a domain name, password protection, a fair number of templates to choose from, space for your photos, and a minimum of six distinct pages. There's no reason to give out your demographic information for anything less than that.

Get What You Pay For

One of the main reasons brides- and grooms-to-be opt not to make a wedding website (besides absentmindedness) is their reaction to the cost. When you're dropping phat cash on a cake that costs almost as much as your rent, a dress that costs as much as a used car, and favors you suspect will be thrown out a few hours after the reception, you're going to be a tad cautious with your remaining dollars.

So many of the freebie sites you'll encounter are going to look like bad hack jobs, which makes it easy to assume that all of the site providers out there are pushing the same product. But the reality is that some are great, some are better than others, and some are so bad you have to see the brutally honest reviews at Weddingwebsites.com to believe it.

After the free trial that most of these services offer, you're going have to pay somewhere in the range of $50 to $100 to keep the site you created in the land of the living. Whether that's all-inclusive or not depends—the baseline price may or may not include permanent web space, a custom domain, and an e-mail address. Prices will also vary depending on the lifespan of your site. For $79, Wedding window.com will host your site for twelve months, outfit your site with a kicky flash intro, help you customize your site's color scheme and layout, send your online STDs, and create an editable mailing list with which you can do what you will. Its prices and packages are similar to those offered all across the board when you're looking at low- and midpriced site options, so your best bet is to go with the site builder that has the templates and colors you actually like.

Fifty bucks will get you a solid, working website that has all of the information your guests will need on its pages. But let's face it: Working with templates can be boring, and the site you wind up with is going to be far from unique. How unique does a wedding website need to be? That's entirely your call. For $580, Weddingorg.com will design a custom, ad-free, full-flash twelve-page website that is all your own. Your money buys you a good-looking site and the convenience of not having to spend your valuable free time fiddling with a site editor. It's also a pretty good deal when you consider that independent web designers can charge as much as $1,500 for a small website.

Only you know what your needs are, so don't feel obligated to spend a bundle on a website if the guests most likely to access your site have already RSVP'd, live near the ceremony and reception venues, and are antiregistry on principle. It's pretty depressing to see a site counter that tops off at eighteen visitors after three months when you spent $300 on web design. You can always make a free site and upgrade later, or play around with your free site until you've got it looking really good. You may even know someone who can whip you up a website and host it for you gratis. All you need to do is drop a few casual hints to let them know that websites make great wedding gifts.

A Little Help Here?

Websites help you help your guests. You get the peace of mind of knowing that the people attending your nuptial celebration aren't going to get lost on their way to the reception site or mistake the groom's ex for a bridesmaid. What they don't do is help you track your budget, manage your guest list, create seating charts, print address labels, or handle all of the details that make planning a wedding so stressful. Luckily, the Internet is more than a collection of unmanned stores that are open twenty-four hours a day. There are, in fact, useful tools floating around the web if you know where to find them. A Google search for "wedding planning tools" will net you more than two million results . . . many of which are about as useful and relevant as those old how-to-be-a-good-wife guides from the 1950s. They're not nearly as funny, though.

Here's the straight dope: A real, live wedding planner will design and execute your entire wedding for about $5,000. Elmsoftware .com's wedding planning package (which has earned great ratings at Cnet.com and Toptenreviews.com) costs $29.95. Planning your own wedding with nothing but software (and this book) at your side will be slightly more stressful than hiring someone to orchestrate the whole event for you, but isn't a little tension in your jaw worth a cool $4,970.05 in your pocket?

Good software should grant you the power to compile customized, dynamic to-do checklists and timelines; organize the names, snail mail addresses, and e-mail addresses of your guests in one place; send out mass mailings, print labels, and tally RSVPs; create seating charts and log meal selections; track your vendors; and design a personalized wedding budget. You should be able to import information from Word and Excel, import general text files, and update your address book. If you have a problem, the company should provide support via phone and e-mail without your having to threaten to file a complaint at BBB.org. And there should be some sort of money-back guarantee mechanism in place so you can recoup your funds if the software turns out to be less comprehensive than it claims.

Unfortunately, not all software is good software, which means you can't just pick the package with the most clever name and expect to be wowed. If you're willing to trust someone else's impression, you can find out which software rules and which software drools at Wedding-planning-software-review.toptenreviews.com. The site's team of reviewers analyzed fifteen pieces of planning software and gave the package at Elmsoftware.com a well-deserved gold rating. Smartwedding.com's software took the silver, and Marziplanner (an Australian package found at Marziplanner.com.au) took the bronze. The lowest-rated software, found at Info-pack.com/weddingplanner, was so bad that the reviewers couldn't even figure out how to use it!

There are also online applications that try to mimic the functionality of the aforementioned software. The sad fact is that these tend to be eleventh-hour add-ons designed to drive traffic to retail sites. In other words, most of them are nothing more than uneditable lists with input boxes easily replicated in any spreadsheet software. It's good to know what you need to do and when it needs to be done, but you can achieve the same ends by printing out one of the hundreds of wedding checklists on the web. Whereas the tools you'll encounter in good software will interact with one another—updating your to-do list automatically when you input your vendor information, for example—online planning tools are usually entirely unconnected. Some, like Ezweddingplanner.com, redeem themselves with e-mail reminders and articles, but the reminders are seldom customizable and the advice is easily found elsewhere.

Overall, the apps at Weddingwire.com are the nicest looking and most useful, and the best part is that they're free. You can create a seating chart, custom timeline, and guest list; track RSVPs, gifts, and vendor payments; manage your vendors and post reviews; and store links to images, websites, and files. Because you're storing the information on Weddingwire.com's servers instead of your own computer, you run the risk of the site's suffering a crash or going under, but that risk is tiny compared with the convenience of being able to access your important info anywhere, at any time.

Then again, a lot of online planning software is nothing more than a bunch of labeled lists. If it's just the anytime access you're after and you're willing to make your own lists, you and your SO can always create a shared, editable planning area at Google.com/notebook, which allows you to take "clippings" of web content—like photos of dresses or limos—and save it in a central location.

Being that you've come so far without launching yourself into the arms of someone seemingly stronger and more capable than yourself, romance-heroine style, it's a sure bet that you're more than smart, talented, and creative enough to get through the next six or so months without lobotomizing yourself or defenestrating your future spouse. The aid you crave is out there, but it's up to you to find it—and to use it. Your website won't do anyone any good if you don't update or advertise it, and the super software you bought won't help you if you don't sit down with it every now and again.

Create a Free Site

- Ewedding.com

- Momentville.com

- Mywedding.com/main/couple_sites.html

- Superweds.com

- Tgwedding.com

- Theweddingvendor.com/WeddingSite.php

- Weddingannouncer.com

- Weddingmuseum.com

Get What You Pay For

- Designourday.com

- Happymoments.net

- Nearlyweds.com

- Ourperfectday.com

- Weddingorg.com

- Weddingpearl.com

- Weddings.myevent.com

- Weddingtracker.com

- Weddingwindow.com

- Wedorama.com

- Wedquarters.com

- Wedshare.com

- Wedstudio.com

Plan Offline

- Rsvpprogram.com

- Smartwedding.com

- Theorganizedwedding.com

- Weddingsoft.com

- Weddingtrix.com/toolkit.php

Plan Online

- Aboutweddings.com/planning_place

- Bridalinsider.com

- Ezweddingplanner.com

- Myweddinghero.com

- Onestopweddingplanner.com

- Onlineweddingboutique.com/member_tools.php

- Ourweddingday.com

- Wedalert.com/content/planning/index.asp

- Weddingsolutions.com/index.cfm?fuseaction=planning

- Weddingwire.com

Chapter 4
Meet Your VIPs

The straight dope is that planning a wedding by yourself can be a total drag. Even if you get no love from your relatives and friends while searching for vendors and vittles, it's still nice to have someone to bounce ideas off of. You know, someone who isn't your future spouse and therefore has no reason not to tell you that the dress you really love is probably going to make you look a little hippy. Enter your VIPs, a helpful group of individuals that can include certain ladies and gentlemen distinguished by honorifics—as well as a whole bunch of parents.

If you've nixed the wedding party idea and your folks aren't really friendly, there will probably still be people you can turn to in times of need. Feel free to substitute "good friend of any gender" for MOH, BM, BMs, and GM. "Parents" can be any person or persons who served as your mentors and are probably older than you by a couple of decades, e.g., the grandmother who raised you or the aunt who took you under her wing. Whatever you call these individuals, they are the ones most likely to recognize that you need a little help, as well as the ones most likely to give it.

In theory, that is. The people you love most are likely less than perfect, and their imperfections may be the sort that interfere with prenuptial harmony. In other words, if your best friend is kind of a flake, don't expect her to morph into Dr. Responsible just because you're tying the knot. If your parents are both artists living from sale to sale, you're going to be better off asking them for design advice than dough. Be nice—when you need help, be anything but demanding. Make your requests as specific as possible to avoid confusion, and if something goes wrong, be forgiving to avoid hurt feelings.

You'll likely discover that you can't avoid ticking people off entirely, because everyone around you will start making assumptions as soon as you announce the fact that you're engaged. Your mom may view you as some kind of control freak if you never ask her for help. Yet she may insist on adding her own spin to your ideas when you do solicit a helping hand. Some attendants may look askance at you for suggesting that they are responsible for anything other than showing up on the appointed day. Others will expect that you're going to foist tasks upon them as soon as you and your intended have set a date . . . and they wouldn't have it any other way.

Ultimately, you can win the war against hurt feelings, but you're not going to be able to win every single battle. If you consistently cater to the whims of parents and attendants while planning, you're going to end up with a wedding that's lovely, functional, and fun, but not quite the wedding you were hoping for. Parents and attendants are individuals, which means they are going to have their

Avoiding Hurt Feelings Was Important to Leah

"I had been involved in several other weddings—I was the maid of honor in my sister's wedding—so I was already familiar with the actual roles various people play during the ceremony, but there were some things that I felt I had to learn to make sure I wasn't going to ask anyone to do too much or hurt someone's feelings by forgetting to ask them to do something. The etiquette protocols surrounding people made me more nervous than anything, I think. I didn't want to offend anyone by forgetting an obscure rule that they knew about but I didn't. Fortunately, almost everyone in my wedding party was super laid back, so things were never in danger of getting out of hand."

own ideas about what should be done and when it ought to happen. When these notions don't gel with your own, you have two choices. You can roll over and let them have their way, or you can stand up to them gently, risking temporary offense.

The easiest way to ensure that everyone is still on speaking terms at the rehearsal dinner is to make sure that all of your VIPs feel comfortable voicing their opinions and concerns. If the MOBs, MOGs, FOBs, and FOGs know that you won't go postal when they make suggestions, they're going to be a lot less likely to invite people or make decor changes behind your back. Likewise, the guys and gals in your wedding party will feel a lot more at ease on your wedding day when you've taken their input into consideration where clothing, flowers, and transportation are concerned. You don't have to gush over every single one of their suggestions—Wear your mom's out of date dress? No. Save money with a cash bar? Nope. Serve a buffet dinner? Maybe—but do be open-minded.

You may even find yourself with some extra VIPs. Before you fret over how to include all your extended relatives and stepparents in your nuptials, count your blessings! You've got all sorts of special people in your life, and that's awesome. Think about asking them to do a reading, sing a song, or light the candles at your ceremony; announcing them at the reception; seating them in a place of honor; or providing them with a corsage or boutonniere that will set them apart from the average Jane and Joe.

Should you feel the pressing need to keep an eye on the progress of your parents, BMs, and GMs, you'll be happy to know that there are checklists that will help you do just that. Visit Americanbridal .com/wedpardut.html if you're looking for a handy list of who traditionally does what in modern weddings, but find someone else to check off each item if you can't bear to leave the spaces blank. There's nothing more distracting than a bride with a clipboard micromanaging from the foot of the aisle.

Of Maids and Men

Why do most brides and grooms take their vows with a gaggle of similarly dressed gals and guys looking on? Go back a few thousand years and you'll discover that Roman marriage laws required that there be at least ten witnesses present at all weddings so that the evil spirits usually found lurking in the vicinity of brides and grooms would get confused. These witnesses dressed in garb similar to that worn by the happy couple, thus initiating a tradition that has gone in and out of fashion for centuries. When bridenapping was popular among Germanic Goths, men with marriage on their minds would kidnap their chosen mates while their closest friends fought off the objectors. In other cultures, the primary job of female attendants was to mockingly deny the groom access to his bride or, conversely, to accompany a newly married woman to the home of her husband.

With the warding off of unseen demons and the fighting off of real live human beings, the attendants of yesteryear had plenty to do. The duties undertaken by modern BMs and GMs are (sadly) not quite as exciting. Swordplay has been replaced by the prewedding swilling of suds in sports bars. Instead of tossing rotten tomatoes at the groom, BMs spend their time assembling tiny paper flowers. There's still plenty for everyone to do, though, provided all involved are amenable to the idea.

Some brides- and grooms-to-be don't want or need outside assistance, and some attendants are just too busy to pitch in. Sites like Theknot.com imply that the only good attendant is the attendant working their way through a long to-do list. This is absolutely not true. A good attendant is whatever you think a good attendant should be. When it comes time to choose BMs and GMs, think about your expectations, the lifestyles and personalities of your candidates, and the size of the venues you're considering. Ten maids and ten men will look great in a cathedral, but they'll be cramped in a chapel. Those same twenty attendants will make a small, informal beach wedding look like a cheesy photo shoot for Mr. Tux.

Brides- and grooms-to-be with small social circles and families get off easy because no one's going to give you the stink eye for getting hitched with too few attendants at your side. But couples with well-stocked families and big groups of friends may find that choosing attendants is a heartbreaking process of elimination. If you're not sure who to choose, you can find a whopping thirty-two-page guide to choosing and mentoring your BMs at Dessy.com/wedding -planner/brides-guide. Choosing your main dudes is apparently less complicated, as most online guides for guys (like this one: Wedding-guide.org/choosegroomsmen.asp) are all of one page long.

What it all boils down to is that you really should choose people who are both close to you and capable of carrying out certain responsibilities. Remember that the duty rosters usually assigned to members of the wedding party are nothing more than extremely loose recommendations. You can ask your maids and men to do just about anything you think they ought to be doing, but there are no guarantees they're going to nod in meek acquiescence. Never forget that your friends and relatives have jobs, hobbies, and families of their own. Presumably, you're choosing your attendants based on your esteem and respect for them, rather than the extra pair of hands they can provide when things get sticky.

Maids of honor are quite often the superwomen of the wedding world. The really awesome ones are there to fix broken favors and mend broken hearts while helping research reception sites and going to multiple dress fittings. Even MOHs who are relatively uninvolved in the planning process will still lend a listening ear to a stressed-out friend as the eve of her matrimony approaches. How much or little she takes on will depend on how much or little you want to give her to do, how much time she has at her disposal, and plenty of other factors. Many MOHs shop alongside the bride-to-be, lend a hand when DIY projects get out of control, hang on to the bride's emergency kit on the big day, and help her dress before the main event. Sometimes this jill-of-all-trades will even run interference while the other ladies are getting gussied up so no uninvited parties inadvertently wander into the bridal chamber.

During the wedding, the MOH holds the bouquet when the bride's hands are otherwise occupied by rings or embraces. And speaking of rings, she may be carrying the groom's ring somewhere on her person if the BM has not been entrusted with both bands. She may sign the license that renders the whole thing official, stand in the receiving line, go on to share a dance with the best man, or give a toast. Sometimes, when the newlyweds are leaving for the honeymoon immediately after the reception, the MOH will take responsibility for the bridal gown, ensuring that it gets to the cleaner's in a timely fashion.

The MOH is also typically the brains (and the debit card) behind the bridal shower and bachelorette party. The lore surrounding the former event involves a Dutch miller who was rich in love but poor in lucre and the uptown girl who wanted to be his wife. Her father chose another for her, stating that she could remain in the family by marrying into wealth or marry the miller and be disowned. He made good on his threat, and she prepared herself for a harsh life in poverty. The miller, however, had always been kind to his neighbors. They responded to his bride's grief by showering the destitute couple with small gifts that would serve them well in their new life together. Eventually, the bride's father came around and bought the newlyweds a house.

Many MOHs feel ill at ease when planning the shower because they aren't sure they've invited the right people or spent enough money. Tell uncertain maids (and matrons and men of honor) that a shower is at its heart nothing more than a party that may or may not have a theme, e.g., lingerie showers and kitchen showers. Whatever they plan will be lovely as long as there is something to eat, something to drink, good conversation, and some form of entertainment—even if it's just watching the bride-to-be open her gifts while the MOH makes a list of who gave what. Allaboutshowers .com/bridal isn't the most comprehensive resource around, but it does address questions commonly asked by novice hosts and explain how to play the most common shower games. You can find a shower checklist to pass along to your MOH here: Simplyweddingstuff .com/brshad.html

The bachelorette party evolved as a direct response to the bachelor party, when friends and relatives of brides began asking themselves why they were sitting in living rooms eating dainty tea cakes while the men were out carousing. As it turns out, women can carouse with the best of them. A Google search for "bachelorette party" will net you more than a million results, and most of those are links to retail sites pushing penis-themed paraphernalia. At Bachelorettepartyfun.com, for example, you'll find Dicky Straws, stud napkins, Pecker Face Plates, naughty cake pans, and Spermies Candy. If these sound more foul than funny to you, let your MOH know that ahead of time so you don't end up feeling obligated to wear a condom veil to your favorite watering hole. You can always gently hint that you'd rather go to a spa instead of getting trashed on girly cocktails.

While the MOH is helping address invites, accompanying the bride to shops and salons, giving feedback on centerpieces, and being a good listener, the best man (or best woman) is probably off somewhere researching accommodations in Vegas. Some BMs no doubt do get involved in the planning side of their friends' weddings, but tradition still dictates that the individual standing next to the groom has a fairly short list of responsibilities. If nothing else, he'll get fitted for and acquire his tux, help transport stuff to the ceremony and reception sites, prod the groom into punctuality as necessary, sign the marriage license, hand out tips, and keep the rings safe until they're on the appropriate fingers. He may even carry the groom's emergency kit or run last-minute errands on the morning of the wedding. Easy stuff, all told.

Frequently, the BM gives a speech at the reception, and this is the duty most likely to cause agitation in the hearts of even the most stolid men. Thebestman.com coaches mic-shy BMs through the toast creation process, with toasting tips, types of toasts, and some canned toasts to help tongue-tied speakers get started. And don't let your best man forget that you want him to work the receiving line—if you plan on having a receiving line, that is.

The best man is also the go-to guy where the bachelor party is concerned, whether you're talking about planning or paying. Be aware that his vision of the perfect prenuptial party may be very different from the groom-to-be's. The groom-to-be can prevent misunderstandings by dropping clear hints well in advance of the night or weekend set aside for this event. Picture the expression on the face of the BM who wants nothing more than to go camping with his soon-to-be married best pal but plans a sordid extravaganza involving strippers, whipped cream, caning, creepy clowns (like Ouchy, from Ouchytheclown.com), donkeys, and a river of booze, when the groom-to-be finally admits he would have much rather spent a sedate weekend in the woods with his buds.

There is no rule stating bachelor parties have to begin and end on a lascivious note. If you and your intended are down with that sort of thing, more power to you. But if you'd rather focus on bonding than babes, let the poor guy know before he gets in touch with the "talent" at sites like Centerfoldstrips.com. At some point, you may find yourself up against a friend, brother, or GM who argues that the customary risqué bachelor party is an established institution that should not be changed. Feel free to remind them that the tradition began as a dinner, not a bacchanal. It was a chance for men to feast with their closest comrades on the eve of a marriage, not an easy opportunity to get in one last grope.

"Often a bridesmaid, but never a bride," read a 1930 advertisement for Listerine. The unlucky subject of the ad was Edna, a halitosis sufferer pushing thirty, and she was apparently unmarried because she wasn't gargling with the right mouth rinse. While Listerine probably snagged the slogan from a song called "Always a Bridesmaid," written by Fred W. Leigh and Charles Collins, its ads certainly helped popularize the idea that being a bridesmaid ain't all that. Superstition even states that a three-time bridesmaid will never be wed!

These oft-derided members of the bridal entourage are generally expected to give the bride and her MOH whatever support they might need, be it decorating the church before the ceremony or tidying up the reception hall after the vows have been declared official. Many maids are invited to offer up their input when it comes time to choose dresses, shoes, and accessories, though not every gal pal is so fortunate. BMs usually attend any and all prenuptial functions, including engagement parties, showers, and the bachelorette bash, and they may end up footing part of the bill for these events if the MOH asks them nicely to chip in. Before the wedding, bridesmaids will need to place their dress orders, go to the required fittings, and pick up whatever accessories you want them to wear. They may or may not offer to do things like craft centerpieces, address invitations, and run errands for you, but be aware that they may be waiting for you to ask them to undertake specific tasks.

How many bridesmaids do you need? Technically, none. But they're fun to have around and will occasionally provide a helping hand, so think about choosing four, five, or six gals for a formal wedding attended by one hundred people. Round up for bigger celebrations, or round down if the ceremony will be more casual. Don't forget to take the size of your venue into account—in a tiny chapel with a correspondingly tiny altar, your eight maids are definitely going to wind up standing on one another's toes.

In the movies, groomsmen are usually irresponsible, party-loving dudes who fear settling down and do everything they can to talk the groom out of getting hitched. Thankfully, real life is nowhere near as dramatic. You may have heard these guys referred to as ushers, but not all ushers are GMs and not all GMs are ushers. Most of the time, these two roles are treated as one, but some couples use the naming disparity as a pretext for including more family and friends in their wedding. Whatever honorific they receive, these guys have it pretty easy, as evidenced by the extremely short list of duties posted at Thegroomguide.com/bestman3.html.

Before the wedding, their primary responsibilities include listening to the groom-to-be vent, giving the chosen formalwear a thumbs-up, and sending their measurements to the tuxedo shop. If the BM asks for a helping hand while planning a bachelor party, the GMs are supposed to assist. They may also be expected to pony up some cash to pay for any prenuptial festivities. On the big day, your groomsmen can hand out programs, direct people to their seats, and keep an eye on the gift table. It's not uncommon for a GM to become the unofficial answer man unwittingly, as guests tend to direct their questions toward anyone wearing a tux. Anticipate this by making sure your GMs know where the bathroom is. Some people even ask their male attendants to dance with any single females at the reception—but this practice is not as common as it once was because being a woman without a dance partner is no longer considered a fate worse than death. When your ushers are not your GMs, you can ensure they don't feel left out by mentioning their names in the wedding program, announcing them at the reception, and seating them with the other members of the wedding party.

How many groomsmen do you need? Like bridesmaids, these guys are, in fact, a nonessential element of weddings. But they look great in photographs and may even prove helpful, so plan on having two or three GMs per fifty guests for a formal wedding or less for an informal affair. If your men have never participated in a wedding before and seem a tad nervous, point them toward Groomgroove

.com/other_players/costs_of_being_a_groomsman.php, where they can learn about some of the duties (and costs) usually shouldered by GMs.

The littlest members of your wedding party have the easiest jobs. They aren't required to host parties or bring gifts, though they should be invited to any prenuptial event that is age-appropriate. Flower girls and ring bearers are lucky enough to be able to call it a night whenever they happen to be feeling cranky instead of having to wait for the last straggling guests to pack up and go home. At the wedding, tykes can toss flower petals and carry ring pillows, as is customary. They can also carry the bride's train or walk up the aisle entirely unencumbered. Sending younger attendants toward the altar in twos or threes can make the experience less stressful for those who are uncomfortable being the center of attention. Make sure there is a familiar adult (and a chair) waiting to receive them. You needn't worry about etiquette too much in this area because kids will be pleased that you're allowing them to participate, so they're not going to sweat the details.

These are the traditional roles, but feel free to gender-bend and refashion the standard wedding party any which way. Call everyone in your wedding party an honor attendant, position them wherever you please, or do away with the hierarchy altogether. Have as many or as few attendants as feels right. A bride whose best friend is a dude and a groom with a best gal pal can have a wedding party that's as mismatched as it needs to be—a best maid and a handful of female ushers may occupy the groom's side while one bridesmaid and the man of honor flank the bride. If your man of honor is feel-

A. J.'s Flowerless Flower Girl

"My FG carried a sparkly wand I made myself instead of a basket of petals, and it really worked with our whole color scheme and look. I came across other good ideas, but the wand ended up looking really fantastic and it was something the FG could keep and enjoy later."

There When Jeanette Needed Her

"I would IM my MOH almost every day when things were rough, just to vent, because she was someone who had solutions to the problems I was facing. That, and she and my sister can't stand each other, and my sister was one of the people driving me absolutely crazy, so it was worth it to complain to her. I really needed someone who would be there for me and listen to me, and my MOH knew that."

ing a little uneasy about his role, point him toward Man-of-honor .blogspot.com—this blog hasn't been updated in quite some time, but it details one man of honor's experience and is a good primer for future male MOHs. Just remind everyone who raises an eyebrow that there are no actual established rules about who is and who isn't allowed to be in the wedding party.

A word of caution: Don't choose your attendants too far in advance, because relationships can change, and there's nothing worse than a falling-out that leads to an attendant dropping out. But do give them enough time to get their wedding-day duds without having to resort to rush orders. As tempting as it is to immediately call up your favorite friends and relatives, consider waiting a month or two before paying them the ultimate honor of asking them to be a part of your wedding party. This will give you time to figure out how many attendants you want on each side and who's best suited to fill each role. The names that initially pop into your head—his sister, her brother, a cousin, or your college roommate—may very well be lodged in your brain because you once dreamed of having them in your wedding and never altered your vision.

Brides- and grooms-to-be often feel a certain obligation to invite certain individuals to be a part of the wedding party. That feeling of obligation may even be the result of outright pressure from friends and family members overeager to be a part of your wedding. Your FMIL may expect you to invite your FBILs or FSILs to be attendants, no questions asked. If you and your childhood best friend promised each other that you'd each be MOH in the other's wedding, you may feel a little guilty not ringing her up even though you haven't spoken to her in ten years. But that pressure you feel? It's ultimately meaningless. You're not going to be a happy camper as you say your vows if you can feel hate waves radiating from the brother who never would have been a GM if your parents hadn't pushed you into adding him to the wedding party.

Pick people you care about, because those are the people who are going to step up to the plate when you need them, no matter what you need them to do.

Remember to be appropriately grateful for whatever services your attendants render! The reason you're inundated with gift sites when searching for information on the usual roles played by maids and men is that most brides and grooms present their attendants with some sort of token of their appreciation, either at the rehearsal dinner or just after the wedding. You can opt for old favorites like cufflinks for the fellows and monogrammed makeup bags for the ladies or explore some of the newer options like personalized meat-branding irons and sleek cookware. If you don't see anything that speaks to you when gift hunting, leave the WIC world behind and shop somewhere you know will have gifts you feel good about giving. Your more seasoned attendants will love you all the better for your decision to go with something other than the usual flasks, picture frames, and novelty key chains.

Mothers and Fathers and Stepparents, Oh My!

Wouldn't it be nice if you could weigh the pros and cons of particular parents when contemplating how to include them in your nuptial festivities? To some extent, blended families have given brides- and grooms-to-be a wider selection of choices. But as the ranks of stepparents grow, many couples are forced to ask themselves how they can avoid alienating, offending, or devaluing their various parental units. If you and your intended plan to say your vows under the watchful gazes of the standard complement of moms and dads, consider yourself lucky. Two moms and two dads can still seem like four too many parents when the going gets rough, but you can at least take comfort in the fact that the tasks they'll carry out before or on your wedding day are pretty well established.

When your parental dance card includes multiple moms and an abundance of dads, don't worry about what anyone else is going to think when you're assigning roles. Etiquette does not, in fact, dictate that mothers must be escorted in by ushers and that one dad must escort one daughter down the aisle. It's perfectly fine to have a dad and a stepdad do the escorting or to walk arm-in-arm with both of your parents. A MOG can escort the groom and give him away, if that's what everyone wants. You can even make up roles for your parents to play if you want to give them something to do during the ceremony. The sky's the limit here, though you may not want to mention that to your folks if you'd rather they just sit down, shut up, and watch the proceedings.

Mothers on both sides of the aisle may offer to help with any and all planning. This can be wonderful or terrible, depending on whether or not the moms decide to overstep their bounds. All moms, whether they be bio-moms or stepmoms, should be included in all appropriate prenuptial parties. It's usually the moms who whip up lists of the names and address of those people who simply must be invited. When guest counts are limited by necessity or by choice, moms may feel offended or even wonder whether their counterparts are getting preferential treatment. The easiest way to avoid potential family feuds is to put MOBs and MOGs in touch with each other ASAP. They can then discuss their dresses, invitees, the ceremony decor, and everything else without turning you and your intended into unwilling middlemen. Theknot.com/moms is one of the few online resources for mothers and by far the most comprehensive.

Ideally, MOBs are right up there with MOHs in terms of helpfulness. They scout for possible ceremony and reception locations, help brides choose their wedding gowns, field questions from family, talk brides-to-be down when they're threatening to cancel the whole shebang, collect important addresses, and attend fittings with those grown-up women who will always be their little girls. They may also book a block of rooms at a local hotel, write checks to vendors, keep track of RSVPs, and greet guests before the ceremony. After the vows have been said, they'll usually stand in a place of honor in the receiving line. Go back a couple of decades, and you'll discover that MOBs were also responsible for buying their daughters' wedding night lingerie. Just be glad that no one does that anymore.

In the past, the MOG's responsibilities were limited to planning and paying for the rehearsal dinner, compiling a list of groom's-side invitees, and getting her butt to the church on time. These mothers of sons are now taking a more active role in the wedding planning process. Being that the question of who pays for what is no longer as cut-and-dried as it once was, you may be pleasantly surprised to discover that your MOG wants to make a generous donation to your wedding coffer. Traditionally, these gals deferred in all things to the MOB, but this isn't 1965, and it's now socially acceptable for everyone to have their say, for better or for worse. Mother-son dances are now a fairly standard part of receptions. MOGs often feel left out, so consider asking for her input or inviting her to help you shop. Or just ask her if there is anything she'd like to do—it's a great way to win in-law brownie points!

Dads—like grooms, best men, and groomsmen—tend to have it pretty dang easy. They can whip out their checkbooks or not and make toasts or not. Sometimes they dance with their daughters, and sometimes they give sage advice to their sons. They stand in the receiving line and chat up the guests. The fact that this role isn't well defined (case in point—Theknot.com/dads currently redirects to the moms content) means that you can make things up as you go along. The FOB is usually expected to write checks, rent the right tux or buy the right suit, and walk his little girl down the aisle. As for FOGs, they typically work with MOGs to think of far-flung relatives to invite, pay for some or all of the upcoming honeymoon, and make some toasts. They can join MOGs in escorting grooms down the aisle. In fact, dads can do anything moms can do if they're up for it and you'd like their help. There's no reason to view fathers as ATMs graying at the temples.

Involved parents add nothing but joy to the wedding planning process—provided they don't become overbearing. If you ask them nicely to give you a hand, chances are they're going to do everything in their power to make you happy. So when you're picking out gifts for your attendants, give a thought to all your many moms and dads. Even if they don't play a particularly large part in your nuptials, they're still a part of your life. The same gifting guidelines that apply when you're shopping for your guys and your gals apply when you're looking for a little something for your MOBs, MOGs, FOBs, and FOGs.

Unexpectedly Isolated

Just because someone is given a role doesn't mean they can play the part well. Once you've chosen the attendants who will eventually stand with you while you're blissfully lost in the process of getting hitched, you may be dismayed to discover that they have no intention of helping you fold programs or address invitations. Their apathy may even extend to the procurement of dresses or suits, shocking as that may seem to you and your SO. Your first impulse will likely be to express your ire as delicately as possible, but passive-aggressive e-mails linking to sites like Badbridesmaid.com or the "Bridesmaids and Beastmen" section of Etiquettehell.com aren't going to make much of an impact on someone who doesn't feel invested enough in your day to get involved on a practical level. Sending the Maidzilla quiz at Beachbride2be.com/page25.html would also be a bad idea. Your second impulse may be to "fire" the offending attendants and be done with them.

However you decide to respond to your apathetic attendants, try to quell your annoyance and irritation. Many brides- and grooms-to-be are surprised to discover that their maids and men have no actual ethical or legal obligation to do anything outside of donning the right duds and showing up on the right day. Sites like Weddingchannel.com, which features lengthy guidelines for wedding party members, would have you believe that attendants are honor-bound to spend hundreds or even thousands of dollars and to host numerous parties. It's even become somewhat de rigueur for organized brides-to-be to hand their bridesmaids long lists of duties months before the culmination of the festivities. But the fact is that as nice as lavish showers and an extra pair of hands can be, attendants have lives, too. Before you give anyone a nuptial pink slip, let them know how their attitude of indifference has hurt your feelings. You may be surprised to find out that your BMs and GMs are keen to help but don't know how, or that they don't have the time or the money to meet what they believe are your expectations. Gently set everyone straight, accept that some people aren't that into weddings, and look for help in other quarters.

As for firing attendants, your power to banish people from your wedding should be used only as a last resort. Criminal behavior, indiscretions of the naughtier sort, and outright cruelty can all be fire-worthy offenses. But know that letting go a bridesmaid or groomsman will more than likely result in the end of a friendship or strained familial interactions for years to come. If your only beef is not getting the planning support you need or the prenuptial parties you were hoping for, find help elsewhere. As for the parties, it may be time to consider hosting a no-gifts, coed stag-and-hen bash with your intended.

Things get thornier when it's your folks who aren't stepping up to the plate. You may not even understand the full scope of your own expectations with regard to your parents until they aren't fulfilled. The stereotypical tear-filled dress fittings with mom or deeply emotive talks with dad may be ingrained in your vision of a "perfect wedding," and now you're starting to realize that your parents are just not that kind of people. After all, this isn't the 1950s, and there is a good chance that you live nowhere near your folks. They may not even live near each other! Before you let hurt feelings lead you down a road you probably don't want to take—no, you can't fire parents, but you sure as hell can try—take a few deep breaths and give your forebears the benefit of the doubt.

Share your feelings with your mom and dad. Help them understand that their attitude is putting a damper on your prenuptial bliss. Once they get it, your relationship at this emotionally tumultuous time of your lives will probably change. You may end up giddily skipping from shop to shop with your mom and enjoying those coveted long chats with your dad. Or you may discover that your parents are more interested in making sure that the bills are paid than in providing any useful input about color schemes or the guest list. You should prepare yourself to adjust your expectations, especially if the parent-child bond hasn't been particularly tight for the past few years. Sometimes weddings will bring people together, and sometimes they won't. If you're hoping that yours will provide you with a means of familial reconciliation, don't bank on it. Check out Conflict911.com, and address long-standing family issues in a nonnuptial context.

Women and, to a lesser extent, men are conditioned from birth onward to think of their eventual nuptials in terms of the help they'll get, the people who will cry tears of joy, the sage advice they'll receive, and the feelings of togetherness that will blossom as the wedding draws ever nearer. The problem is that these ideas are constructs that belong in the same file as the myth of the perfect prince on his white horse and the wedding where absolutely nothing goes wrong. Real life may or may not mirror the myths, but people are people. Your relationships will likely unfold as they always have. Helpful friends will be helpful, sweet in-laws will be sweet, and cranky relatives will be cranky. Express your expectations in no un-certain terms, take what you can get, forgive others their faux pas, and you'll be a happier newlywed for it.

Share a Link with the Ladies

- A-bridesmaid.com
- Allaboutshowers.com/bridal
- Bachelorette.com
- Blissweddings.com/wedding_planner/bridesmaid-guide.pdf
- Bridal-showers.net
- Bridalshowergamesatoz.com
- Bridesmaid-gifts.com
- Bridesmaidaid.com
- Bridesmaidessentials.com
- Chicblvd.com/wedding/bridesmaid_guide/birdesmaid _guide.html (not a typo)
- Ebridalshowers.com
- Maidofhonoradvice.com
- Theknot.com/moms
- Wedding-guide.org/bridesmaids.asp

Get the Guys Online

- Adventurebachelorparty.com
- Bachelorblowout.com
- Bachelorparty.com
- Bachelorpartytips.com
- Blissweddings.com/library/toasts_engine.asp
- Ehow.com/articles_5166-groomsmen.html
- Groomsmen.com/groomsmen.html
- Groomsmen411.com/groomsmen-advice.html
- Soverywrong.com
- Thebestman.com
- Thebestmanspeech.com

Find Gifts for Your Gals . . .

- Americanbridal.com/bridgif.html
- Goweddinggifts.com/bridesmaid-gifts.html
- Idaclaire.com
- Mybridesmaidsgifts.com
- Shoploveme.com
- Sistersylvie.com
- Thepashminastore.com
- Weddinghankies.com

- Weddingish.com

- Weddingstand.com

. . . Or Gifts for the Groomsmen

- Cufflinksdepot.com

- Eflasks.com

- Flaskshop.com

- Groomsmen.com

- Groomstand.com

- Mygroomsmengifts.com

- Pubsignstore.com

- Steakbrands.com

Chapter 5
Your Wedding, Your Way

A great-looking wedding starts with a few good ideas. Where do good ideas come from? Sometimes they originate in the heart, sometimes they originate in the head, and sometimes they originate on the pages of other people's blogs and websites. Even the most original ideas were inspired by something someone saw or heard. Take, for example, the Tiffany-blue wedding. The first person ever to base their nuptial colors on the iconic blue box had a good idea. Tiffany's provided the seed of inspiration, but that doesn't mean that first Tiffany-blue wedding was anything less than original. If you put your own unique spin on the Tiffany-blue wedding, that can be original, too.

Why all the talk of originality? Brides- and grooms-to-be spend a lot of time and energy looking for the right colors, the right themes, and the right stuff because they want their nuptial celebrations to be in some way representative of their personalities and interests. People who have well-defined likes and dislikes can turn to their preferences without ever doubting that they'll be anything but happy with the results. When blue and silver are your favorite colors, it makes perfect sense to use them as your jumping-off point in the planning process.

Some people don't have a favorite color—or a favorite season, sport, historical period, holiday, or hobby. Maybe you're just not that into butterflies, snowflakes, Victoriana, or country living. There's always flowers and lace, but both get old fairly fast when you're thinking about how you're going to embellish your tabletops, spruce up the walls, and outfit your wedding party. It's easy to get discouraged when you're trying to make what you and your sweetie consider to be fairly important decisions and nothing is coming to mind. Don't get discouraged—being original does not have to mean plucking ideas out of thin air.

Back in the day, choosing the matrimonial decor was a lot simpler. Your wedding was a reflection of your parents' tastes and your social class. If your family wasn't in the upper echelon, sisters and aunts would get together to slap some tulle and ribbon on the walls of your home or the VFW hall. If you were some sort of debutante, the decorations got fancier and the venues got more expensive. You gave out some Jordan almonds and tossed a modest bouquet. It's not that people didn't want choices, but rather that no one had yet thought to market personalized wine labels, flameless tea lights, or heart-shaped measuring spoons.

Choice is definitely a good thing, but with so much to choose from, zeroing in on that perfect color combo or theme is going to take time and research. You can draw a complete blank in the early days of your engagement and still end up with a wedding that looks like a million bucks. Patience and persistence will be your two best friends for a while, because you're going to be doing a lot of browsing until you figure out just what sort of wedding you'd really like to have. Luckily, scoping out wedding swag can be fun; when you're not drooling over really amazing floral arrangements, you can laugh at the atrocities on sites like Stupidweddingcrap.com.

Your first two stops should be Flickr.com and Images.google .com. Search for "weddings" or "wedding reception" with or without quotes, and you'll be in wedding voyeur heaven. Try some variations like "purple wedding" or "modern wedding" to narrow your results, but don't expect that these pics will be the antidote to indecision.

You may start your hunt for the perfect table settings, reception decor, and stuff for your ceremony on sites like Brides.com because that's where your search parameters take you. It probably won't be long, however, until you discover that it's a lot more satisfying to see the same colors and products in snapshots taken by guests, coordinators, and site managers at actual weddings. Try searching for the same stuff on Flickr.com. Even the flimsiest stemware and the gaudiest seat covers look great in pictures taken by pro photographers with specialized lighting and expensive image-editing software. When something looks good under crappy lighting conditions in a slipshod snapshot, you can bet it will look even better in person.

Mind Your Themes and Hues

After looking at hundreds of pictures of other people's weddings, you may start to wonder what exactly a theme is in the context of matrimony. When two people love something almost as much as they love each other, they often choose to make that thing the focal point of their ceremony and/or reception decor. Budgetdream weddings.com does a good job of bringing together items suited to certain themes, which means that you can get a sense of how colors and products come together without clashing. Wedthemes.com outlines the basic components of themes, from "Artists of the world" to "Tiptoeing through the tulips." Take2weddings.com/themes/default.asp outlines your basic Star Trek– and biker-themed weddings. Some of the themes you'll encounter will definitely be on the lame (or just plain weird) side, but there's a lot to be said for figuring out what you don't like.

Charity-themed weddings are slowly catching on, though they're not particularly popular and consequently don't get a lot of play in most online planning guides. You can learn how to plan a wedding that benefits one or more animal organizations at Ehow.com/how_2030218_plan-wedding-benefit-animal-organization.html. If puppies and kitties aren't your thing, you can adapt most of the eHow info by choosing a human or environmental charity. You can make donations in your guests' names in lieu of favors and ask guests for donations in lieu of gifts. The hardest part is working the theme into your decor, though some charities will provide you with personalized favor cards—see examples at Diabetes.org/support-the-cause/make-a-donation/wedding-favors.jsp.

Some brides- and grooms-to-be have strong ties to their cultural heritage and transform their family histories into unexpectedly compelling themes. There's no shame, however, in borrowing from other traditions if you come from a family full of mutts (what's the best way to indicate you're 1/16 Egyptian) or think the wedding traditions of your predecessors rather odd. Perhaps your family hails from Sudan, but you have no desire to burn seven broomsticks. Or you're Hungarian and have no inclination to be escorted to your ceremony in an elaborately painted cart. Have a look at World weddingtraditions.com, a site that outlines cultural and ethnic wedding traditions from all over the globe. You could do worse than to plant a pair of pine trees like some Norwegians do!

Green—as in ecological, not Kermit—weddings are also on the

Jeanette Inadvertently Went Green

"We weren't particularly focused on being green and never really considered it as a theme, but our wedding wound up being low-impact nonetheless. All the leftover food was carted home by my family instead of being tossed out. They had a second party later that night since everyone was already around and they had plenty on hand to eat. My mom and Chris's aunt took home all of the centerpieces that didn't go home with other guests. Mom was hoping to reuse some of the silk flowers when outfitting my sister's wedding, and I'm talking about flowers that had already been used in a friend's wedding! The decorations that weren't part of the hall itself were donated to a church group, which was fine by me.

"As far as the dresses were concerned, one of my bridesmaids got her dress early enough to wear to her prom before wearing it in the wedding. In fact, she loved it so much she'll probably end up wearing it again. Another bridesmaid donated her dress for my wedding along with the dress I wore in her wedding to a charity drive at the school where she teaches. Most importantly, we had the wedding and the ceremony in one place, so no one had to drive too much, and a lot of my guests carpooled, which helped even more. I also tried to limit my guest list—mostly for budgeting purposes—but it did mean that we didn't have fifty people crisscrossing the country in planes.

"Even though it totally wasn't intentional, you could say we did a good job being green. I think that most lower-cost weddings are probably going to err on the green side, because there is just no room in the budget for anything disposable!"

rise. It isn't always easy to go green because so much wedding swag is considered disposable, and the lack of instant gratification turns some couples off. As much as you're doing for the earth by buying biodegradable bamboo dinnerware made by Bambuhome.com and serving a locally sourced, organic vegetarian meal, it can be dismaying to know that your guests may not be able to guess your "theme." Nonetheless, Portovert.com is just one of the many sites dedicated to introducing brides- and grooms-to-be to nuptial products and services that are as responsible as they are lovely.

Of course, there's nothing wrong with choosing straight-up marriage as a wedding theme. The tulle and the ribbons that made the weddings of yesteryear so delightful are still plenty pretty. Weddings with narrowly defined themes usually come complete with a rather limited range of color choices. Wedding-themed weddings, on the other hand, can be as colorful or monochromatic as you'd like.

> ## Jeanette's Challenge: Incorporating Her Man's Tartan into the Decor
>
> "Picking the right colors to match the tartan was about as annoying as you could get. The site we eventually bought this surprisingly expensive fabric from was nice enough to sell small samples of the material so we could see it in person. The samples weren't free, but they were cheap. Making this particular tartan a part of our color scheme meant that we either had to go with the dullest wedding colors ever, a patriotic theme, or colors usually associated with Christmas. We ended up going with Christmas colors and toned down the green as much as we could. Thankfully, I don't think anyone even made the connection between our colors and the holiday."

This is obviously the point at which you're going to want to think long and hard about whether you have a favorite color. If the answer is no, you can find the colors you *prefer* easily enough using a photograph, piece of artwork, or movie still you really like. Grab a snapshot of it or download it, then upload it to Flickr and paste the pic's URL into the box at www.Degraeve.com/color-palette. The site will generate a custom color palette that might just provide you with the inspiration you're looking for.

Nailing down your wedding colors is particularly important because you can't sit down with a florist, baker, or reception-space decorator for a meaningful conversation until you have. Ask yourself whether you prefer bold, primary colors or soft pastels. Take a gander at your closet—your black-and-white wardrobe may give you a window into your partialities. Your favorite flower or gemstone can form the heart of your scheme. Or take a look around your house or apartment, because the objects and artworks that attract you can provide you with a blueprint of your likes and dislikes. Whether your favored style is quirky, funky, traditional, girlish, intellectual, or sophisticated, there is a color scheme that will complement it.

Go with your gut. Just because everyone you know is expecting you to go with brown and gold because you are known far and wide as the brown-and-gold gal does not mean you cannot, just this once, give in to your secret love of mint green. Sign up for a free account from Colorschemer.com/schemes to search through user-generated palettes by keywords like "vintage," "soothing," "romantic," and "French." Think up a keyword that describes your simmering wedding vision and someone out there has probably created a palette for it.

When you have a rough idea of the colors you might like to incorporate into your wedding, don't get too matchy-matchy in your mind. Apple green is a lovely hue, but too much of it will grate on the nerves of even the most color-starved guests. Think of accent colors that could complement your main choices, and ask yourself how you could use them in a bouquet, centerpiece, or attendant ensemble. You can learn about color theory and color harmony at Colormatters.com/colortheory.html, a site that explains why some colors just look right when placed side by side. If that's too technical for you, the app at Wellstyled.com/tools/colorscheme2/index-en.html lets you scroll through scientifically harmonious color combos.

If you're unwilling to experiment with colors, vary shades or tones until you find two or three that flatter one another unexpectedly. You'll know you've hit on a spectacular combo when your colors come together effortlessly. Don't worry, however, if your colors don't seem to mesh. You can incorporate as many colors as you like into your matrimonial palette, but choose one to be your main hue. That one color should appear in most of your decorations, flowers, and apparel, meaning it should be identifiably dominant. Your other color choices can be incorporated into your wedding celebration however you see fit.

The Sincerest Form of Flattery

Don't worry too much about the ethics of "borrowing" ideas from wedding blogs and websites. There's no reason to feel weird. After all, that's what they're there for! Even if you went so far as to plagiarize an entire wedding from start to finish, it's pretty unlikely that you're going to run into the person whose nuptials you appropriated or that an account of your ceremony and reception will get back to them. For the most part, the creative and talented people who post pictures of unusual wedding finds and descriptions of entire weddings are sharing their finds because they want to inspire brides- and grooms-to-be to step away from the matrimonial mold. In the online wedding world, most sites can be crammed into three basic categories: retail, advice, and inspiration. Inspirational sites can be divided into two more categories: stuff and design.

The majority of those in the stuff category highlight unique swag in a context-free way. One or more times per day, sites like Weddingbee.com and Manolobrides.com—whose editor, Never teh Bride, happens to be the author of this very book—will present you with another cute set of hand-drawn invitations, another gravity-defying cake from a master baker, another elegant gown from a little-known designer, or another set of gorgeous gold bands. The recommendations may just scratch the surface of the product or vendor highlighted, but there will almost always be a link to the item or service in question. Sites that talk about stuff (and are searchable by keyword or tag) can help brides- and grooms-to-be looking for a perfect cake knife set or groomsmen gift, because the articles and posts tend to be specific.

Design sites—like Ohjoy.blogs.com/my_weblog/here_comes_the _bride and Stylemepretty.com—take inspiration to the next level by putting their finds together in an organized and aesthetically pleasing way. If you're wondering how your chosen colors are supposed to come together gracefully when they seem so dang different, look no further. It's here that you're going to see stunning collages of decorative items, clothing, venues, and just about everything else associated with weddings. Perusing any sites that focus primarily on event design will help you get a feel for how colors and patterns work together within the context of an actual event.

Being that most people are engaged for eight to fourteen months, you'll probably have more than enough time to shop even if you give yourself a whole month to acquaint yourself with the many matrimonial muses that call the Internet home. Should you begin to feel like a plagiarist because you just can't stop pulling ideas off the web, keep telling yourself that you're putting your own spin on them. People have been tying the knot for thousands upon thousands of years—you can only get so original before you realize that your innovative notions regarding nuptials have probably already occurred to others.

Folders Within Folders

Keeping track of the hundreds of totally sweet links you're going to find can be a real hassle, as your Bookmarks (in Firefox and Safari) or Favorites (in Internet Explorer) menu will soon become almost impossible to navigate without the help of a magnifying glass and a pair of tweezers. When you're still in browsing mode and unsure of where your tastes will ultimately take you, folders labeled with categories like "Centerpieces," "Flowers," "Gowns," and the like can ensure you don't lose a single link. But if you stumble across more stuff you like than stuff you dislike, even your tagged folders can get crowded. Differentiating between what you really, really like and what you just sort of like is the answer.

Whether you employ a complicated system of subfolders (Reception stuff ⟶ Centerpieces ⟶ Candles ⟶ Tea lights) or distinguish your favorite links with asterisks (***Mike's Amazing Cakes***), you will never experience the horror of discovering you've misplaced the URL for round mirror tiles that are not only the perfect size but also half price. When you're ready to start shopping and making reservations, create a new set of folders so you can easily review what you've purchased and reserved thus far. Buying online means that everything from flatware to favors is going to spend some time in transit, and it will be a lot easier to coordinate colors and styles if you can go back and review what you've bought without having to do an exhaustive search.

Putting all of your links in the same place will save you time and jog your memory when you have trouble bringing up a mental image of your upcoming wedding. Bookmark everything that excites you, even if it's too expensive to contemplate buying or really doesn't go with anything else you like. Sites that feature products and services that are inaccessible to you for whatever reason can serve as a blueprint you use when you're shopping elsewhere or attempting to produce a stellar DIY creation. If you can't find a cheaper alternative or make it yourself, you'll likely find a similar version somewhere else. You may have hundreds of sites bookmarked by the time your wedding day rolls around, and each and every one of those will have provided you with a wealth of ideas.

Catch Spam as Catch Can

If you're planning to change your name once you're hitched or you want a fresh e-mail address, feel free to use your current one to sign up for the ubiquitous wedding site mailing lists. But if you're attached to your current address or need to continue using it for business purposes, it's high time you created a spam catchall e-mail address. As soon as you sign up with any of the big wedding sites, major online registries, or national chain dress shops, they turn around and sell your info to direct mailing companies. Avoiding the deluge is close to impossible because so many sites won't let you look at their really juicy content until you've told them who you are, where you live, and what kind of wedding you're planning to have.

Welcome to the world of unsolicited matrimonial mail; it's going to be a long time before the spam stops rolling in. You may have already noticed the flyers from bridal shops, bridal expos, and vendors showing up in your real-life mailbox each day. Other than creating a PO box that you use for the duration of your engagement or using a fake address each time you sign up with a site, there's little you can do to stop the influx, so get your recycling bin ready, because some newlyweds are still fielding adverts and shady contest notifications a year or more after becoming husband and wife.

The same spam delivered daily by the mailman is probably already flooding your inbox, and if it isn't, it will be soon. Sign up for an account with Gmail, Hotmail, or Yahoo! and use that address as your default when registering with wedding websites and wedding retailers. Gmail is a particularly good choice for brides- and grooms-to-be because it has searchable folders and is fairly good at rooting out what is obviously spam-with-a-capital-S. Wedding spam occasionally proves useful; adverts for under-the-table erectile dysfunction medicines seldom do. Once the wedding is over and you've settled into married life, you can forget all about the e-mail address you created while it continues to collect unwanted e-mails for all of eternity.

The wedding industry is not only huge, it's also hugely competitive, with a vast sea of vendors competing to attract the attention of a limited number of brides and grooms each year. Add to that the unsavory companies who want nothing more than to capitalize on the trusting nature of people delirious with love, and you inevitably end up struggling to tell the scammers from the legitimate service providers. You can bypass the baddies by following this simple rule: When in doubt, toss it out, whether that means throwing out a piece of potential junk mail or hitting Delete. There will always be another videographer or bakery looking for your business, but once a time-share outlet or marketing firm discovers you're a receptive customer, there is no going back.

As for your phone number, keep it to yourself. Even if you don't particularly mind getting scads of real and virtual junk mail, giving one company permission to contact you via phone is like giving every company on the planet permission to reach out and touch you. The sale and exchange of telephone listings is a big business, and no one wants to receive telemarketing calls 24/7, but that's exactly what you'll set yourself up for if you fill in your real phone number when confronted with the forms you'll encounter at expos, in stores, and on websites. Unless you like being woken up at seven on a Sunday by someone telling you that you've just won a Caribbean vacation, (123) 456-7890 should be your phone number for the foreseeable future.

A Promise Is a Promise

People who haven't seen the inside of a school building in decades occasionally have nightmares about arriving at an exam only to realize that they're entirely unprepared . . . not to mention naked. As scary as that sounds, realizing that you've forgotten to write your vows on the night before your nuptials is even worse. It reads like something that could only ever happen in a cheesy romantic comedy—panic and hilarity ensue as the groom-to-be searches frantically for a scrap of paper and a pen—but you'd be surprised how many people intentionally and unintentionally put this relatively simple task off until the last minute instead of taking care of it early on.

If you and your intended have decided to exchange some form of personalized statement—vows or otherwise—during your ceremony, you should start thinking about your contribution right about when you begin contemplating color choices. Even individuals who get a real kick out of playing with words can find themselves struggling with writer's block when it comes time to compose what will be a very public declaration of love. Your theme and decor will set the tone of your wedding, which means that you should consider the relationship between them and your words when you start mulling over what you might like to say to your sweetie.

Lighthearted and silly vows work best at lighthearted and silly weddings. Really serious, straightforward, and romantic vows will work best at elaborate, formal affairs. That's not to say you should limit yourself, but you may want to consider leaving the sci-fi references out of your ceremony unless you've decided that a Star Trek, Star Wars, or Dr. Who wedding is right for you. Then again, if your guests aren't going to get the references anyway, why worry? Be aware, however, that some religious marriage rites don't allow the couple to interject their own sentiments into the ceremony. If you have your heart set on saying your piece but your religion doesn't allow it, get on the mic at the reception.

Vows should come from the heart, but feelings don't always translate very well into plain language. Plus, writing can be a real chore—there are plenty of people in this world who would rather paint a fence than write an essay. Luckily there is help online for everyone, from the tongue-tied to those who simply hate to pick up a pen, in the form of sample vows (like Myweddingvows.com) and how-tos (like Theweddingnetwork.com.au/writingvows.htm), as well as quotes and verses you can throw in for added oomph.

You Really Haven't Already Won

That Caribbean vacation? The vacation itself is legit—if you want to consider a three-day long excursion with massive restrictions and no airfare included legit—but you have to sit through what amounts to a high-pressure cookware or time-share demonstration to get it. Sometimes the payoff is a $500 shopping spree . . . that can only be redeemed at the company's own website which is full of overpriced, crappy stuff and charges insane amounts for shipping. Be wary if you get a call from someone telling you that you've won a contest, because what they don't tell you is that everyone who ends up on their lists is a "winner." And know that these companies change their names frequently because they tend to end up on the wrong side of BBB.org. If you "win" a contest you never entered, do yourself a favor and look up the business name on Ripoffreport.com. You may just save yourself a little aggravation and a whole lot of cash.

There's even a list of popular vow vocabulary at Electpress.com/ loveandromance/wvg-vow3.htm, just in case you find yourself at a loss for words.

It may help you to remember that your vows are basically an assertion of the emotions you feel, the stuff you plan to do when you're married, and what you promise to be as the years pass. Leave out anything embarrassing, personal, or otherwise inappropriate, and keep your vows under three minutes long. Your guests—as much as they love you—will thank you for your brevity.

Play with Color

- Bighugelabs.com/flickr/colors.php
- Blissweddings.com/wedding%2Dcolor%2Dpalette
- Brides.com/weddingstyle/receptions/colorstudio
- Colorhunter.com
- Colorschemer.com/schemes
- www.Degraeve.com/color-palette
- Weddingbycolor.com

Be Different

- Bondmag.net
- Earthfriendlywedding.blogspot.com
- Ecochicweddings.typepad.com
- Ethicalweddings.com
- Greatgreenwedding.com

- Handfasting.info
- Indiebride.com
- Offbeatbride.com
- Portovert.com

Be Traditional

- Buddybuddy.com/mar-trad.html
- Celtarts.com/WEDDING/traditions.htm
- Chcp.org/wedding.html
- En.wikipedia.org/wiki/wedding_traditions
- Gagirl.com/wedding
- Travour.com/weddings/world-wedding-traditions
- Victoriana.com/bridal/bridal-welcome.htm
- Weddingdetails.com/lore
- Weddings.pirate-king.com/wedcultures.htm
- Worldweddingtraditions.com
- Yourwedding101.com/ethnic-wedding-traditions

Let Others Inspire You

- Aboutweddings.com/realweddings
- Elegala.com/go/real.weddings
- Insideweddings.com/real-weddings

- Projectwedding.com/photo/browse

- Weddingannouncer.com/gallery

- Weddings.theknot.com/odb/Results.aspx

- Weddingstylemagazine.com/featured

Find Your Voice

- Brilliantweddingpages.com/couples/sample_vows.asp

- Elegantvows.com

- Marriagevowworkbook.com

- Myweddingvows.com

- Theknot.com/vows

- Weddingdialogues.com

- Weddings.about.com/od/yourweddingceremony/a/personalizevows.htm

Chapter 6
Money and Matrimony

Money comes just after love on the list of ingredients that make up a successful wedding. Without love, you haven't got a leg to stand on. Without money, your guests are going to get awfully hungry. Whether you plan to drop a cool $100,000 on your nuptials or you're dragging your best buds to the courthouse to act as your witnesses, someone is going to need to pay for something. You and the people who share your big day will probably need to eat at some point, no matter how lavish or thrifty you choose to be. Maybe you see getting married as the perfect excuse to spring for some new shoes or that debonair crystal-topped cane you've always wanted.

The cold, hard truth is that even the dreamiest, most romantic weddings are still backed by the power of the almighty dollar. In the movies, ceremonies and receptions just seem to happen—everyone gets a luxe matrimonial celebration because, heck, don't they deserve it? They're getting married, after all! Yes, it would be nice if everything unfolded so perfectly in real life, but in real life bills don't just pay themselves. The money comes in and the money goes out, and the smartest brides- and grooms-to-be keep track of (and probably contribute to) the flow.

This isn't particularly surprising, considering that the average groom is about twenty-seven years old and the average bride is somewhere around twenty-five. There's a good chance they're living together, and they've either pooled their finances or are sharing their expenses in an equitable fashion. Unless they're pursuing further education, school is nothing more than a distant memory, though the loan bills arrive on time once a month. If they're lucky, they have a little dough saved up for a rainy day and are making ends meet on a consistent basis.

You may have heard that the average cost of a wedding in the United States hovers somewhere around $20,000 to $30,000. To many, that figure sounds shocking, but think back for a moment to your grade school math classes and the lessons you learned about averages. Those numbers are tossed around in bridal magazines, books, and blogs, but sources are seldom cited. You can't be sure that they're not grouping together everything from the courthouse ceremonies that cost nothing more than the price of the license to the biggest multimillion-dollar events thrown by celebrities. The averages are furthermore skewed toward the prices in major cities, because of population density, and tend to include everything from the engagement rings to the honeymoon.

The prices break down a little something like this:

- 50 percent goes toward the reception and includes site fees, nonfloral decor costs, and the price of food and drinks.

- 10 percent goes toward all of your flowers, including those used decoratively at the ceremony and reception.

- 10 percent goes toward the cost of a gown, menswear rentals, and accessories.

- 10 percent goes toward your photographer.

- 7 percent goes toward your band or DJ and any musicians that play during the ceremony.

- 6 percent goes toward unspecified extras that are different for each wedding.

- 4 percent goes toward stationery costs, including STDs, invitations, and thank-you cards.

- 3 percent goes toward your wedding rings.

The best way to get a handle on the cost of wedding services and stuff in your area is to e-mail vendors and peruse products. The price breakdowns you encounter at sites like Bridal associationofamerica.com/Wedding_Statistics are educational, but the geographical location of your wedding is going to have a huge impact on the prices you encounter. How much does the "average" wedding in your area cost? Plug your zip code into Costofwedding. com to find out how much your neighbors and coworkers may have spent on their nuptials, but take the figure the generator spits out with a grain of salt. That's not to say that $30,000 weddings aren't taking place all over, because they are. The difference is that while some people happen to have an extra thirty grand lying around, other people see that number everywhere they look and start planning around it.

It's not hard to see why—if you're told over and over again that weddings cost $40,000 in your area, you're going to assume that you need to spend that amount to make your wedding as beautiful and fun as it can be. That's the amount you'll budget for, and that's the amount you'll ultimately spend. Whereas five years ago, you would have balked at spending forty grand on anything other than the down payment on a house, it now seems like an entirely reasonable price to pay for a party.

There is no right or wrong where money and matrimony are

Christa Terry

The Assumptions Weddingchannel.com Made About Leah

"You put your budget into the site's calculator, and it slices it up based on an average percentage for each product and vendor category. It then gives you an easily editable budget based on those numbers—you can add and delete items, and the application updates your budget accordingly. That was nice.

"The suggestions you'd receive in response to your changes weren't always so fantastic. I didn't have much in the decoration budget slot because we were getting married in a castle, and the site suggested that we enlist the help of friends or family members who could loan us some decorations. That was sensible, but sometimes the suggestions seemed almost condescending or just plain sad. For instance, I stated on my budget that I wanted to spend less than $500 on my dress, and the suggestion I received basically read, 'Those expensive boutiques aren't for you, so perhaps you should look into finding a wedding dress in an alternate place.' What does that even mean?"

concerned. Admit that your budget is that big in some of the more progressive wedding forums, and the response you'll likely receive will be indignant at best. Ignore the haters. You shouldn't let anyone make you feel guilty for wanting to spend eighty thou on your wedding. And if your budget is relatively small, don't let all the "But it's your big daaaaay" hype discourage you from throwing the bash you can afford.

The first question most engaged couples ask when they stumble upon the usual sums is "Who the hell is going to pay for all this?" Thirty thou is an awful lot of cash for one day's worth of wedding, and not even an entire day at that! Sites like Ourmarriage.com/html/who_pays_for_what.html can give you an idea of who used to pay for what back when weddings were relatively simple affairs with cake and punch and gifts of shiny new toasters. If your parents or the parents of your intended have offered to foot the bill and they've given you a number to work with, it's time to whip up a budget.

If, however, all you've received are hearty congratulations, then you may need to come right out and ask whether your parents or other relatives plan to provide a little prenuptial assistance of the financial kind. It used to be that the FOB in tandem with the MOB automatically doled out the cash necessary to make their little

{80}

girl's dreams a reality. Those dreams were a lot less expensive than the dreams of today, and that's with inflation taken into account. When did some of the onus to pay for the wedding drop from harried parental shoulders? Probably about five minutes after tales of proud mamas and papas who took out massive loans to pay for their progenies' nuptials started hitting the newswires. Nowadays, it's common for the bride- and groom-to-be to take on some if not all of the responsibility for financing the wedding.

Whatever your monetary circumstances, embrace them. If money from Mommy and Daddy isn't forthcoming, try not to feel as if you're being robbed of your birthright. The misconception that everyone is having these ultraexpensive, fabulous, perfectly styled weddings can mess with your head and make you feel a little glum when you find out that you're going to have to depend on your own savings. If the bank account you share with your SO is bone dry, consider a prolonged engagement. You'll have the time you need to get your thrift on at sites like Stretcher.com and blogs like The simpledollar.com while you sock away mad cash.

The WIC knows that weddings are as emotionally taxing as they are expensive—in fact, it's banking on it. It's a double whammy that can easily become a recipe for disaster. Retailers love brides- and grooms-to-be who give themselves financial free rein because it's *their special day.* Of course it's your special day, but do you really want to be paying off that special day for the next five years because you decided to put your fairy-tale wedding on your credit card? Is realizing your nuptial vision worth knowing that your parents had to take out a second mortgage on their home?

You're likely planning your wedding online for a variety of reasons—make one of those reasons the fact that you can get married in the most expensive parts of the country using stuff you bought in the cheapest parts of the world. When you're in a brick-and-mortar store, you're a captive audience. Smart sellers hire persuasive retail assistants to make sure that customers who enter shops don't leave until their debit cards have seen some action. When you're sitting at your computer desk with a cup of coffee, there's no pressure to buy anything. If you browse with your budget open in another window, you'll know at a glance whether the deal in front of you is as good as it seems.

The Basics of Budgeting

Budgeting and thrift are not synonymous, so expel any visions of paupers from your mind. No matter how stacked your matrimonial coffer is, you're going to want to spend more money in some areas than in others, meaning that there's no reason to shop blindly. You may scoff at the idea of spending more than a thousand bucks on a cake or ten thousand to hire a photographer, even though you have enough cash to easily do both. Your preferences, your desires, and the amount you're willing to spend are all represented in a thorough budget, and you can get more for your money by paying attention to the numbers in front of you.

Keeping track of a budget can mean a lot of things. It might mean making a spreadsheet that tracks your wants and needs, the potential costs, the actual prices you paid, who you've paid so far, and how much you've spent altogether. Because so many vendors will ask you for checks rather than let you pay over the phone—archaic, yes—you should probably include check numbers in your spreadsheet so you can track your cash flow (i.e., balance your checkbook) more easily.

Look over the figures at Costhelper.com/cost/wedding/wedding.html before you start running numbers. The site lays out the general price ranges associated with everything from reception site rentals (the average hovers around $1,300) to officiant fees (expect to pay between $50 and $400) to the rehearsal dinner (anywhere from $30 to $70 per person is considered reasonable). Use the info you find there when you're deciding how much you think you'll allocate toward specific expenses, adjusting as necessary.

If having perfect prints is important to you, think about devoting more of your money to photography costs. On the other hand, if you're a total sucker for a good cocktail, put aside some extra cash to pay for a bartender who will astound your guests with signature drinks he designed just for you. The breakdown of costs described previously is nothing more than a recommendation based on the aforementioned averages. Clothes-crazy brides and grooms who consider themselves gourmands might choose to devote 90 percent of their $20,000 wedding budget to the finest apparel and just over 9 percent going toward the most luxurious food and libations for two. As for the leftover money, they'll use that to pay for the marriage license and courthouse fees at their elopement.

However you divvy up your dough (and seriously, you can divvy it however you like), you can keep an eye on all these numbers without resorting to some crazy envelope system, because the apps you seek are all online. Of course, not all budget tracking apps are created equal. The collection of data boxes at Foreverwed.com/ planner/weddingbudgetcheck.htm may tout itself as a wedding budget worksheet, but it's no more useful than a piece of lined paper. No, wait, that's doing a disservice to paper, which you can come back to repeatedly, reasonably sure that no one has erased what you've written while you were gone. When you navigate away from Foreverwed.com, your input disappears into the ether.

You'll be better off sticking to sites that have actual working calculators and are editable, like Ourdreamwedding.com/index .cfm?page=wedding_budget_form_1&crid=7. Partypop.com/budget _calculator.htm looks odd, but it's useful because it allows you to choose between basic, average, good, better, and best goods and levels of service for your wedding size, date, and location. While it won't let you keep track of any of your actual costs and the pricing seems to run a tad high ($683 for an average officiant?), the targeted recommendations the site displays next to your choices may just help you find your vendors. Being able to save your data online is also nothing to sneeze at, so don't automatically discount wedding tool sites that ask you to create an account, like Weddingwire.com.

If you feel a little uncomfortable inputting what amounts to an intimate survey of your nuptial finances into a website, you can always make your own budget in a document or spreadsheet. The upside is that the spreadsheet you create is fully customizable and is stored on your own computer instead of someone else's servers. You can track payments and create new expenses as you plan. The downside is that you'll have to look at sites like Foreverwed .com to get a handle on the costs you're facing and then input all of those costs into your spreadsheet. Most people use Excel for their spreadsheet needs, but if you don't have it, you can download what amounts to the exact same program at Openoffice.org for free. The premade wedding cost comparison and calculation spreadsheet at Weddingsaffordable.com/budgettool will work in either program and save you the trouble of typing up a lengthy list of expenses. If you happen to be a Gmail user, you can make a spreadsheet, edit it from anywhere, and share it with your sweetie at Spreadsheets .google.com.

Making a simple spreadsheet is easy . . . unless, of course, you've never made one before. To start, list the products and services you'll be spending money on in the leftmost column. The next column over is where you input your anticipated expenses in each area, and the column to the right of that is where you input your actual costs. Additional columns can be devoted to anything from deposits made to balances paid. Videos like the one found at Video.about.com/ weddings/Wedding-Budget-Spreadsheet.htm can help you familiarize yourself with the process. Or search for "wedding" and "budget" on YouTube, where you'll find a couple of spreadsheet tutorials along with a lot of emphatically presented advice that comes straight out of the mouths of actual brides.

Though you can make your budget as straightforward or as detailed as you like by simplifying categories or breaking them down into their component parts, most basic budgets are broken down like this:

{
Engagement party

Rehearsal dinner

Bridesmaid luncheon

Ceremony and officiant fees

Organist
}

{
Guestbook

RB pillow

FG basket

Dried petals

Ceremony decor

Other ceremony accessories (unity candle, programs, etc.)
}

{
Stylist

Manicure and pedicure

Bridal gown and alterations
}

Christa Terry

{
- Veil or headpiece
- Accessories and underthings
- Jewelry
- Shoes
- Groom's tux

{
- Stationery
- Postage
- Website
- Marriage license
- Wedding rings
- Attendants' gifts
- Parents' gifts

{
- Reception decor
- Seating chart and place cards
- Photographer
- Videographer
- Florist
- Caterer
- Baker
- Bartender
- Band or DJ

{
Transportation

Valet

Favors

Rental items

Gratuities

{ Honeymoon travel, accommodations, and extras

On the off chance that paper is actually your thing, there are printable budget worksheets all over the place that are pretty similar to the one you'll find at Stylishweddingideas.com/files/wedding -budget.pdf. Just hit up Google and search for the words "printable," "wedding," "budget," and "worksheet." Voila! You now have all the links you need to make a kickass budget, whether you want to save your digits on someone else's server so you can access them from anywhere, keep them locked up tight on your own computer, or put them in a three-ring binder.

Spending While Saving

You can budget without saving money, but you can't save money without budgeting. When you're dealing with limited resources, your budget basically forces you to set firm price caps, curb your spending, and get creative. It's a lot harder to go overboard when you know you have this much—and *only* this much—to spend on your flowers or the limo. You'll know how much you've spent and how much you have left at a glance, further minimizing the chances that you'll go on a spontaneous shopping spree with an already overloaded credit card.

Christa Terry

Cutting costs is no picnic, however, and many brides- and grooms-to-be find that saving money is a much more arduous task than planning the actual wedding. Receptions eat up most of the matrimonial money, high-profile wedding shops mark up their merchandise, and people have been taught that a wedding isn't a wedding without favors, tiered cakes, big poufy gowns, and fresh flowers. If you're serious about saving, you're going to have to adjust some of your expectations. You'll be no less married if you walk down the aisle carrying silk blooms—or nothing at all.

There are entire sites dedicated to budget nuptials, though you're usually not going to see them sitting pretty in the top ten results of a Google search. Cheap-chic-weddings.com (home of a rather well-known annual toilet paper wedding gown contest) is one resource that every bride- and groom-to-be can use. You don't have to be a Martha Stewart clone to make simple bouquets that save you hundreds, craft elegant centerpieces using stuff from the supermarket, or print your own wedding programs using templates like those at Weddingboutique.us/templates.html. Craftier brides- and grooms-to-be will feel more comfy over at Diybride.com, which has projects, guides, podcasts, and videos designed to aid those who'd rather make than buy. And there are savings suggestions on almost

Got Budget Woes Like Jeanette?

"I would have loved to find more sites sharing information pertinent to the weddings-on-a-budget crowd. Not everyone has $50,000 to spend on a wedding, and not everyone has the time, energy, or imagination to come up with ways to do everything on the cheap. I'm sure we could have done everything more cheaply, but I didn't have the resources I needed to make that happen. I wish, for example, that I'd found some ways to cut costs without actively slashing my head count, which was already limited.

"I wound up feeling like a lot of things came off as being too cheap, and that's a big part of why I wish I had come across more tips for making things feel like a million bucks while only costing a couple. Maybe I just didn't know where to look for that information, but I feel like lower-budget weddings are a lot more common now, so you would think that things like that would be a little more mainstream and a little easier to find."

every wedding site, though they can usually be whittled down to one piece of advice: Have a smaller, simpler wedding.

Trimming the guest list is indeed the easiest way to cut wedding costs, though many brides- and grooms-to-be find taking this step more difficult than nixing the top-shelf liquor. You may feel hugely guilty as you contemplate excluding certain people from your nuptial celebration, but try balancing your huge guilt against a huge bar tab, huge catering and cake costs, and the price of a huge reception hall. Choosing an off-season wedding date is another (less heartbreaking) way to cut costs, but don't risk cancellation by blizzard or tornado to save a few bucks if you're marrying in a locale known for its severe weather. There are off hours, too, meaning that a lunchtime wedding on a Sunday will be less expensive than a dinnertime wedding on a Saturday.

Retailers of mass-market noncustom wedding goods carry nearly the same stock when it comes to ceremony and reception goods, invitations, clothing, accessories, favors, and packaging, but their prices differ quite a bit. You can capitalize on that if you're patient. Just because you found the perfect flower girl basket or unity candle at one online shop doesn't mean you have to whip out your wallet to feel the immediate buzz of consumer satisfaction. When you have a real eureka moment, it's time to start scouring the Internet for alternate stores that carry the same items at lower prices and ship for free. Save the wallet-whipping for those moments in which you stumble upon a sale price that is too good to last or a one-of-a-kind accessory that is just too unusual to adequately replicate.

The raw materials of food and cake are cheap, but you pay a premium for the handiwork of caterers and cake designers. Slice and dice reception costs by having a buffet instead of a sit-down meal, serving brunch or lunch instead of dinner, and pairing pretty prop cakes (see 'em at Cakerental.com) with behind-the-scenes sheet cakes. Chow that's dropped off is cheaper than chow carried about on shiny platters by begloved waiters. Booze-free affairs are just as fun as lush events, but if you want to get your drink on, skip the bartenders and let people pour their own cocktails.

The sky's the limit when you're looking for ways to save. Shop around for the best prices—look at nonwedding retailers, check eBay and Etsy.com, and look on classified boards like Craigslist.com. You may find what you want for nothing at all on Freecycle.org, though you have to post a few offers before you can solicit specific items from other members. Lose the fluff—most wedding favors get thrown out. If you're not willing to pay full price for services rendered by expensive vendors, you can do it yourself, delegate the duty to someone who cares enough about you to do it right, or hire cheap labor in the form of college students or novices looking to pad their portfolios.

Whether your wedding's shaping up to cost a little or a lot, start comparing prices as early as possible, especially when it comes to vendor services that tend to be reserved well in advance. You may not know your final guest count or the specifics of what you want, but you can guesstimate. Check out sites like Decidio.com to find listings of all types of vendors in your wedding locale, and then get in touch with any that strike you as interesting. Tell them your anticipated wedding date, where the party is happening, how many people you expect, and the services you're looking for. Then ask them what services they offer, how much they charge, who does the work, and whether or not they deliver.

An e-mail to a vendor might read like this: *I'm getting married on the evening of March 20th of this year at Mulberry Mansion, and I anticipate 75 guests, including the wedding party and our officiant. We are looking for a baker who will provide us with an edible top tier on two tiers of decorated foam "cake" along with enough sheet cake to accommodate all of our guests. If you don't offer this type of service, do you have any other budget-friendly options? How much do you generally charge, and who actually creates and decorates your cakes? Also, do you deliver?*

If you feel weird tossing a big list of questions and demands at caterers, site managers, or print shops, remind yourself that you are, in essence, interviewing potential freelance employees. You can save time by creating a template e-mail for each service you need so you don't have to write the same information again and again and again. Feel free to knock vendors who are dismissive or elusive right off your list—they obviously don't want or need your business. Vendors who actually care about their customers are quick to reply, friendly, willing to answer your questions, and honest about their options and prices.

You can be as up front or subtle about your monetary concerns as you want when pricing vendors, but realize that your choice to lay your limits on the line will give them a chance to work with you to come up with lower-priced alternatives. Your offer may be low, but it's probably not the lowest number they've ever heard. And just because someone usually charges a thousand bucks for four hours of DJing doesn't mean that they'll necessarily be opposed to taking $650, especially if the wedding is taking place during the slowest part of the year.

Sometimes saving sucks, but remember that you're not alone. Nearly every newlywed couple has to operate under some form of limitation while planning, and yet they end up just as married as the handful of people for whom the sky is the limit. Some people have to cut their guest counts because of space constraints. Others are limited as to what they can wear, say, or do because there are strict codes of conduct in their faith. Still others have limited financial flexibility and have to work around it when making purchases and reservations.

The plain truth is that the WIC has spent millions in advertising dollars to convince brides- and grooms-to-be that they can throw rational economic thought out the window because they're only going to get married once. Put aside the statistics that say a lot of those guys and gals will be making a second or third trip down Matrimony Lane, and it still doesn't make sense for couples to go crazy with their cash. It doesn't matter how much money you have—let's say you do have all the dough in the world at your fingertips; do you really want to spend $5 for something that's worth, at most, two bucks when you can find it for $1.50 on sale?

Two simple rules will help you avoid almost all monetary pitfalls, whether you're planning your wedding or just living your life. The first is don't spend money you don't have. Credit card debt is becoming a national epidemic, and the unsecured loans you can get from lender outfits like Bridalloans.com amount to the same kind of liability. "In the hole" is not a great place to begin married life. The second? Never spend exorbitant amounts of dough on stuff that doesn't matter to you. Retailers, advertisers, and service providers should not have a say in where, when, or how you plan your wedding, no matter how hard they pressure you.

Create a Budget . . .

- Bridalinsider.com
- Bridallinks.com/planning.asp
- Brides.com/myweddingplanner/tools/budget
- Dressupyourwedding.com
- Ehitched.com/wedding_planning/create_budget_list.htm
- Money.ninemsn.com/saving-and-spending/tools/wedding-planner.aspx
- Numsum.com
- Ourdreamwedding.com/index.cfm?page=wedding_budget_form_1&crid=7
- Partypop.com/budget_calculator.htm
- Riwedding.com/wedding_worksheet.asp
- Stylishweddingideas.com/files/wedding-budget.pdf

. . . And Stick to It

- A-budget-wedding.com
- Brides.com/planning/budget
- Budgetdreamweddings.com/weddingplanning
- Cheap-chic-weddings.com
- Diybride.com
- Stretcher.com/menu/topic-r.htm#weddings
- Tenthousandonly.blogspot.com
- Thriftyfun.com/weddingsforless_1125.html
- Weddingsaffordable.com

Do Some Preliminary Pricing

- Bridepros.com
- Decidio.com
- Elegala.com
- Onewed.com/vendors.php
- Respond.com/weddings-and-events/browse-match.html
- Weddingsolutions.com/wed_reviews
- Weddingwire.com

Chapter 7
The Biggest Party You May Ever Plan

Unless you're planning to party down in your own backyard using all your own gear after you tie the knot, your reception is going to eat up a hefty chunk of your budget. Consequently, the cost of your postnuptial shindig can have a huge impact on how much money you can spend on everything else you want. In-demand venues book up fast, but that's not the only reason to make finding the right one a priority. The look and feel of your reception venue will also affect your final color choices, your decor preferences, and the mood of the event itself. For example, if you've always dreamed of getting married in one of the striking antique barns you found at Thebarnjournal.org/resource/event _barns.html, how likely is it that you're going to give out dainty art deco roses as favors?

But don't get ahead of yourself—have you even set a firm date? Weather patterns are pretty important, because climatic conditions have the power to make guests happy or tick them off. As beautiful as your favorite mountain chalet is during the height of blizzard season, your attendees may not appreciate having to trek up the side of a peak in driving snow. Outdoor venues and wintertime weddings do not mix, unless you're saying your vows someplace sunny. And that very same open-air spot can give your guests heatstroke in the height of summer if you don't provide relief in the form of shade, fans, and air conditioners running nonstop.

Look at Weather.com/activities/events/weddings/setthedate/index .html for a graph of average high and low temperatures for your wedding zip code. You can also explore precipitation trends and compare the climates of two locales. The people behind Bridal weather.com/OWWI_top.html will even track down the best dates weather-wise for your location—for a small fee, of course.

Once you know where and when you're having your reception, it's time to think about time. The romantic riverboat that looks so lovely all lit up at night may not be quite so beautiful under the sun's angry glare. The public garden that is so alive with birds during the daytime may attract the wrong sort of "wildlife" after dusk. If you're planning on partying the night away indoors, the numbers on the clock won't have as much of an impact on your festivities, but maybe you're a morning person. Perhaps you tend to prefer brunch over lunch. These are all things to think about.

Then there's scale. Fifteen guests plus a bride and a groom will fit comfortably in the back room of a restaurant or pub. Two hundred guests can spread out nicely in a country club ballroom. Know that there are benefits and drawbacks to celebrations of all sizes if you still haven't nailed down your guest list. A small reception allows you and your new spouse to enjoy some quality time with each of your guests in an intimate setting, whereas a large reception gives you the freedom to invite *all* of the people closest to you. However large or small your venue turns out to be, your guests are going to need more than a footprint's worth of room. Do everyone a favor and give them the space they need to schmooze, grab a bite, hit the bar, and shake their moneymakers.

When's the Big Day?

August could easily be called the month of marriage, as more people get married in August than in any other month. June comes in at a close second and was in fact the top marriage month for many a decade before being kicked out of the number one spot. Historically, June came out on top because the weather is fairly mild and because the Romans chose to honor Juno (the goddess of marriage, among other things) by getting hitched in droves during her month. But June's not the only month with scads of superstitions surrounding it, as is evidenced in this folksy rhyme:

> Married when the year is new, he'll be loving, kind and true.
> When February birds do mate, you will wed or dread your fate.
> If you wed when March winds blow, joy and sorrow both you'll know.
> Marry in April when you can, joy for maiden and for man.
> Marry in the month of May, and you will surely rue the day.
> Marry when June roses grow, over land and sea you'll go.
> Those who in July do wed, must labor always for their bread.
> Whoever wed in August be, many a change are sure to see.
> Marry in September's shine, your living will be rich and fine.
> If in October you do marry, love will come but riches tarry.
> If you wed in bleak November, only joy will come, remember.
> When December snows fall fast, marry and true love will last.

Some days are apparently better than others, too.

> Mondays for health,
> Tuesdays for wealth,
> Wednesday best of all,
> Thursday for losses,
> Friday for crosses,
> Saturday for no luck at all.

According to lore, the ideal wedding would take place on a Wednesday in November. The luckiest brides would encounter a lamb, a dove, a chimney sweep, and a black cat just before their ceremonies, which would of course take place on the rainiest days. If you want to plan a by-the-book wedding—where the book in question is a book of folklore—look no further than sites like Oldsuperstitions.com/wedding.html and Secular-celebrations.com/weddings/superstitions.htm.

Now ask yourself what sort of wedding venues speak to you and your future spouse. Do you picture yourselves saying "I do" under a starry, open sky? How about amidst priceless relics from a long-lost age? Forget the country clubs and look into parks, arboretums, and charter boats, or museums and mansions. Those spaces may be too predictable for you if you've always imagined yourself saying your vows under garlands of cobwebs and the watchful gazes of leering gargoyles. Don't discount wackier venues if that's what you're into. Your reception space is just as much a part of your decor as the centerpieces, which means that location really is a *big deal*.

Do you feel at ease when you're the one calling the shots? Then you may want to opt for a venue that doesn't have dedicated caterers, bakers, and decorators, whose repertoires may be more limited than you'd like. While some venues let you work with almost any vendor, others will demand that you use their in-house vendors or choose from their short list of "approved vendors." If you absolutely adore a venue, be prepared to balance your love of the location against your apathy toward its vendors. The freedom to choose your own vendors can sometimes be bought with hefty fees, but be prepared to get the stink eye from the managerial staff whose routines are being mucked up by your individuality.

Even if you're utterly sure that the answer you get will be no, ask for what you want when speaking to venues and vendors. Try aiming directly for managers and owners, because they're the ones who can satisfy your desires. Yes, some staffers will bend over backward to fulfill your requests, but they may be bound by company policies that limit their ability to give discounts and throw in extras. Rather than get these lackeys in trouble by asking them to do what they don't have the authority to do, hedge your bets and reach out to higher-ups right off the bat.

You can even make demands if you're ready to accept that the response you receive may be overwhelmingly negative. Venue owners, managers, and staff members—like all people whose livelihoods are inexorably bound to the WIC—have learned over time to bully brides- and grooms-to-be into making what they consider to be the right choices. It makes sense—they want you to spend as much money as possible for as little as possible. But technically, you're the boss, because you're the one paying the bills. Act just the tiniest bit entitled and you may find that you no longer have to deal with people desperately trying to get you to choose crystal over glass. They'll be able to sense that you're not going to budge.

If you push a little and a venue pushes back hard, it's time to move on. You don't need to be dealing with pushy people when you've got busybody relatives riding your butt and you're trying to figure out how to come in under budget. Outlining your specific needs does not make you a 'zilla. Sure, getting a great deal can mean clamming up when the hors d'oeuvres aren't exactly what you ordered, but you shouldn't settle for substitutes when you're dropping a great big wad of dough on your reception space, your menu, and your booze. You owe it to yourself to speak up when your expectations aren't being met. All business-savvy venues and vendors will hit you with the upsell, but the really good ones will do everything they can to make sure that you walk away from your wedding day completely satisfied.

Think of the reception venue amenities important to you. Do you want a built-in PA system so toasts will be heard over the hubbub of guests going for seconds at the buffet? Would you prefer a venue with a dedicated bridal chamber where you can change or relax a bit before hitting the dance floor? Will there be children in need of supervision and entertainment at your reception? Are you planning to incorporate lit candles into your decor? Creating a list of wants, needs, and wishes before you ever even talk to a potential venue rep can help you decide what questions you should ask. Don't hold back—there's almost nothing you can ask a manager venue or a vendor that they haven't heard before.

Knowing what kind of space you'd like to reserve, the number of guests you plan to wine and dine, and how fancy the shindig will be will help you get cracking on a task that brides- and grooms-to-be love to hate: the creation of the reception seating chart. This may seem like a duty that can be safely put off for another few months, but ask yourself whether you really want to scramble to put yours together two weeks before the wedding, when most of your RSVPs finally roll on in. Even if you're not entirely sure who will attend your nuptial affair, you can probably think of some people who should under no circumstances sit together and other people who will be really offended if you seat them separately.

If you create a really well-thought-out seating chart, no one will end up sitting alone at the unpopular table, which means that no one will feel left out. The usual mad dash for seats and eats will be a little less mad, if only because people will have to locate their names and table numbers on a lengthy list. Multicourse meals won't be too much of a burden on your waitstaff. And people generally like to know that they're still going to have a seat waiting for them when they return from a long trip to the bathroom.

Seating chart software turns a tedious task into a slightly less tedious task by ensuring that your kitchen table won't spend the next five months buried under varying configurations of paper slips bearing your guests' names. You can upload a guest list you create in Excel into most seating chart programs, sparing you the wrist cramps. Access to Toptableplanner.com costs a cool $20, but there's no software to download and you can rearrange your seating plan as often as you want to using a simple drag-and-drop interface. Perfecttableplan.com lets you seat guests and track their RSVPs, meal selections, and seating preferences, and once you've created a seating plan, you can check the male-to-female ratio, make sure that guests who should not be seated together are far apart, and track seatmate compatibility.

Standard etiquette rules suggest placing beloved relatives and friends at the tables closest to the newlywed's own seats, but that doesn't exactly work when you're closer than usual to your extended family. There's also the rule about seating people in alternating male and female patterns, but it's not really a rule at all. All that alternating testosterone and estrogen makes for a nice photograph, but your boy/girl seating chart may not sit well with gay couples, good friends of the same gender, or those invitees for whom "and guest" is a sibling, parent, or pal. The happy couple's folks are traditionally seated at the same table, but why tempt fate if there's tension there? The fact is that you have no control over whether guests will feel comfortable talking to one another. You can pair off people in similar professions or group people by age and interest, but after you've done your best, it's up to the guests themselves to make the chitchat.

To please 90 percent of your guests, put two couples and four singles at each table. Make sure that each guest at a specific table knows at least one other guest at the same table. Make it two or three other guests if you can, but aim to combine cliques so everyone invited to your wedding has a chance to make a connection with someone new. Kids should sit with their parents, and you should populate any tables that include children with people who can tolerate them. Be sure to have your finalized seating arrangements printed up in legible lettering so guests don't have to grab for their bifocals. Plenty of online printers—like Lisaselegantthings.com and Calligraphia.com, for instance—create unambiguous and readable charts.

For civility's sake, do not seat all of your single relatives and friends at one table because you feel like playing matchmaker. It won't work. Weddings can be painful for those single people who don't really want to be single and for people who have recently ended relationships. The table of alternating unacquainted male and female guests without dates or wedding rings screams single, so don't think you're going to make five matches made in heaven at a ten-person table. It happens in the movies—it doesn't happen that way in real life. In real life, it's nothing short of embarrassing.

Of course, if the whole idea of telling grown-up people where they ought to sit makes you a little uncomfortable, feel free to assign tables but not seats, or to nix the chart altogether. Free-for-all seating works best at smaller receptions where a buffet meal will be served. Be ready for some confusion as guests scan the room for table numbers and place cards, and then be prepared to see people mingling at will during the whole of the evening. You may want to keep an eye on any attendees who don't know anyone except for you and your spouse. If you see someone sitting alone, do the right thing and chat with them for a minute or two before introducing them to that one friend of yours who can get along with just about anyone.

As an aside, you can save some dough without sacrificing quality *or* trimming your guest list by holding your ceremony and reception at the same site. This will necessitate your finding a venue with space enough for a ceremony and an officiant to perform the rites, but weigh that against how out-of-control the required donations and officiant fees at houses of worship can get. Be aware that some venues will charge you extra if you're also using the space for a rehearsal, but you may be able to avoid paying by staging your run-through during off-peak hours. And there are even some venues that will charge you to move chairs and tables around. Ask if you can assign helpful loved ones to the task instead of using venue staff. The worst thing they can say is no, and the added fees will probably still be cheaper than the cost of saying your vows in a different location.

Fabulously Prefabricated

Venues tend to be pricey, and refreshments come at a premium when they're being prepared by a professional catering staff. The average reception hall will run you about $1,300—a figure that may or may not include the space itself, tables and chairs, linens, and tableware. All in all, that doesn't sound too bad until you consider that you may also be paying out of pocket for parking, decorations, waitstaff, liability insurance (like that offered at Wedsafe.com/event -liability-insurance.html), or security personnel required by the venue itself. If you're set on a certain venue, there's usually no way to get around those costs. Still, it's nice to know where your money's going when you could have used that cash to pay off a chunk of your student loans.

Before you ever dream about the ultimate space, picture the ultimate reception in your mind. How many people do you see attending your postnuptial party? Are there lots of decorations, complete with lit candles and helium balloons? Will there be dancing? Is your fête going to be rowdy and raucous or sophisticated and subdued? Do you envision a cozy, family atmosphere or something more modern? There are, as usual, no right or wrong answers. These questions will help you get a handle on the size, shape, and type of venue you should be looking for.

The words "reception" and "hall" go hand in hand in the collective consciousness, but that doesn't mean you should limit yourself to the traditional wedding venues when searching for reception spaces. Browse historic hotels at Historichotels.org/meetings _events/75 or scope out someplace snootier at Countryclub receptions.com. Smaller affairs can be held in theaters, historic buildings, pubs, or restaurants—a particularly nice choice when you're a food and wine aficionado. And there are always the old standbys: church basements, VFW posts, and banquet halls. The image you choose to project is up to you, but remember that you and your guests will have fun whether your venue's walls are draped in dupioni silk or strings of $1.99 Christmas lights.

Some venues have websites, and the really great websites have walkthrough tours that you can take without ever leaving your seat. Try to look at the whole picture and maintain your perspective when you scope out potential venues in person. Ugly walls can be camouflaged with swaths of tulle or low lighting. No one's going to remember the color of the carpet or the weird-looking light fixtures. It's easy to reject space after space because some look a little run down or others don't set your heart aflutter. Yet what you need is not the perfect space or the most beautiful space, but rather a workable space. Some venues stock a whole range of decor options, so it's worth it to ask whether your tablecloths will necessarily be maroon like the ones on display. If you don't ask, you may never find out that the venue has tablecloths *and* topiaries *and* tulle in every color under the sun.

Things that can't be prettied up with a little lace and a lot of creativity include bad lighting, crappy acoustics, rooms that are shaped oddly, a lack of accessible electrical outlets, funny smells, mold and mildew, and a bitchy waitstaff. These things should definitely be considered deal breakers.

This is not the time to make assumptions—every venue is different, and the road to hell is paved with the best guesses of brides and grooms. The venues you fall in love with may very well have policies you hate, so be forthright with your queries and get as much information as you can in writing. In fact, get everything in writing, preferably in the form of an itemized list. When you've just started looking, print out brochures and price lists from venue websites. If you visit any of those venues, take your printout with you and take notes on it. You can call reps on price discrepancies and make sure you're being offered everything the brochure says is part of the standard package. What's a standard package? Some halls hook you up with absolutely everything for one flat rate. Most charge on a sliding scale based on your particular needs and wants.

Once you have confirmation that the venue you like is free on your wedding date, it's time to dig a little more deeply into the specifics. Don't take anything for granted, because doing that is a recipe for disaster. Imagine finding out after your wedding that your uncle Jim busted a bunch of glasses and now you're responsible. Sites that lay out the questions brides- and grooms-to-be should ask venue representatives are usually incomplete, so look at a variety of them. Combine the lists you'll find at Weddingplanning.com/tips/content/wedding_facilities.html, Hitched.co.uk/venues/askvenue.aspx, and Elegala.com/reception-questions.html to see what a really comprehensive set of questions would look like. If you're not sure you'll remember them all, copy and paste them into a document, print that doc, and bring it with you whenever you're speaking to someone in person. When you're communicating via e-mail, just paste them into the text box. Here are the basics:

- Find out how many years the venue has been hosting weddings, and request a list of previous clients who are willing to share their experiences.

- Make sure that yours will be the only wedding taking place or that the venue has enough staff and space to accommodate multiple events.

- Inquire as to how many guests the venue can hold, and ask about the ratio of waitstaff to guests—you can't go wrong with one to a table.

- Ask for a list of services and stuff the venue does not provide so you can anticipate the extra cost.

- Check to make sure that tables, chairs, linens, and tableware are provided or rentable, and ask whether any decorations will be provided.

- Request a written cost breakdown for package prices, and familiarize yourself with the venue's policies concerning special requests.

- Find out whether your venue requires that you use its

on-site vendors and, if it doesn't, whether there are setup or corkage fees.

- Ask about any potential discounts, extras, or added services that interest you.

- Inquire as to how many cars can be accommodated in the parking lot and whether there'll be a valet on hand.

- Find out if you'll need to pay for insurance, security, or other unexpected fees and if you'll need to tidy up at the party's end.

- Determine how early in the day people can arrive to set up and when you'll be expected to vacate the premises.

Book the venue you settle on as early as possible. How ticked are you going to be if you've planned your decor around a particular space and that space is now booked because you decided the deposit could wait? That deposit can be almost any amount, so don't be surprised when one venue asks for half up front and another asks for a mere quarter of the total bill. If you're up for it, give haggling a try. Some venue managers will risk losing a reservation because they want their money when they want it, no exceptions, thank you very much, but it never hurts to ask.

Before you book, look around for reviews of your preferred venues. Search for them on Yelp.com to read what other people are saying, or put the name of each space and the word "review" in Google to see if anyone cared enough either way to post about it on their blog. The first review you find may very well be a negative one, but keep looking. One bad evaluation should not be damning—everyone has their bad days, from reception staffers to newlyweds writing reviews. Should you find yourself reading dreadful review after dreadful review, walk away. As painful as it is to have to start your whole search over again, your reception is too big a part of your matrimonial celebration to leave to chance. And if you've been saving your search results, it's not like you'll be starting from scratch.

While you're skimming reviews, examining spaces, and talking to managers, you should also be familiarizing yourself with some of the ins and outs of contracts. If a vendor—any vendor—does not immediately offer to draw up a contract when you've agreed to work with each other, tell them you expect to see one ASAP. Contracts protect both you and your vendors, and you may very well be putting your John Hancock on a lot of dotted lines before you say "I do." The most unnerving part of any contract is typically the perplexing language—how are you supposed to know what's what when you can't even process the verbiage? Take a look at Wikipedia.org/wiki/ Contract in case one of your vendors tries to use legalese to scam you, but know that most of the contracts you'll be asked to sign as you plan your wedding are going to be way less complicated than the Wikipedia article itself. The basics of wedding contracts can be found at Weddingfanatic.com/signing-on-the-dotted-line.

A. J. Got Acquainted Online

"Looking at pictures of a venue online is so hard, because you just know it's going to look different in person. But the Internet helped us to acquaint ourselves with different kinds of venues, and I really appreciated being able to see what was out there in terms of menus, pricing, and services.

"Matt didn't like that there were very few reviews of wedding reception venues, besides those venues' own brag books. I couldn't agree more. In a way, it makes sense, because of course venues are only going to post the most favorable reviews. But I wanted to know about the good, bad, and ugly. If a previous client really loved a venue and loved its staff but thought the food was blah, I could have planned accordingly if I needed to.

"We looked at menus online whenever we could. Most of the affordable venues we checked out had the usual wedding foods prepared by an in-house catering staff. Some people probably look for more variety, but we liked the consistency because my MIL is a very selective eater. It was fun to imagine serving shot glasses of hors d'oeuvres or other funky culinary creations, but we decided that we really wanted our reception to have a cozy, family feel, so we went with the ultimate traditional meal: a Thanksgiving dinner."

Venue contracts should include your name and your intended's name; your wedding date; the duration of the reception, including setup and breakdown times; the name of the venue and the room name or number (if any); the name of your primary contact at the venue; deposit amounts and due dates; the date on which the full balance is due; a detailed and comprehensive list of rentals and equipment being provided by the venue; the services being provided by the venue; usage limitations; and the venue's refund and cancellation policy. Always aim for the loosest refund policies possible, regardless of what vendor you're dealing with. And wherever you can, pay your deposits with a credit card, because your credit card company will help you make your case in the event that things go totally wrong and you have to fight to get your money back.

Assembling a Wedding Piece by Piece

When you're building a wedding from the ground up (i.e., utilizing a space that does not include any amenities), you have to think about more than tables and chairs. It doesn't matter whether you're getting hitched in a local park, on your grandparents' property, or in some indoor space that's not traditionally used for nuptials—you're going to have to train yourself to think like an event planner. The trade-off is that you get complete control over the look and feel of your celebration when you're picking out everything from the tent to the silverware pattern. You don't have to work around a venue's outdated color schemes or agree to use its in-house vendors; you can be as picky as you want to be.

Before you rush off to start comparing prices on monogrammed napkins, you should know that the outdoor wedding isn't always going to be the cheapest wedding. Building your own nuptials sounds like the least-expensive option when you're thinking you can set up a tent, get some seating, slap together a meal, and be done with it. You can indeed save some dough by hosting a wedding in your very own backyard, but your costs will be dependent upon a whole lot of factors. Do you have enough bathrooms to accommodate your guests, or will appropriately upscale port-o-johns be in order? Can everyone fit in your house if it rains, or will you need to rent a tent? There are also linens and plates and centerpieces to think of. If you want to hire a caterer who provides anything above and beyond drop-off service, be prepared to pay premium prices. And then there are generators for electricity, portable dance floors, trash cans, valets, PA systems, food prep supplies, coffee carafes, chocolate fountains, coolers, and the booze . . . not to mention plates, glasses, mugs, forks, knives, and spoons.

How many of each? You'll likely sit eight or ten guests at each round table. Then you'll need a longer rectangular head table if you plan to seat your wedding party away from the hoi polloi. Top that list off with a table for the buffet (if you're having one), a table for the cake, a table for the booze, and a table for any gifts brought in under the arms of attendees. Get at least three dinner plates, two dessert plates, and six cups per person. Save yourself the trouble of counting and snag as many napkins and as much cutlery as you can afford. People drop stuff and lose stuff, and you'll enjoy your wedding day a whole lot more if you're not worrying about whether your grandma has a fork.

This shouldn't discourage you from having the ultimate plan-it-yourself reception. If you're up to the task, more power to you. The first thing you need to do—after you've decided on the actual location of your reception—is get in touch with rental outfits that specialize in large events. They'll have most of the raw materials you'll need, from tables to tablecloths and everything that goes on top of them. Go to Gatheringguide.com/event_categories/party _rentals_tents.html and check out the party rental listings they have for your state. If nothing's close by, pop your zip code into the search box at Rentalhq.com/findstore. You'll have to wade through power tool and heavy equipment rentals to find what you're looking for, but the site's listings are pretty comprehensive. Look for party rental companies with websites so you can peruse their price lists at your leisure.

Then again, you could always try renting a tent and more entirely online at Weisertent.com, a company with nationwide delivery and setup. Sound nuts? You can also rent linens online at a number of sites. Take Distinctivedetails.com, for example. It ships everything from napkins to tablecloths to chair overlays right to you, and you send 'em all back dirty using the boxes and shipping labels provided. Tabledecor.com rents out a small selection of table lighting (e.g., little lamps) on its website. There are also all the sites that sell stuff like ready-made decor—expensive ready-made decor, that is. If you're not keen on spending ages assembling centerpieces to match your dinnerware, you can pay a premium at sites like Social couture.com for all the elements of a perfectly coordinated table.

You can find everything you'll need for your reception on the Internet, but don't forget about shipping charges and shipping times when you're putting together your budget and your to-do list. Give yourself plenty of time to find the right stuff and the right prices. Don't forget that you *will* need to enlist the help of friends and family members, because you'll need warm bodies to move chairs, announce dinner, help people find this or that, dole out food, cut and serve the cake, and pack everything away once the last guest has gone home.

The most budget-friendly plan-it-yourself weddings usually take place in spots that have their own natural ambiance. Expansive waterfront properties overlooking beautiful bays, large woodsy gardens overflowing with flowers, and wide sculpted lawns with shrubberies save you the trouble of decorating. A buffet-style cold luncheon that's dropped off by a caterer who graciously provides premium disposable tableware negates the need for chafing dishes, cooking facilities, plates and silverware, and waitstaff. No lamps are necessary at daytime receptions, and you can skip the valet if you've got plenty of room for parking. You can even cut the bartender from your budget if you put your booze in buckets and make sure you have more than enough ice on hand.

Leave 'Em Satisfied

Wherever, however, and whomever you marry, you have to provide some manner of refreshments for your guests. This is one of the few wedding elements that is entirely 100 percent nonnegotiable unless you are eloping. It's simply not nice to say, "You watched us get hitched, you gave us some gifts . . . now get out." What *is* completely negotiable is the menu. If your budget allows for nothing more than cake and punch, know that many a loving and long-lived marriage has been celebrated with just that. Casual people with casual tastes planning casual weddings should feel free to serve casual food and drinks. As in almost all things wedding related, let your event's formality level be your guide. Yes, you can serve sliders at your black-tie event; just call them gourmet mini-burgers and top them with luxe condiments like marinated Korean pears.

The menu you create will largely be a product of two factors: your tastes and the dishes offered by your particular caterer. Before you start looking for the master chef of your dreams—or opt not to look for one at all because you're planning on asking someone you know to dish up something tasty—mull over that first factor. You shouldn't feel obligated to serve certain foods (e.g., the tired old pasta primavera, salmon, or filet mignon) because you associate them with weddings or think people won't enjoy themselves without them. The lengthy article at Weddingzone.net/px-pl042.htm outlines how to plan a vegetarian wedding menu, with examples of crowd-pleasing soups, breads, salads, hors d'oeuvres, entrees, and desserts.

Jeanette's Lucky Venue Find

"Before we found out that our favorite restaurant in the whole world also does catering, I did a lot of research online and checked out about five different locations. I had very precise needs—I had to find a venue that could host the ceremony and the reception. They needed to be able to either cater the wedding or coordinate the catering for me, because I had no desire to plan all of that myself. I basically used and abused as many resources as I could, from online reviews to Yahoo! Yellow Pages listings to local bridal mailing lists.

"We found our site after finding our caterer because the restaurant listed the venues it works with on its website. I saw one I liked online, then I fell in love with it in person. It was just a stroke of luck that the venue we chose had a virtual tour on its site. It was a great way to show the venue to my brother, who was DJing, so he would know how to set up the musical equipment. There was no way he was going to get to the venue before the day before the wedding, but he could look over the layout, and that really helped him draw up a plan.

"As far as choosing a menu went, we were incredibly limited by our budget. While it was nice to browse the ideas at Foodnetwork.com and places like that, most of them were just too cost prohibitive. I really wish that I'd come across some menus that were creative and inexpensive so I could have seen what people were doing with limited means."

Even if you're a slave to the DIY spirit, think twice about cooking and setting out your own refreshments. While you can find fantastic menu and drink ideas at Epicurious.com/recipesmenus/holidays/wedding/menus as well as a handy timeline outlining what can be prepared ahead, ask yourself if you really want to be marinating lamb chops and whipping up a yogurt sauce the day before your wedding. When it comes to edibles, you should delegate to your heart's content without feeling the slightest twinge of guilt. Feel free to micromanage your menu after drooling over what you find when you search for "wedding" at Epicurious.com, Foodandwine.com, and Foodnetwork.com, but let someone else slave away in the kitchen.

Your menu can be as wedding-y or as wacky as you want it to be. Toss out the three-course dinner template and serve food family style at each table if you don't want to limit guests to certain entrees. Dish out a piping-hot breakfast. Divvy up the buffet, creating multiple themed serving stations. Or incorporate your ethnic heritage into your menu with a buffet based on the meals your ancestors ate for centuries. If you're into the sort of haute cuisine that is barely identifiable as food (see some at www.Lenclume.co.uk/food), know that you're going to a pay a premium for your meal once you find a caterer equipped to serve up dehydrated and gelled edibles. Your guests may also be somewhat confused by the little globs of jelly and piles of froth that appear on their plates.

When you know what sort of food you want, it's time to start interviewing caterers by e-mail. Look for potential candidates on sites that group vendors by category instead of using dedicated search tools like Localcatering.com, because bigger sites attract more vendors. Feel free to step outside of the WIC world by searching on sites like Citysearch.com/allcities. If you want to know the skinny on a particular caterer, check Weddingwire.com for listings paired with honest reviews and ratings left by former brides. You can even do a Google search for the caterer's name in quotes and the word "complaint," which will help you find any patently negative reviews lurking out there on the web. Should you discover that you are bound by your venue's policies to use its caterer, go ahead and interview its catering manager.

Tell potential caterers how much money you want to spend and what you hope to get in return. Ask for sample menus and references. Then hit 'em with these questions:

- Can my intended and I come in for a tasting session so that we can experience the flavors and presentation of your dishes?

- Do you specialize in certain meals or certain styles of food? Can you also provide a wedding cake?

- What is your price range and how is it calculated? Do you charge a flat or per-item rate?

- Are taxes and gratuities included in your prices? Are drinks, linens, and tableware included?

- Is your food prepared from fresh ingredients? Can you use local or organic ingredients upon request?

- Can you accommodate dietary issues such as veganism and gluten allergies?

- Do you base your prices on guaranteed numbers, and will we have to pay a fee if our final count is higher or lower?

- Will there be an additional fee if you have to supply your own cooking equipment?

- Who will prepare the meal? Will a catering manager help coordinate any reception events involving food, such as meal service or the cutting of the cake?

- Will ours be the only event you're working that day?

- Do you offer less expensive, less elaborate vendors' meals?

When you've got the details nailed down, it's time to sign yet another contract. This one should list the caterer's company information (including contact info and license numbers), the name of your contact, the date and time of your reception, the address and room where it will take place, the type of service to be provided, a detailed list of foods and beverages that will be served, the staff-to-guest ratio, the full price along with the deposit schedule, the date the final payment will be due, the date the final head count will be needed, compensation for cancellation by the vendor, and the company's full cancellation and refund policy. Dispute any inconsistencies in the contract *before* you sign it, lest you end up eating rubber chicken instead of chicken a la king.

And then, of course, there are beverages to think about! It's best not to skimp on water, tea, and coffee, as a rule. Soft drinks tend to be the favored drink of both the kiddies in attendance and those guests who, for whatever reasons, aren't down with the booze, so make sure there will be plenty on hand. Nonboozaholic beverages are often included in your catering costs, even if you opt to use a drop-off service. If you're building your nuptial celebration from the ground up, get someone you know with a warehouse club membership to pick up the sodas, cups, ground coffee, tea, and water. You may end up with lots of liquid leftovers at the end of the day, but you probably won't have any trouble unloading them on friends and family.

Ask a sizable group of people what they like most about weddings, and you're going to hear the words "open bar" more than once. Before you give an automatic thumbs-up to all-you-can-drink top-shelf liquor, consider that it is perfectly possible to plan an enjoyable reception that does not include a single drop of booze. If you're worried that your festivities won't be quite festive enough without the firewater, a quick Google search for "nonalcoholic punch" results in hundreds of thousands of links to recipes. Some brides- and grooms-to-be who don't mind a wee drop now and again serve only beer and wine, or they have a limited bar selection that includes beer, wine, and one or two cocktails.

Or even, perhaps, one or two signature cocktails. A true signature cocktail is a chic custom drink designed for you and just for you by a professional bartender. This, however, is a service that the best and most creative bartenders usually provide to restaurants and bars for a hefty price. If you can afford that sort of thing, wonderful. If not, you could always try creating your own signature cocktail. The search box at Cocktaildb.com lets you find recipes based on your favorite ingredients. Find a drink you dig, modify it to make it yours, and then give it a snappy name that fits in with your matrimonial theme. Want to pay someone else to do it for you? The people at Signaturecocktails.com will create one for you for about seventy bucks, and they'll even whip you up some custom recipe cards to give out to guests who are understandably impressed.

Open bars (with or without signature cocktails) are super keen, but the plain truth is that open bars can get really expensive really quickly, depending on how you're being charged for your booze. Most open bars—be they full, premium, or super premium with regard to liquor quality—are priced on a per person/per hour scale. What this means is that you pay a set price for each guest for each hour the bar is open. Sounds like a good deal, right? It doesn't matter if every guest from your grandma to your cousin's new baby has seven stiff ones every half an hour—no one is going to drink you into bankruptcy. But you're going to pay the same per person/per hour price if the only person with glass in hand is your aunt Margo . . . the one who likes straight tonic water.

Cutting expenses where bar bills are concerned is usually a matter of either having a limited cocktail hour with an open bar that shuts down when mealtime arrives or providing your bartender with a preset monetary cap like $1,500 so that they know to shut down the bar when guests have imbibed fifteen hundred bucks' worth of the hard stuff.

Cash bars are indeed an option, though you may get the stink eye from guests who think it's just too tacky. In some locales, cash bars are practically the norm, but there are many places in which they're frowned upon. One upside to cash bars is that some guests who might otherwise kick back two too many curb their drinking earlier in the evening because they don't feel like busting out their wallets yet again. That is, if they even have cash with them—cash bars fulfill a function, but it never occurs to many people that they're going to need to bring drinkin' money. If you're including reception information on your website, consider letting people know the deal regarding drinks.

Some venues charge abominable prices for atrocious house wines and lowbrow beers. Consider going the BYOB route with sites like Mywinesdirect.com and Bottletrek.com. Even with the ridiculous corkage fees some venues charge, you may spend a lot less for quality libations when you buy them yourself from a beer distributor or liquor store. How much sauce do you need if you're stocking your own nuptials or making sure your guests aren't being subjected to bad booze? There is a beverage needs calculator at Bridallinks .com/planning.asp, but there's no one foolproof formula. Country weddings.com/receptionvenues/liquor.shtml has created a guide based on a guest list of one hundred, and you should be able to adjust that accordingly.

Don't let anyone pressure you into over-ordering liquor when more than half of your guests are self-proclaimed teetotalers or under-ordering when you know for a fact that the majority of your loved ones can really tie one on. You know how your family and friends respond to oodles of free alcohol—plan your bar accordingly. If you're worried about drunk driving or disorderly conduct, you can limit the cocktail hour or arrange for a shuttle service.

Never forget to tip your bartenders . . . and your maitre d', catering manager, and waitstaff. Tipping in this context means giving labeled tip envelopes to the best man before the event so he can dole out cash as appropriate. How much you tip will mostly depend

Leah Said No to Assigned Seating, but Yes to an Open Bar

"We didn't have assigned seats at the reception, and we didn't hear any complaints about that. We have a lot of friends who come from all over the place, but they have a lot in common. Because of that, we didn't feel any pressing need to make people mix or keep anyone apart. Our venue was relatively small, so no one was isolated from anyone else.

"Will was in charge of the alcohol for the reception because he's really into liquor and beer. Not just drinking it, but also how it's made and what tastes best. I gave him free rein in that area. One of the few temporary sticking points was that we wanted an open bar. Our parents were briefly against the idea—they were specifically worried about drunk driving because the venue was a castle in the woods rather than someplace in town. Once we told them that the hotel could run a shuttle service to and from the wedding and reception they retracted their objections."

on how much you spent, and you should ask if you've already paid out a gratuity in your bill. You don't need to tip the owner of a business, though you can if you like. Tips are traditionally reserved for those service professionals who will only see a small percentage of the money you gave to the big boss. Tip your maitre d' around $150, tip your catering manager about 15 percent of the total bill, tip your bartender 10 percent of the total liquor bill, and allocate $20 or more each to waiters and waitresses. If this seems irksome because you've already spent so much, remember that these are the people who usually end up working the hardest.

Oh, and feed your vendors, too. Whether you let them dine on full-priced dinners alongside your guests or serve them a less-expensive vendor meal somewhere out of sight, give them a break and something to eat. Weddings usually take place during mealtimes, and a well-fed vendor is a content, industrious vendor. A hungry, grumpy vendor isn't going to do you any good.

As for you, you're probably going to be hungry and thirsty and maybe even a little grumpy after saying all those vows, but most newlyweds do not get to make a beeline for the buffet and bar. If your reception space happens to have a separate bridal chamber, wonderful. While guests wander in, you can relax and have a light snack and a mimosa to tide you over. When you're confident that your guests have arrived and are eager to load up their plates, you and your sweetie should join the receiving line—if in fact you're planning to have one because your wedding is formal enough to necessitate it. The traditional and most formal receiving line is made up of the MOB, the MOG, the bride, the groom, the MOH, and the BMs. No men other than the groom are required. But these days, FOBs and FOGs get in on the action, and there's nothing wrong with asking Grandma and Gramps to join in the tedium. Yes, tedium . . . thanking two hundred guests on an empty stomach is not an activity most people would classify as fun.

If the many individuals who contributed something to the success of your nuptials all want to get in line, keep in mind that short really is sweet. Your guests are probably more than ready to hit the dance floor. Your nerves may still be all a-jangle. Consequently, everyone involved will thank you for putting a cap on the number of people in the receiving line. In the event you decide to forgo this tradition altogether, you and your spouse absolutely must go around and visit with each table sometime during mealtime. Your guests took the time to honor you with their presence at your wedding, and now it's time for you to repay them. This can be just as tedious as standing in the receiving line, but hey, at least you'll have had a chance to have a few mouthfuls of the food you yourself picked out!

Scope a Site

- Banquetfacilities.com
- Countryclubreceptions.com
- Eventective.com
- Historichotels.org/meetings_events/75
- Nps.gov
- Weddinglocation.com
- Weddingsolutions.com/vendor_search/search_reception _sites.php
- www.Ultimatevenue.us

Create Top-notch Tables

- Perfecttableplan.com
- Seatingarrangement.com

- Simpleseating.com

- Toptableplanner.com

Find Someone to Provide Foodstuffs

- Chowbaby.com/defaultcatering.asp

- Citysearch.com/allcities

- Directcatering.com

- Findqualitycaterers.com

- Gatheringguide.com/event_categories/caterers_catering .html

- Localcatering.com

- Weddingwire.com

Stock Your Party

- 4yourparty.com

- Cateringsupplies.com

- Chocolatefountainrental.com

- Distinctivedetails.com

- Gatheringguide.com/event_categories/party_rentals _tents.html

- Lineneffects.com

- Munkeboelinens.com

- Nationwideparty.com

- Platesandnapkins.com

- Plumparty.com

- Qualitychaircovers.com

- Rentalhq.com/findstore

- Royalrestrooms.com

- Socialcouture.com

- Tabledecor.com

- Tobeenamed.com

- Weisertent.com

Plan a Personalized Cocktail Menu

- Barmeister.com/drinks

- Cocktailatlas.com

- Cocktaildb.com

- Drinksmixer.com

- Extratasty.com

- Fineliving.com/fine/great_cocktails

- Supercocktails.com

Chapter 8
With This Click

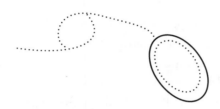

Contrary to what the wedding rags and the WIC would have you believe, you don't actually need to weigh down your wedding with a ton of stuff. A lot of newly engaged couples start planning their weddings by saying that they are not going to buy and give away a lot of useless junk. Their resolve usually weakens around the time they start reading up on weddings, because they inevitably encounter advice mavens stating that brides and grooms *must* give their guests favors to thank them for their presence and *must* light a unity candle during the ceremony. Furthermore, they *must* serve a full dinner on real china. The bride *must* wear a traditional wedding dress and the groom *must* be dressed in a tux. As brides- and grooms-to-be get saddled with more and more musts, they forget that etiquette is about making people feel comfortable, not buying the right stuff.

The intentions of these matrimonial advisers are probably good; the problem is that their information is just plain wrong. For example, you do not have to give your guests wedding favors. Your guests turn up to support you as you say your vows, and you express your gratitude by throwing a kick-ass party. Plenty of guests would rather not go home with bubbles, woven baskets of Jordan almonds, or a mini bamboo steamer in tow—they know that these things will sit around for a socially acceptable amount of time before someone takes the initiative and chucks 'em. There are useful favors, but the most useful favors are usually the most expensive. People used to give out monogrammed matchbooks that cost a quarter, and those were useful until everyone realized that smoking was just plain unhealthy.

Need some more examples of what you don't have to do? You do not have to print wedding programs so your guests have something to do before the ceremony starts. If they really want to know who's who in the wedding party, they'll ask as they move through the receiving line. In a perfect world, all of the paper products that go hand in hand with weddings would be made of quickly renewing resources like bamboo and end up in the recycling bin instead of the trash can. Too bad this isn't a perfect world. You do not have to do anything other than speak your vows while the marriage is being formalized. This means that you don't really have to buy a great big candle or two different colors of sand.

You'll be just as married if your guests have no guestbook to sign and your RB walks down the aisle with no satin pillow in his grubby little hands. At the reception, you can get away without having any sweets at all if you're serving plenty of dinner, and you can skip the savories completely if the focal point of your party is champagne and cake. You don't have to serve a meal's worth of hors d'oeuvres or a bar's worth of spirituous liquors. Cake toppers are by no means a necessity, and guests will be more than happy to toast with plastic cups. You can nix the place cards if you assign tables only or let your guests seat themselves.

Whatever you do, don't let anyone fool you into thinking that you're a bad bride or groom because you've decided not to buy certain mass-produced goods. Conversely, don't let anyone tell you that you're some kind of superficial tool of the man because you really want Jordan almonds or big floral centerpieces. For the most part, human beings like wedding stuff—the fact that the WIC hasn't gone out of business proves it. Feel free to look at all of the stuff associated with modern matrimony, but make your own decisions about what's important to you and what isn't.

The online wedding market does business to the tune of $7.9 million a year, which sounds like a lot until you compare it with the $70 *billion* that the WIC takes in each year. What's the deal with the low digits? An estimated 77 percent of engaged couples turn to the Internet when trawling for wedding day ideas, but a scant 13 percent buy or reserve products and services online. These are likely the same people who buy everything from DVDs to living room sets on Amazon.com, but something is keeping them from fully committing themselves to the idea that buying wedding swag on the net is totally sweet. Two factors are probably at work here. The first is that weddings are generally regarded as being more important than the average shindig, so no one wants to do anything that's going to compromise the planned flawlessness of the ceremony and reception.

The second factor may very well be fear. As you'll discover a few chapters from now, the ladieswear division of the WIC has made it its mission to discourage brides and bridesmaids from buying dresses online by sharing horror stories of mixed dye lots, counterfeit gowns, shoddy sewing, and dresses forever in transit. Because people preparing to be wed tend to be emotionally invested in the idea of perfect fairy-tale nuptials, they can be easily frightened into making an appointment with a bridal salon and, by extension, visiting print shops, scheduling trips to party supply outlets, and visiting with jewelers.

Before you go any further, repeat the following sentence to yourself to banish pessimistic and panicky thoughts from your mind: "I can buy wedding goods online with confidence." Sounds hokey, doesn't it? That's because it is. Wedding retailer shipping times may seem outrageous in a day and age when you can get almost anything you want overnighted to your door, but the wedding industry moves a lot more slowly than other industries. That's just the way things are for now. Waiting six weeks for a product sucks, but think back to the halcyon days of your youth. You probably waited that long and then some for cereal box giveaways where the prize was nothing but a dinky plastic toy.

Know, however, that retailers pad shipping times, so the estimated six weeks usually turns out to be more like two. If a seller doesn't actually keep merchandise in stock, but instead orders it from a larger distributor when you place your order, that seller will overestimate shipping times to make sure it doesn't get bitten in the butt when the order that was placed is delayed. Other sellers, like Weddingshowergifts.com, make made-to-order products that take time to put together. How quickly you get your stuff depends on how many orders the seller is currently handling.

This is especially important to remember when you're buying from a seller on Etsy.com or eBay. Stuff on Etsy is handcrafted—usually by hobbyists or crafters who haven't yet made the pros. A lot of the sellers on eBay are hobbyists, too. The person handling your order may have a full-time job, three screaming tots, and a home to manage, which means that shipping times will vary quite a bit. That

Leah Wouldn't Have Shopped Any Other Way

"I hit up Internet stores for almost every single thing we used in the wedding and at the reception. Working a full-time job while I was planning a wedding meant that I spent a lot of lunch hours at my desk, browsing for things online. Not having to leave the office to shop was really great. Besides, I'm a big fan of multitasking, especially when I'm working under a tight deadline. Shopping online also opened up the possibilities—there are almost no limitations other than the occasional website written in Japanese.

"There were some things I bought IRL [in real life]. Since I'm a printmaker, I really wanted to give all of the wedding guests little framed pictures as favors, but I was having trouble finding frames I liked and could afford online. Then I got a call from my mom in Alabama. She told me that Target had these little silver frames in their dollar bins, so I drove to the nearest Target. The frames were perfect, and I emptied those bins."

shouldn't scare you, provided you give yourself plenty of time to browse, buy, and wait for the mailman.

If your wedding is going to be anything like the average wedding, you'll be buying some stuff really soon. The time to start looking is right now. The big wedding sites all dedicate some part of their server space to their retail pages—do yourself a favor and visit these only for idea-gathering purposes. Overpriced is overpriced whether or not it fits into your larger financial plan. When you find something you like that is way out of your price range, search for the product by name, then the item number, and then by any defining characteristics that jump out at you. Most of the online retailers selling favors, ceremony swag, and reception gear online have the exact same merchandise in stock. The only variable is the price.

Some brides- and grooms-to-be arrive at this point in the planning process and discover that they have absolutely no idea what they want. Oh, they know that they want to give their guests a little something or to spruce up the tables in their reception space, but that's as far as their preferences have taken them. If this sounds like you, Images.google.com is here to help. Just plug whatever it is you're looking for into the search box, and you'll be bombarded with more pretty pictures than you can shake a stick at. A search for "favors" brings up more than nine hundred thousand results, with everything from baby trees (Plantamemory.com) to chocolate mice (Burdickchocolate.com) to personalized music (Soundexpression greetings.com).

When you first start browsing for stuff, keep your search parameters as wide as possible. Searching for "favors" instead of "wedding favors" means you'll never miss out on little gifts that are exactly what you want precisely because they have nothing to do with weddings. Almost everything you could want for the ceremony and reception can be found in a nonwedding version for less dough. An FG basket is just a small basket covered in something silky—look for something in white wicker instead. Just about anything decorative can be made into a centerpiece. The whole unity candle setup is really just one hefty candle and two thinner ones—and how much do you really want to spend on something Wikipedia says was made popular by characters on a soap opera?

To some extent, a good shop is any shop that has what you need. No one is going to know where anything you buy came from unless you are just so damn excited about getting a great deal that you can't help shouting about it from the rooftops. At the same time, some stores are just plain safer than others. The best retail sites tend to be those that look professional—the owners either took the time to design a site with a quality layout and color scheme or they paid someone else to do it. It's not a perfect yardstick by which to measure shops, but you can usually safely infer that someone who has invested time and money into their business will give reasonably good customer service.

An online shop may be shady if . . .

- The website is overrun with long lists of keywords or just looks plain cheap.

- There's no phone number or the posted phone number doesn't work.

- Your only means of contacting customer service is via web form and the form is broken.

- You find lots of complaints about it on Ripoffreport.com.

- The shop itself is located overseas, in a country known for bad business practices.

- There are no return, refund, or privacy policies posted anywhere on the site.

- Merchandise listed as brand-name appears to be counterfeit.

- The pictures of posted items are blurry, dark, or obviously Photoshopped.

- Product descriptions are incomplete or overblown.

- There are no signs that the site is encrypted or secured—look at the encryption symbols at Familysafemedia.com/how_safe_is _buying_online_.html.

- The seller wants you to pay via cash, check, or money order.

- The seller requests that you take your transaction off-site or asks for payment info via e-mail.

At the same time, a store that sells its stuff at a steep discount simply may not have the moolah to pretty up its web space. The biggest drawback to shopping online is that the buyer has to rely on the photographs and descriptions provided by the seller. Browse through an aesthetically pleasing online shop and you'll probably feel more confident putting your faith in the seller's portrayals of its featured products. A cheap site can make even the most upscale items look crappy. Buy only from sellers and sites that don't set off warning bells in your head. If you're already worrying about whether or not you'll get your merchandise before you've even hit the Buy It Now button, back away from the keyboard.

People with their hearts in the right place may advise you against buying anything at all for your wedding online because they fear that you will fall prey to all sorts of scams. The truth is that most of the scams you'll hear about are accounts of people who got screwed because they failed to read the fine print. Whenever you're buying anything online—wedding related or not—you should find out where the seller is located; what the seller's shipping, return, and order

Say Cheese: Taking a Screenshot

What happens when you print your receipt but then find yourself up against a problem that requires showing that receipt to someone six hundred miles away? Then there are all those dress designers who madly use Flash on their websites, making it impossible to bookmark pages or download images so you can look at them later. Screenshots are the answer. If you need to dispute a charge, a screenshot of the purchased item along with one of your receipt can help you prove your case. And taking a screenshot of a web page is way easier than copying and pasting every piece of info into a document. How's it done?

In Mac OS X

- Command-Shift-3 snaps a pic of the whole screen, turning it into a PNG or PDF file that appears on the desktop.

- Command-Shift-4 does the same thing but lets you select the area of the screen that will be captured.

- Command-Shift-4 plus Control snaps a pic of the whole screen and places the file in the clipboard.

- Command-Shift-4 plus Spacebar snaps a pic of the selected window, turning it into a PNG file that appears on the desktop.

In Windows

- Hit the Print Screen (which might also be labeled PrtScn or PrtScrn) button on your keyboard to copy an image of the entire screen to the clipboard.

- Print Screen plus Alt will do the same thing for an active window.

- In Vista, use the Snipping Tool in the Accessories menu to capture rectangular or freeform images of any part of your screen, and the image you snip will show up in the program's edito.r

There are free screen-capture apps you can download at Wisdom-soft.com/products/screen hunter.htm and Mirekw.com/winfreeware/mwsnap.html, but you may as well just do it yourself.

cancellation policies are; who pays for return shipping and any associated fees; and how you'll be getting your money back. Some shops will provide you with a monetary refund, while others will give you some form of store credit, just like in the real world.

Seller policies can change, of course, which is why screenshots are a good thing. Don't feel as if you have to capture every policy on every site you buy from in JPEG form, but a screenshot can serve as an added bit of insurance when you're spending a few hundred or a few thousand dollars on the Internet. Just snap one of the shop's refund policies and one of the items you bought. Should you later request a refund only to be told you can't have one because of a relatively new return policy, your evidence that the policies were quite different when you made your purchase may give you the leverage you need to come out on top. For much the same reason, it's a good idea to save receipts sent via e-mail and to take screenshots of printable receipts.

Unless you're dealing with a seller that is completely up-front about its curmudgeonly no-returns-whatsoever policy, the paper-less paper trail you've created will usually get you the refund you deserve. And if the seller won't give you one? That's why you should always pay with a credit card. If you've got a leg to stand on in your disagreement, you're protected under the Fair Credit Billing Act, meaning you can dispute charges and withhold payments at will. Just so you know, debit cards look an awful lot like credit cards, but they seldom offer the same protections.

A Token of Your Thanks

No one knows exactly when the tradition of giving guests a little thank-you got off the ground. The popular theory is that European aristocrats would give bombonieres (i.e., boxes of stuff) made out of gold, silver, or precious gems to their party guests. The stuff in those boxes was typically something made out of a heaping helping of sugar, as the bombonieres were a way for newlyweds to pass some of their own sweetness and luck on to their guests.

Modern wedding favors basically come in two categories: edible and inedible. You can expand these categories in any number of ways. Inedible can be broken down into useful and not useful, breakable and not-so-breakable, or serious and silly. Edible can be broken down into sweet and savory, ingredients and snacks, or homemade and store bought. You're going to come across the same favors repeatedly as you search, like the omnipresent miniframes, Jordan almonds, coasters, candles, and silvery spoons. Then there are soaps, salt and pepper shakers, key chains, bookmarks, and bottle stoppers.

That, mind you, is in the United States. Wedding guests in Malaysia look forward to beautiful hand-decorated eggs, while guests in Italy munch on rich marzipan fruits. It's common in a number of cultures for brides and grooms to give their guests tins or bags containing five candies representing health, happiness, wealth, longevity, and fertility. If you want to do the whole five candies thing, Confettiflowers.com offers a chic delivery system in the form of flowers made of tulle, lace, satin, and netting.

Favors are, as mentioned earlier, entirely optional, but most brides and grooms give them out, so there's a good chance you've already been browsing sellers' websites. See anything you like? The best favors are reflective of your and your intended's personalities, long lasting, and practical. A tiny ivory ceramic basket can be useful, provided the majority of your guests happen to have tiny ceramic cats that will enjoy sleeping in them. Some wedding books and blogs will tell you to analyze your wedding style when choosing favors, but what you should really be looking at is your personal style. Ask yourself what kind of favor you would like to receive—a question that's particularly important because you're going to end up with plenty of leftover favors.

A search for "cheap wedding favors" reveals bombonieres that cost less than a dollar apiece. A search for "upscale wedding favors" results in links to wedding favors that will run you $60 and up! That should tell you a little something about the wide range of costs you'll encounter in your search for the perfect token of thanks. You won't be able to please everyone who picks up one of your favors, so don't think you can win over picky people by spending as much money as possible on something that screams "wedding."

You can convey your interests, outlook, and personal philosophy through your favors without giving the WIC one red cent. Think about what part of your life you might like to share with your family and friends, and then think of small gifts that reflect that aspect of yourself. Favors do not have to be covered in hearts and flowers to make good gifts, just like they don't have to be labeled "favors" to make good favors. If, however, you do decide to buy from a wedding-specific retailer, know that the listed price isn't always the price you will pay. Sites like Myweddingfavors.com adjust their prices when buyers adjust quantities, and they list the lowest prices first to capture customer interest. When you see a product listed for "As low as $1.90," that really means that the unit price will be a buck ninety if you buy one hundred or more of them. On some sites, you'll only get the best price if you purchase a ridiculous and unrealistic amount of favors.

If little knickknacks aren't your bag, you may be one of those rare brides- or grooms-to-be who gravitates toward charitable favors. When you give charitable favors, you take all of the cash you budgeted on favors and you either donate it to a charity or use it to purchase a charitable gift through a site. Let's say you have $600 budgeted toward favors—you can make a lump sum donation to Diabetes.org or buy an emergency rescue kit for a vulnerable community through Oxfamamericaunwrapped.com. The American Diabetes Foundation will print your favor cards for you; buying the rescue kit means you have to find some way of letting guests know what you've done on their behalf.

There are also green favors, like the seed-filled paper keepsakes from Botanicalpaperworks.com. The paper itself breaks down in the soil, and wildflowers sprout from the seeds so that guests are reminded all summer long of your nuptials. If you can't find anything you like in the small eco-friendly selection at favor shops like Beau-coup.com and Blissweddingsmarket.com, search for eco-friendly party supplies. Going green isn't always easy, so this may be the right time to think about the virtues of DIY. You could always buy some recycled gift boxes and fill 'em up with fair-trade coffee from Groundsforchange.com or organic dark chocolate miniatures from Greenandblacks.com.

On your wedding day, favors can be distributed to guests in one of two ways. You can put one favor per place setting at each table—a move that works particularly well when you've decided to go with assigned seating so no one double dips. Or you can put all your favors in one basket, virtually guaranteeing that guests will double dip. Remember to buy plenty of extras.

As You Say "I Do"

Some ceremony spots come complete with all the decorations you could ever want. There are religious institutions that are decked out with beautiful floral arrangements twenty-four hours a day, seven days a week. There are places outdoors where Mother Nature has truly outdone herself. Stately mansions and museums have their own unique charm. The point is that decorating these places would be gilding the lily. Other ceremony spots are nice and there's nothing wrong with them, but they'll definitely need a little sprucing up before they're wedding worthy.

You may be wondering if you really need to buy all sorts of ceremony accoutrements. The definitive answer is that you don't. It's easy to talk yourself into buying something you never knew you wanted when you're looking at the beautiful hand-painted aisle runners at Aisleart.com and the custom wedding rugs at Wedding rugs.com. Then again, maybe you want a long piece of cloth with your name on it because it'll look classy *and* hide your ceremony space's ugly puce carpeting.

Things like pew bows and flower cones, garlands, white pillar candles on thick brass candlesticks, fresh flowers, and whatever else it is you're into can take an everyday, blah space and turn it into a self-contained wedding wonderland. The appropriate decor can heighten the matrimonial magic in a big way. As far as larger decorative items go, there are plenty of wedding arches on eBay, and the shipping is nowhere near as bad as you might suppose. You'll also have no trouble finding a custom chuppah on the net at sites like Mpartworks.com/e-chuppah.htm.

The usual rules apply with regard to buying from online sellers. You'll want to wait until you know where you'll be holding your ceremony before making any purchases, lest you end up with pink tapers that clash heinously with the deep ocean blue of the carpet you'll be standing on. Pay close attention to posted shipping times and give yourself plenty of wiggle room so you don't end up tying the knot without those twenty strands of faux ivy you so desperately wanted.

If you're introducing modern secular rituals into your traditional rites, you've got to have the right tools. The aforementioned unity candle has become the darling of the wedding world, though quite a number of venues aren't exactly keen on letting people play around with open flames. This trio of tapers is easy to come by because of the popularity of the unity candle ritual, and most wedding retailers stock the candles themselves as well as stylized candle stands. There is even a surprising number of sites dedicated to personalizing unity candles, like Personalizedweddingcandle.com and Printedcandle.com.

Unity rites vary from culture to culture. Some brides and grooms break bread while others jump over brooms. Some are lassoed together with rope while others exchange salt. There are water ceremonies and sand ceremonies, where newlyweds pour colored liquids or particulates into a single container to symbolize the blending of their lives. Some brides and grooms exchange roses, and fresh-flower retailers abound on the web. In one wine ceremony, newlyweds pour wine from two carafes into a single chalice and take consecutive drinks. In another, the bride and groom drink at the same time using a German wedding cup, a drinking vessel so dangerous that it's also known as a wager cup because guests place bets on whether the bride and groom will spill wine all over their fancy duds. Intrigued? They're usually found at German specialty shops like German-toasting-glasses.com /german_wedding_cups.html.

Feel free to make up your own imaginative ceremonies to demonstrate how your lives have become forever intertwined. If you can't envision anything original, just be thankful that most of the stuff used in the standard ceremonies is easy enough to come by, whether you're buying from online wedding shops or stores that carry regular old consumer goods. After all, salt is salt and sand is sand, right?

A. J. Saved a Little Here and There

"The favors from Botanical Paperworks were exactly what I wanted, and I know I wouldn't have found them at a bridal show or store. The paper was handmade and beautiful, and I know from talking to people who attended the wedding that the seeds sprouted quickly into great flowers. I felt like we were giving people a memory of our love that would grow over time.

"Because I shopped online, I got a slight discount for each item I purchased, but those discounts added up fast. I'm sure we saved a nice chunk of change by buying stuff online. But that aside, I don't think I would have known where to shop in the real world for what I ended up purchasing. You can't tell from a name or address what a store carries. When it came to my butterfly decorations, I found boxes of mixed colors at a local craft outlet, but all I wanted were the blue ones. It was a lot easier to order them online instead of buying tons of butterflies in colors I couldn't even use. I was so happy when I finally found the right ones online—it took a lot of searching but they were the perfect color!"

The Party of Your Dreams

Your guests will notice your reception decor. They may not realize that they're noticing it, but they're still getting a big fat eyeful of all the cool stuff you picked out. That means that decor is important—maybe not as important as the dress or the food or even the music, but still pretty important.

The first question you should ask is how do you take a generic space and make it your own? Wonderfulgraffitiwedding.com/index .html creates monograms and messages on its special contact paper so you can leave your mark on everything from your centerpieces to the dance floor. As far as personalization goes, it opens up some interesting options—provided your reception venue is cool with your slapping stickers all over the place. Wreaths, floral swags, balloon arches, and tulle bows are all plenty easy to come by on-line and a lot less likely to piss off venue managers who are trying not to get fired. If your bridal party is large enough and will be carrying some big bouquets, you can always spring for vases, bottles, and jars on eBay and turn the bouquets into instant centerpieces. Voila!

The best part about buying for your reception online is that you may very well end up buying in bulk, and bulk buying is an area in which the Internet truly shines, even when you're talking about stores influenced by the heavy hand of the WIC. Those unit prices that make favor pricing so deceptive can make buying fifteen centerpieces far less painful. As a rule, unit prices drop much more quickly on higher-priced items, so the unit price on one high-end centerpiece may be a lot higher than the unit price for ten of the same exact product. On eBay, look for "lots" of the item you're hoping to buy in bulk, like "vases lot" or "dried flower lot."

And for the love of all things matrimonial, shop around. The first price you come across may seem like a bargain, but until you've done some searching, you can't really be sure you're getting a good deal. That's the whole point of buying online. In a brick-and-mortar store, you pay the store's price, or you leave and hope that there's another shop that's still open at 7 p.m. because you just don't have time to go back into the city later on in the week. When you shop on the Internet, you can look at twenty different stores in less than an hour at five in the morning if you feel like it.

It's up to you whether you want to get toasting flutes, cake knives and servers, card boxes, wishing wells, and all the other products associated with the traditional wedding reception. The problem won't be finding the wedding stuff you want, because the WIC has its tendrils in every corner of the Internet. Your time will be spent comparing prices, wading through search results to find better-quality items, and looking for shops that have multiple items you want so you don't get punched in the gut by hefty shipping costs. On that note, here's a neat trick: When you're searching for something you want on Google, be it dresses, serving spoons, or blooms, add "free shipping" to your search parameters to find the sites that will gladly cover that cost for their customers.

With Your Own Two Hands

Lots of wedding stuff is made out of other stuff. Boxed candy wedding favors, for example, became boxed candy wedding favors when a paid employee of the company selling said favors put some candy in a box and tied it up with a ribbon. When you buy boxed candy favors, you're not only paying for the candy—you're paying for the box and for the wages of the person who put the candy in the box. Now presumably you're smart enough and dexterous enough to put candy in a box on your own time. You are free to choose whether you want to pay someone else to box up that candy.

That is, in a nutshell, the motivation that drives brides-and grooms-to-be to explore the wonderful world of DIY. Whether you're the next Martha Stewart in the making or a total klutz, you can DIY with a little patience. The fact is that most of the projects you'll find floating around the web are easy enough for beginners to tackle without much trouble. A lot of people who have never before considered themselves crafty suddenly find that they're motivated to craft when they realize they can save serious money on favors, centerpieces, and all sorts of other nuptial accessories.

Before you actually decide to DIY and order a hundred or so dollars' worth of supplies, ask yourself if you have the time and the fortitude to spend half a Saturday tying 150 slippery ribbons around 150 bubble bowls. Some people get really pumped when they think about impressing their guests, but that initial enthusiasm deflates rapidly when the reality of the task sets in. You may lead a relatively stress-free lifestyle that leaves you with plenty of leisure hours that you can devote to the manual creation of all the wedding stuff you want and need. Conditions are perfect—get a nice flat surface ready. On the other hand, if you work seventy hours a week at a high-stress job, DIY may not be for you. When making your own decorations and gifts is more frustrating than fun, put down the bows and unplug the hot glue gun.

Let's say you have the time, the inclination, and the help to delve right into DIY. Your first step should be to look for the instructions you need if you're planning to do anything more complicated than, say, wrap Jordan almonds in tulle. Thankfully, there are tutorials all over the web, on sites and in blogs. Visit DIYbride.com for project ideas with directions, crafter's resources, and planning advice. Look at Craftster.org, DIYnetwork.com/diy/cr_wedding, and other searchable crafting sites for inspiration and instructions. If reading printed instructions gets too confusing, head over to YouTube and search for things like "wedding favors," "DIY wedding," and "make

Jeanette, the Hunter

"I think that eBay was the resource I turned to most when looking for all of the DIY supplies we used and the stuff we bought. I definitely paid less than I would have at Michael's or other craft stores for the things I needed. Incidentally, I pretty much refused to shop on the big wedding sites—everything was way too expensive! I would see these great little favors on Weddingchannel.com, and then I'd look for them on eBay and find them for a quarter of the price!

"DIY was everything in our wedding. We just didn't have the money to pay people to do things for us. We assembled our own centerpieces with my mother's help, my bridal party was sweet enough to put together our favors, and we printed our own invitations. My favors were too simple to need a tutorial, but I did do a lot of research on how to make favors on a limited budget, which was very useful. A lot of people expect couples to spend quite a chunk of change on something most people won't even keep. The best piece of advice I can offer is this: You'd better like your favors, because you're going to be stuck with a whole lot of them!"

centerpieces," with or without quotes. DIY gets a lot easier when you can actually see people in action.

The raw materials you're going to need will be a lot cheaper if you buy from craft stores instead of wedding retailers. Save-on -crafts.com and Factorydirectcraft.com stock just about everything crafty brides- and grooms-to-be need to make stuff for their nuptials, but they are by no means the only source of raw materials online. Search anywhere and everywhere for the component parts you need to realize your DIY dreams, and you'll inevitably end up paying the lowest prices for the best supplies.

So what can you make? How about:

- Truly easy favors—Bridalchoice.com/wedding_how-to/easy _favors.html

- Centerpieces—Weddingflowers.freeservers.com

- Wineglass lamps—Save-on-crafts.com/wincanlamfro.html

- Fancy ribbon roses—Offray.com/106a.html

- Garters—Wedfrugal.com/projects/garterssimple.html

- Guest books—Ourhouse.ninemsn.com.au/ourhouse/fact sheets/db/craft/07/783.asp

- Pew bows—Offray.com/pewbows.html

- Cone pew markers—Save-on-crafts.com/pewmarkers.html

- Twinkle tents—Todays-weddings.com/crafts/archives/craft _tent.php

- Unity candles—Unitycandle.com/makeUnityCandles.html

- Homemade candles—Craftbits.com/viewProject.do?projectID=283

These links represent only a tiny sample of the many hundreds of instructionals out there on the web. If you want to make it—whatever "it" is—you can bet that someone has posted directions somewhere. Just remember that you don't have to bury yourself in piles of silk flowers and faux pearls for the next six months if that's not what you're into. Hit up Google and search for "wedding favor kits" and "wedding centerpiece kits" to find examples of the easiest in easy DIY. But don't actually buy the kit! Spend a little time analyzing the item in question, then go buy the components from an inexpensive online craft store. Here's why: The centerpiece kits at Surroundings.com are made out of flameless tea lights, glass crystals, and votive holders that you can buy cheaply all over the Internet. Invest the money you save in your catering costs—your guests will probably forget your thoughtfully chosen table decor, but they'll almost always remember what you fed them.

Find Gifts for Guests

- Beau-coup.com

- Bellaregalo.com

- Botanicalpaperworks.com

- Cookiesinbloomweddings.com

- Cutiepiecookie.com/customs.htm

- Delvecchiodesigns.com

- Ecoparti.com

- Exclusivelyweddings.com

- Favoroutlet.com

- Favors.weddingstar.com

- Favorsandflowers.com

- Favorsdirect.com

- Favorstudio.com

- Greenworldproject.net

- Hansonellis.com

- Icandywrap.com

- Inspirasiancreations.com

- Myjeanm.com

- Mymms.com/customprint

- Myowncookie.com

- Plantamemory.com
- Weddingthings.com

Stock Up for the Ceremony (and Reception)

- Balsacircle.com
- Candles.com
- Everythingbutthevows.com
- Findajp.com/chuppas.htm
- Jewelrybyrhonda.com/webpages/cakecharmsmenu.htm
- Kensingtonclassics.com
- Loveandvows.com
- Myspiritualwedding.com
- Sayido.com/wedding-keepers/shop
- Theweddingoutlet.com
- Weddingcakecharms.com
- Weddingdepot.com
- Weddingmountain.com
- Weddingrugs.com

Decide to DIY

- Craft-o-mania.com/weddings/index.html
- Diynetwork.com (search for "wedding")

- Factorydirectcraft.com
- Frugalbride.com/frugalcrafts.html
- Marthastewart.com/wedding-decorations
- Michaels.com/art/online/static?page=wedding
- Offray.com
- Papermart.com
- Printmyribbon.com
- Save-on-crafts.com
- Stencil-library.com
- Surroundings.com
- Wedcraft.com
- Wrapsmart.com

Chapter 9
Don't Leave
Them Guessing

???

In a perfect world, the people who care most about you and your intended would know exactly what you want and need at this moment in time. No one would think of buying you, the consummate meat-and-potatoes couple, an encyclopedic tofu cookbook. Repeat gifts would not be a problem because each guest would come up with a creative and thoughtful gift idea all their own. Guests would not walk helplessly through department store aisles wondering if you already have a lobster pot. You, in turn, would not have to force a gracious smile as you open your gift, thinking all the while about how much you hate lobster.

Because it's not a perfect world, there are gift registries. The idea that brides- and grooms-to-be should just ask for what they want originated in 1924, when some smart cookie at the Marshall Field's department store in Chicago figured out that personalized registries would be a great way to get warm bodies into the store. Registries also took the guesswork out of gift selection, endearing them to clueless gift givers. Everybody involved benefited—stores with registries got a little free advertising and engaged couples could be reasonably sure that the gifts they received would be to their taste. Other department stores jumped on the idea, and the retail world hasn't looked back since.

You can create your registry in one of two ways. If your idea of a well-spent Saturday involves walking around and around giant superstores with a scanning gun, an in-store registry may be for you. You and your intended can wander around, zapping what you like, and your selections will end up in the store's database. Actually, make that two or three Saturdays, because most brides- and grooms-to-be need to make a few trips before they feel like their registries are complete. If, however, you think that sounds like a colossal waste of time, you should explore the hundreds of online registry opportunities out there. Almost all of the big housewares and home improvement stores will let you register on the web.

Spend some time browsing Lnt.com, Homedepot.com, Crateandbarrel.com, Target.com, and Tiffany.com to figure out what sort of gifts you might like to receive. You should keep in mind that guests tend to favor registries at larger stores with locations all over the United States—even if they're shopping at 4 a.m. from the comfort of their home office. In the unlikely event that there is some sort of major issue with one of your wedding presents, the giftee knows they can drive to the nearest location and complain in person. Start creating your registry as soon as you get engaged, because you never know when some kind soul will decide it's time for presents. The great thing about online registries is that you can edit them whenever and as often as you like.

Be aware that there is a subtle song-and-dance brides- and grooms-to-be must do when the subject of gifts comes up. You create a registry to let loved ones know what you're pining for, but it's considered very, very bad manners to spread the word yourself. You can make a list of what you want, but you can't actually ask for what you want. Any information related to your registry or registries must be passed along via word of mouth by your parents and friends. If someone asks you directly where you're registered, it's all right to give them the specifics as long as you also imply that you'll absolutely adore anything they give you. Some stores still encourage those who are soon to be wed to include registry cards in their invitations, confusing engaged couples who thought they had the etiquette rules all figured out.

Registry etiquette is actually simple and straightforward. You and your intended can create a wedding registry and share it with relatives or your attendants without incurring the wrath of the etiquette gods. There is no rule stating that you can have only one registry, and there is no reason you shouldn't register for as many items as you can think of. The bigger your registry, the better the chances your loved ones will find an item they can feel good about buying for you. Just make sure you don't overload your registry with pricey presents that the majority of the people you know will have to struggle to afford. Your loved ones may very well spring for that fancy countertop rotisserie, but expect that acquaintances

Jeanette

"One of the things that Chris and I share is a love of food. We both grew up in big Italian families, where half our lives and all major events revolved around food. Hell, my entire life has been focused on food, because I grew up on a fruit and vegetable farm! We both developed a love for cooking, and it's one of the special things we do together.

"A lot of the cooking equipment that we had amassed as a couple was cheap, came to us as hand-me-downs, or was battered from overuse. When we talked about putting together registries, it was only natural that we think, 'Hey, maybe we can ask for all the stuff we've always wanted but couldn't afford or would never buy for ourselves!' We imagined our dream kitchen, and then we asked for all the things we envisioned by way of our online registry.

"We got a lot of the things we asked for. Not everything we wanted—we received only three or four china settings, for example—but we now have a phenomenally more complete kitchen than we ever had before. A lot of guests used the registry as a guideline and bought other stuff based on what we'd asked for. I loved the recipe gifts we received—the giver would assemble all of the hardware we needed to make a certain recipe and include the recipe as part of the gift. Very thoughtful!"

will buy smaller token gifts. You'll cover all your bases when you stock your registry with plenty of low-priced, midrange, and up-scale stuff. Don't be surprised when someone splurges on you unexpectedly!

The plain truth is that guests are not bound by nuptial law to buy you something from the registries that you and your sweetie put together. In fact, your guests are not even obligated to give you a gift, though gift-giving is considered an important social nicety. You can be as miffed as you like that people aren't buying the items on your carefully created registry, but please don't let it show. Most people who go out on a limb and pick a personalized present do so because they wanted to get you something a little more meaningful than a mixing bowl, so cut them some slack. Gifts that just don't do it for you can easily be returned, donated to charity, or hidden away in the darkest part of your basement. It's a lot harder to mend the feelings of the people you hurt when you get pissed at them for turning a blind eye to your wish list. When your bohemian SIL asks if you like the macramé planter she made just for you, do the right thing and lie through your teeth.

Where there are registry dos there must also be registry don'ts. Do not, under any circumstances, include the aforementioned registry cards in your wedding invitations, because that is just tacky as all get-out. Do not go blabbing to anyone and everyone that you've created a registry to make your guests' lives so much easier. And never assume that the value of the gifts you receive must be equal to or greater than the cost of the gift giver's meal.

To some extent, weddings are a chance for brides and grooms to rake in some choice loot, but common courtesy dictates that you pretend otherwise. Try not to drop too many thinly veiled hints when discussing the wedding with future guests. They will see right through you as you sing the praises of Potterybarn.com's registry system, so don't sing too loudly, lest you discourage gift givers from giving generously. Be realistic when you create your registry. Choose gifts that you'll use—like a good chef's knife—instead of gifts you think you'll use someday when you finally get around to learning how to make crème brûlée. You do not need double old-fashioned glasses just because the list at Bedbathandbeyond.com/regchecklist .asp says you do.

Maybe you want cash, not stuff. It's okay to think of money as the perfect gift. Furthermore, there's nothing wrong with giving registries a pass because you're hoping to encourage your guests to throw some dough your way. But you really ought to be subtle about it, the same way you'd be subtle about spreading your wedding registry info around. Faux pas happen when excited brides- and grooms-to-be forget that money is a gift like any other. It really doesn't matter that you've got two toasters, sixteen oven mitts, and enough tea towels between you to fill a closet. You wouldn't include a note in your invitations stating that you really only want green-and-gold striped placemats from Bedbathandbeyond.com, so do not assume that it's a-okay to include a poem like this one:

> *So what do you get*
> *For the bride and groom*
> *Whose house needs things*
> *In every room?*
> *When shopping for a present please don't be rash*
> *As there is always the option*
> *To just give cash!*
> *We hope you don't find*
> *Our request to be funny*
> *But we really would appreciate*
> *A gift of money.*

In the end, you simply cannot dictate what people will buy, because they will make gift-giving choices based on all sorts of factors you won't be able to anticipate. What you can do is use all of the craftiness and cunning in your repertoire to make sure that guests are informed of your preferences. Those guests will then decide for themselves what makes a good gift and whether they will abide by the gift-giving etiquette rules found on sites like Beau-coup .com/gift_giving_etiquette.htm. Once the gifts start rolling in, it will be your responsibility to try as hard as possible to be grateful for every gift you receive—even if it's something you really don't want—because each of those gifts is a reflection of the love others have for you. When a gift is just so dang bad that there can be no justification, fake it.

Of course, where there are dos and there are don'ts, there are also exceptions. The same registry information that ought never to appear in an invitation can be safely posted somewhere on your wedding website. Put your site address on your STDs, and your guests will eventually stumble onto your registry without your ever having to breathe a word of it to anyone. Your MOH can also include your registry information in the shower invitations, provided you didn't have a hand in planning the event.

What do you do if your registry says that guests have bought you all sorts of lovely things but your mailbox remains suspiciously empty? Search engines may actually be to blame—every now and again online registries get indexed by search engines, which means that someone scouring the net for the best prices on butcher block cutting boards can accidentally purchase something listed on your registry. That awesome cutting board won't ever land on your doorstep, but it will show up as "purchased" on your registry. When it seems as if you're getting an awful lot of no-show presents, get in touch with the shop handling your registry to find out who's been buying what and where exactly those goods have been going.

And don't forget to check the return policies associated with your registry. A lot of stores give preferential treatment to their registry customers because they assume that there won't be a lot of returns, but you never know. It's better to be safe than screwed!

Traditional Registries Still Rule

As brides and grooms get older and spend more time living on their own before tying the knot, the less relevant registry checklists like the one found at Elegala.com/registry-checklist.html become. Unless you've been living the ultimate bachelorette's existence and eating one-pot pasta every night, you likely already have a decent set of cookware, plenty of towels, and all the flatware you need to get by. But as registries are part of the traditional WIC package, a lot of couples feel pressured to replace everything in their kitchens, bedrooms, and bathrooms with newer and nicer stuff. It's up to you whether or not you want to trade up, but if you do decide that you want to swap out your tired old household accessories for something more sophisticated, this is the time to do it.

Traditional registries are all about housewares. That means stuff like plates, pans, toilet paper holders, that fuzzy rug thing some people like to put on their toilet seats, pillowcases and the pillows that go in them, and silver-plated three-tiered serving trays that hardly anyone ever uses anymore. The sky's the limit when you're setting up a traditional registry, because everyone will expect you to pad your wish list with crystal pitchers and wall sconces. You're supposed to be stocking up for the future, so don't feel obligated to limit yourself to two of everything. Your little family may very well grow in the not-so-distant future, and even the child-free-by-choice community entertains now and again.

If you need a little help, there are plenty of online guides that will take you through the process of registering for housewares. There are individual tutorials for glassware (Flawlesswedding .com/bridal-registry/registering-for-glassware), dinerware (Flawless wedding.com/bridal-registry/registering-for-dinnerware), cookware (Flawlesswedding.com/bridal-registry/registering-for-cookware), and flatware (Flawlesswedding.com/bridal-registry/registering-for

A. J. Stayed Firmly on the Right Side of Etiquette

"We got into the whole online registry thing but stuck with the typical Crate and Barrel and Bed Bath & Beyond stuff. We originally went all traditional and registered for actual china, but it wasn't long before we realized that we don't actually have any use for china. No one was buying it anyway, so we took it off our list. Right around that time, I was tempted to start deleting other stuff, because people were buying gifts off the registry but they weren't the gifts I really wanted. I'm still tempted to go back and get more of the towels we loved because we got only a few."

-flatware). Have a look at the online checklists mentioned previously in the chapter—you may not be planning on rebuilding your kitchen from scratch, but you might find some more obscure items you probably would have forgotten about. After all, how much time do you spend thinking about splatter screens and steam vacs?

With so many items and so many options, it's really easy to get carried away. Be a little discerning as you register, lest you end up with asker's remorse. Some couples register for everything under the sun instead of focusing on what they actually need or want and then find themselves inundated with countertop-hogging appliances they'll never use, an overabundance of dishes that don't quite fit in their apartment-sized kitchen cabinets, and all sorts of other things they'll never actually get around to opening.

Preventing that sort of sorry situation is a matter of going from room to room in your home with a notepad so you can make a list of anything you actually need. The word "need" is fairly subjective, so you have a lot of wiggle room. If you're really into sports, you might need a huge flat-screen television. Once you've figured out where the gaps are, think about all of the fun stuff you want but really can't justify buying. As much as you want to avoid offending anyone you care about, realize that your guests will probably not judge the contents of your registry.

Have a second look at the checklist at Bedbathandbeyond.com/regchecklist.asp and ask yourself some pointed questions. Do you really eat or make enough layer cakes to make storing a full-size cake dome worth it? How often is that gravy boat actually going to come out of the darkest recesses of your pantry? If the urge to whip up a pizza from scratch has never struck you, why exactly do you need a pizza stone? Griddles, woks, slow cookers, and stock pots are pretty big, so where do you plan to store all of these culinary tools? If you're still not quite sure what you want, try taking the silly quiz at Lifestyleregistry.theknot.com. You probably won't learn anything about yourself, but you may just get a few inspiring ideas.

The standard, unexciting housewares registry is typically the kind of registry that guests like to see. Yes, there are those old folks who can't believe that anyone anywhere would have the audacity to register for anything, but registries are, for the most part, so ingrained in the collective consciousness that people will just assume you have one.

When Your Kitchen, Bedroom, and Bathroom Are Stocked

Traditionally, a bride filled her registry with stuff for the home because she and her mate-to-be were going to be building a home from the ground up. You, however, probably have almost all of the kitchen, bedroom, and bathroom accoutrements that you need. If it happens that you don't feel particularly inclined to replace everything you own because you're getting hitched, there are other things you can register for. But be prepared to get the stink eye from some of your more conservative guests when you register for anything other than housewares. Just so you know, there's actually nothing wrong with alternative registries; they're no more or less gift-grabby than any other type of wedding registry. Make good etiquette your focus, and you'll be fine.

The simplest nontraditional registry is probably the Amazon .com Wish List. You can stock this unorthodox wedding registry with books, DVDs, CDs, furniture, toys, clothes, and just about everything else imaginable. The site does have a separate wedding registry app located at Amazon.com/gp/wedding/homepage, but if one of you already has a wish list in progress, you can use that instead. Amazon does link to a fairly comprehensive selection of wedding planning articles from its registry page, so you can read up on nuptial niceties if you do decide to make a fresh list. Amazon will even provide you with the HTML you need to put button-style links to your registry on your wedding website.

Sites like Yourweddingregistry.com provide almost the same service, but you can register for any item, from any store, anywhere in the world. You pay a fee up-front for this all-encompassing password-protected registry, and that fee is based on the number of invitations you plan to send out. One benefit to this rather pricey service is that you can turn to the company's live customer service in the event that a gift doesn't reach you or your registry isn't functioning as expected. The downsides are the fees and the etiquette-unfriendly registry announcements the company will send to all of your guests.

You can always forget the fee and go with services like My registry.com or Felicite.com. Myregistry.com is pretty much a clone of Yourweddingregistry.com, except it's free to set up a registry and the interface is nowhere near as clunky. Felicite.com is the more limited service in that the company works with affiliate merchants, but the list of stores it works with is fairly long and includes Amazon.com. Or just search online for what you want and the word "registry." You'll find furniture registries, travel gear registries, jewelry registries, and lingerie registries, though do you really want your grandma picking out your underwear?

Then there are the online honeymoon registries. If you go this route, you'll have plenty of registries to choose from—a Google search for "honeymoon registry" yields over two hundred thousand results. Make sure you choose a site with no setup fees, like Honeymoonwishes.com. Know, however, that most of the sites will deduct some sort of fee from the 'moon money your guests give you. When you set up a honeymoon registry, the descriptions of each gift should be specific and creative. A "Moonlit Venetian Gondola Ride" sounds a lot more appealing to guests with dough to spend than "$50 for Venice." And the usual rules apply where the numbers are concerned: Make sure your big-ticket items (like, for example, plane tickets, train tickets, etc.) are balanced out by smaller gifts, like $20 for "Gelato for Two."

Don't think you need to register for a tropical vacation or a European tour if that's not what you're into. Sites like Aftthe weddingday.com let you register for things like tickets to sporting events and the movies, massages, golf outings, and camping trips. But when it comes down to it, all of the fancy descriptions you'll write as you create your honeymoon or activity registry are just for show. You don't actually book your vacations and jaunts through the registry sites! You're technically registering for the cash to do all the things you want to do, but when the gifts start rolling in, you can use the money you've accrued to buy a car or a boat. To keep gift-givers happy, however, you should probably go on the trips. They may ask for photographic evidence that you enjoyed your presents.

Your choices don't stop there: Homeregistrysolutions.com, a registry service created by two Realtors, lets your guest deposit gift money into an escrow account that you can then use to finance a new home. You'll have to pay $25 up front, but that $25 is actually the initial deposit used to open your escrow account. If you'd rather not have your gift money managed by a couple of dudes from Arizona, search for "mortgage wedding registry" to find more reputable home registries, like the one offered at Suntrustmortgage.com/bridalrg.asp. Guests who balk at the idea of buying you a book may not blink an eye when contributing to your new house registry.

Semitraditional registries made up of gift cards are a useful compromise. You should never, ever ask for cash, but who's going to notice if there are a few Bed Bath & Beyond gift cards listed at the tail end of your Bedbathandbeyond.com registry? You're still getting what amounts to money, and your guests know that you'll be spending it on something for your home. Sure, gift cards are one step away from straight cash registries like Reebles.com, but they're a lot more etiquette-friendly because they're associated with stores your loved ones are familiar with.

As for those straight cash registries, stay away from them unless you know that your relatives and friends won't be offended. As much as cash registry services like to claim that they are tasteful ways to ask for cash, the only truly tasteful method involves asking your loved ones to let anyone who inquires know that you and your intended would really prefer monetary gifts. Are cash registries convenient? Certainly—Aperfectweddinggift.com even uses PayPal as its dough delivery system. But it's really not that hard to cash a stack of checks after your wedding day.

Nontraditional registries are a fairly new thing in the online wedding world, so protect yourself by doing a little research. When in doubt, look up the registry company on BBBonline.org. In the event that nothing good or bad comes up in that search, plug the company name and "complaints" into Google and see what comes up. You can also look for the company name and "reviews" as a last resort. The average bride and groom pull in hundreds if not thousands of dollars' worth of wedding gifts—don't risk losing it all by working with a shady, fly-by-night registry service.

Gifts That Give Back

Presents in general are awesome—whether they help you beautify a home or help you buy one—but the most awesome gifts are usually the ones that make the world a better place. Someone in recent history decided to improve upon the conventional gift registry, and so it was that the charitable registry was born. If you like the idea but want guests' gifts to go directly to your charity of choice, you can always bypass the whole registry thing and put links to the organizations important to you on your website. You can entice people to donate by adding a note about why you care so much about the associated issues, but be prepared to field questions about how exactly people can make a donation in your names.

Charitable registries come in two flavors. There are direct donation sites like Justgive.org that let you choose a from lengthy list of charities when creating your registry. Guests can give monetary gifts on your behalf to those people who need them most without having to go through the rigmarole of figuring out how to make a donation in your name. You'll receive an e-mail notification each time one of your guests donates to one of the charities listed on your registry, ensuring that you know that it's time to write up another thank-you card. Just make sure that 100 percent of the charitable gifts given in your name will reach the charities important to you before signing up with this type of service.

Some registry services will automatically add fees to any donations your guests make on your behalf. For example, Idofoundation .com appends a 4.75 percent sliding fee to all gifts, while Justgive .org adds a $5 tax-deductible fee, no matter how large the gift. Gift givers pay the fee on top of the donation so that none of the money intended for those in need is used to pay the registry's operational costs. Fees suck, but they're a necessary evil—nonprofit charity registries pay the credit card companies to process transactions, and that expense gets passed on to you or your guests. Of course, some charities will let you set up a fee-free registry directly so your guests can avoid dealing with middlemen. If your favorite charity offers this service, they may even provide you with icons you can put in the registry section of your website.

Doing good should be its own reward, but the thought of all the traditional wedding bounty rolling in can make even the most magnanimous future newlyweds a little bit greedy. You can satisfy your selfishness while still doing something nice for your fellow human beings by opting to set up the second type of charitable registry. It works like this: A generous guest buys you that really sweet stand mixer you've been coveting from Cooking.com through your Ido foundation.com "Gifts That Give Back" registry. Up to 10 percent of the purchase price of that item will be donated to your chosen charity, making it a win-win setup. You get your $400 mixer and the charitable organization of your choice gets forty bucks. Everyone gets what they want!

And here's one more piece of registry advice: You may not be a traditional bride- or groom-to-be with traditional needs, but that doesn't mean your guests don't feel strongly about the value of the time-honored gifting traditions. Do the right thing and register for *some* housewares so your more conventional loved ones don't feel slighted by what they see as your outlandish choices. It may seem as if you're pandering to the mores of the past, but there are just some people who don't regard matching Vespas or donations to the SPCA as appropriate wedding gifts.

Create a Traditional Registry

- Bedbathandbeyond.com/regHome.asp
- Bloomingdales.weddingchannel.com
- Crateandbarrel.com/gr/default.aspx
- Fortunoff.com/br_home.asp
- Gifts.com/ideas/wedding
- Lnt.com
- Macys.weddingchannel.com
- Potterybarn.com/registry
- Target.com/clubwedd
- Tiffany.com
- Williams-sonoma.com/registry

Help the World

- Changingthepresent.org/weddings
- Globalgiving.com/gifts/registries.html
- Heifer.org
- Idofoundation.org
- Justgive.org
- Tenthousandvillages.com/catalog/registry/index.php

Score Something Different

- Aftertheweddingday.com
- Amazon.com/gp/wedding/homepage
- Aperfectweddinggift.com
- Felicite.com
- Gogift.com
- Homeregistrysolutions.com
- Myregistry.com
- Rainfallofenvelopes.com
- Reebles.com
- Vow2save.com
- Yourweddingregistry.com

Fund Your Honeymoon

- Buy-our-honeymoon.com/usa
- Forthemoon.com
- Honeyluna.com
- Sendusoff.com
- Thebigday.com
- Thehoneymoon.com
- Travelersjoy.com

Chapter 10

A Dress to Dream About

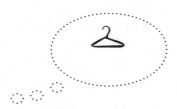

Many brides-to-be believe, and rightly so, that the bridal gown is one of the most important aspects of the matrimonial celebration. Over the years, the woman's wedding costume—once nothing more than a bride's Sunday best or a new but fairly practical dress that would be dyed and reworn—has evolved into a sort of centerpiece of frivolity around which the entire nuptial ceremony revolves. And it's no wonder! A drop-dead gorgeous couture bridal gown can cost as much as the services of the caterer, baker, and photographer combined. Heck, even a moderately priced gown will set you back $800 or so. Either way, if you're paying that much for a dress, you're going to want it to stand out.

Yet while the dress you wear on your wedding day can be as much of a showstopper as the wedding cake and the reception decor, it will not exist in a vacuum. The typical bride is responsible for choosing both the attendants' dresses and the flower girl's dress. She may even have a hand in helping the MOB and MOG choose their wedding-day wear. That might sound like a lot of work, but choosing your gown and your ladies' attire does not have to become an expedition into some frightening territory filled with bubblegum-pink crinoline and leg-of-mutton sleeves. If you do some basic research, you'll already know what you want by the time you begin browsing the virtual (or real) dress racks.

Many women start envisioning their dream wedding dress before they are fully capable of pronouncing the word "nuptial." Some dream of wearing mom's gown, only to discover that the de rigueur dresses of yesteryear have become horrifyingly dated. But most women, whatever their matrimonial assumptions, have never given a second thought to the sort of waistlines, hemlines, and necklines found on your average gown. A little knowledge can mean the difference between looking fabulous on your wedding day and looking like an overpuffed marshmallow, not to mention the difference between attracting the admiration of your bridesmaids or earning their undying ire.

If you've already taken a virtual peek at what is currently fash-

Leah's Gown Search

"To find a gown I loved I went straight to the archives at Weddingchannel.com, which has that neat scrapbook capability and tons of pictures catalogued by wedding type, style, color, and more. I liked that I could add the pictures of the gowns I liked best to my scrapbook so I could view them whenever I wanted. I also looked online for the best style of dress for my body type (i.e., short and curvy) and made sure I was making good choices.

"Once I'd done all my research, I went with my mom and my FMIL to a local salon and picked out my dress in less than half an hour! I was frustrated, however, by a lot of the designers' websites, because it was almost impossible to find a really good picture of each gown online and, on top of that, the sites wouldn't tell you how much each gown cost. Sure, I could have waited ten weeks for a local boutique to order a sample, but in an age when I can get shoes *overnighted* to my door, it shouldn't take that long!

"Generally, I was surprised and saddened by the state of wedding dresses online—it seemed as if they really wanted to make sure that the boutique was the only place you could actually see the dresses. And then you might not even be able to try them on for six weeks! They don't seem to realize that you can keep your specialized appeal and still sell to an online audience these days."

ionable in the wedding world, you may have noticed the distressing lack of "Add to cart" buttons on dress designers' websites. The fact is, up until now, the dressmakers had a good thing going with the bridal salons. The designers get paid full price for their wares, while the salons charge brides-to-be and their attendants a hefty markup. Online discounters interfere with that age-old partnership by allowing future brides to buy from businesses that don't need to cut paychecks for shop clerks or pay rent for prime storefront locations—and the savings are passed on to the buyer.

While you may get treated like a queen at a full-service salon, you'll more than likely pay full price (which means suggested retail and then some) for the privilege. Gowns at online retailers typically cost 20 to 50 percent less than those found in traditional stores. And though some designers will warn you that you'll lose money on your online discount when it comes time to pay for alterations and pressing, the truth is that plenty of real-world retailers charge extra fees for those services anyway. As for the myth of costly shipping charges, you'll seldom pay more than $30 for shipping when buying a gown online, and you can avoid paying sales tax by buying from a retailer located out of state.

Nonetheless, always be somewhat wary when buying your gown from a web-based seller. Some, like Houseofbrides.com and Aria dress.com, represent the online presence of real-world shops. The former is an authorized retailer of the gowns it stocks, and the latter is the website of Aria Bridesmaids, which creates and sells its own designs. Other designers and manufacturers operate exclusively online and acquire their gowns from questionable sources, like sweatshops. Still others will craft you a designer imposter version of the dress you adore. Gownbidder.com is a seemingly unregulated auction portal that handles nothing but discontinued gowns and floor samples.

Go with your gut—if a site's layout looks cheap, the fine print seems calculated to confuse, or you're unsure where the merchandise originated, don't hesitate to find another retailer. The mantra "better safe than sorry" definitely applies where dresses worth hundreds or even thousands of dollars are concerned. If you're comfortable buying an inexpensive gown that unapologetically mimics a pricier designer frock, you may want to give the legality of your purchase a second thought—wedding gown designs are generally not copyrightable unless they have very distinctive lacework, but "counterfeit chic" remains a legal gray area. Additionally, be aware that the dress that arrives on your doorstep may be made of inferior materials shoddily sewn together by seamstresses making pennies on the dollar. Of course, most legitimate gown manufacturers outsource, and there is no guarantee that the more expensive dress of your dreams wasn't sewn in similar conditions.

Some things to keep in mind:

- Many bridal salons both online and offline will take steps to prevent brides-to-be from finding out who manufactured or designed the gowns with which they are enamored. This is supposed to stop them from trying on a dress in the salon (or finding one on a nonretail website) and then price-shopping at other salons or on retail websites. In brick-and-mortar salons, store employees rip the tags out of gowns—a practice that's lawful but annoying. Online stores often make up their own style numbers and assign them randomly to otherwise unbranded dresses. The easiest way to get around this is to visit big-name sites like Brides.com and Weddingchannel.com, which let you search their image archives using specific criteria like length, style, color, and fabric, so you can ID the gowns you like that way.

- Don't fib about your size and don't let your attendants fib about their sizes. While some ambitious brides-to-be buy their gowns a few sizes smaller as an incentive to lose weight before the big day, that type of thinking is a recipe for heartache. One, your future spouse loves you just the way you are and is likely looking forward to seeing a healthy, happy woman walking down the aisle. Two, if you plan to lose weight and that plan goes awry, you may be left with no other choice than to buy a second dress when your seamstress informs you that your gown's seam allowance prevents it from being let out any further. Three, if you do lose weight, it's a lot easier to make a dress smaller than it is to make a dress bigger. Be aware, however, that stiffer fabrics can only be sized down so much before they start to distort.

· Wedding gown sizes usually differ from street clothes sizes by one or two sizes. And that's one or two sizes up, mind you. If you wear a six in street clothes, you'll probably be looking at size eight or size ten gowns. If you're a twelve, check out the fourteens and sixteens. Before you buy, have a professional seamstress (or tailor) take your measurements and recheck the manufacturer's size charts, just in case. Never, ever guess your size, as most wedding gowns are nonreturnable. When you are ready to order your dream dress, choose your size based on your largest measurement. Again, it's easy to alter down but often impossible to alter up.

· Don't assume that the perfect gown—the one that moves you to tears *and* is the perfect color *and* fits your budget— will still be there in a month, a week, a day, or even an hour. The line might be discontinued. If it's on sale, it may be snapped up by some other bride-to-be. It might even be a one-of-a-kind sample. When you find the perfect gown, buy it, even if you have to put it on your credit card. In fact, do put it on your credit card, because credit cards almost always offer some form of buyer protection.

· If you buy your gown (or your attendants' dresses) online, you'll be responsible for scheduling your own alterations. Be aware that some seamstresses—particularly those with connections to real-world bridal salons—will overcharge you for alterations if they know you bought your gown online. If your seamstress inquires as to your dress's origins, feel free to say you bought it out of town. Technically speaking, that's the truth!

· Always, always, always read the fine print and be sure you understand an online retailer's policies regarding shipping, returns, deposits, fees, taxes, and buyer privacy. Take a screenshot of the web page containing product information and the shop's refund policies. Print those receipts! And always pay with a credit card, because if your gown arrives damaged or your headpiece shows up in your mailbox two weeks after your wedding, your only recourse may be to have your credit card company contest the charges.

The Dress

Timing is everything when it comes to choosing, ordering, and altering a gown when you plan to buy online. The good news is that there are so many fabulous resources on the web for brides-to-be who aren't looking forward to going from bridal salon to bridal salon with a gaggle of female friends and relatives in tow. However,

Jeanette Knew What She Didn't Want

"I wasn't interested in anything trendy or even particularly traditional. I also had additional considerations, as I was looking at plus-size gowns. And a lot of the gowns I loved either didn't come in my size or were way out of my budget range. But for the most part, it was easy to find styles I loved and could afford once I'd done a little research about gowns in general and had a solid idea of what I was looking for. I do wonder if I kind of took the fun out of it for my mom, because looking at gown after gown online meant that she and I weren't visiting bridal salons together. But when I think of the time and money I saved searching and buying online, I figure it was worth it."

just like store-hopping brides-to-be, net-savvy brides should start shopping for their gowns at least nine months before the wedding and purchase their gowns at least six months in advance.

You'll save yourself a big heap of stress by ordering well ahead of your nuptials—just grab yourself one of the huge fabric-safe garment bags from Heritagegown.com and make some closet space. The fact is, if you're not in a rush, shipping delays can't become fuel for panic attacks. On the other hand, if you *are* in a rush, Bridecouture.com keeps gowns on hand and almost always ships in two to four weeks, while Gownsales.com can expedite certain orders. And don't rule out vintage or secondhand gowns! Check out the in-stock selection at Cherishedbride.com, Vintagegown.com, and Vintagewedding.com.

Whether you fall asleep at night dreaming of poufy princess dresses or this is your first foray out of the land of jeans and T-shirts, you'll want to consider a few things before you begin to browse. Take a moment to think about your body type, your skin tone and undertones, the formality level of your wedding, and your everyday personal style. While a majority of women still opt for fairy-tale-style puffs and poufs, there is no reason your wedding day look can't reflect the same individuality you project every day. Don't ever change, because, baby, you're fabulous.

Start your formalwear education at Store.tjformal.com/fashion_glossary, which has a short illustrated primer that describes

Good Things Come to Those Who Wait

Whatever your shopping style, give yourself as much lead time as possible to ensure that shipping problems, gown issues, and fittings don't become a source of panic. If you know what to expect before buying or bidding at a particular store, you won't be surprised when your gown shows up three days after you place your order or three months after you place your order. Shipping times vary in a big way.

- Houseofbrides.com (which purports to be the world's largest online wedding store and offers free shipping on almost all orders) suggests the orders be placed as far in advance of your wedding date as possible.

- Bridalonlinestore.com ships all in-stock orders within five days, but nonstock items may not be shipped for eight to ten weeks.

- Netbride.com can ship in less than eleven weeks or more than sixteen weeks, depending on factory delivery times.

- Ebridalsuperstore.com ships in four to sixteen weeks, so cross your fingers but be prepared to kill some time.

- Thebridalshop.com has a standard twelve-week delivery time, meaning you won't have to wait impatiently for each day's mail call.

- Bridepower.com usually ships gowns in three to five weeks, but will put them in the post earlier whenever possible.

- Sellers on eBay's wedding apparel section can dictate their own shipping times, so ask *before* you bid or buy.

Never hesitate to reach out to the company that sold you your gown. Accidents happen, so don't just assume your gown is still in the mail. Once the estimated ship date has come and gone, it's time for you to find out just where your dress is, and fast.

common necklines, waistlines, bodice styles, sleeve styles, skirt styles, and fabric types. That way, when you're comparing gowns on sites with pictures that are utter crap, you'll still be capable of picturing an organza A-line gown with a boat neckline and bell sleeves.

"Body type" refers to body shape, a rather unforgiving concept that has been reduced to a standard package encompassing four traits: bust, waist, hips, and height. The assumption here is that you likely won't be showing off your legs—though never say never—and that you will choose a gown with sleeves if you absolutely despise your arms (for a quick tutorial on sleeves and necklines, visit Mybridaldresses.com). Remember that just because a gown is available in your size doesn't mean it will complement your body type. Be honest with yourself and you can save yourself a lot of buyer's remorse later on. Don't miss the bridal buying guides at Usabride .com and Confetti.co.uk, but do make a note of this brief summary of the best gowns for specific body types:

- If you're busty, look for styles without a lot of embellishments in the bust area. Straps set widely apart and V-shaped or off-the-shoulder necklines can both diminish the visual impact of a large bust, while corset-style, elongated bodices can ensure your assets stay put. Look for A-line gowns and ball gowns, as fuller skirts can balance out your figure. Avoid, at all costs, empire waistlines, cinched fabric around the bustline, and beadwork concentrated around the upper bodice.

- If you're absolutely not busty, you can always create the illusion of bust with padding. But if you'd rather not enhance yourself, consider a gown that has intricate embellishment in the upper bodice area. Contrary to popular belief, strapless necklines look fabulous on less-endowed brides. Choose a jewel or bateau neckline, but steer clear of bodices made of stiff fabric that hold their own shape. They can leave you struggling to cover up an embarrassing gap.

- If you are of average weight, height, and shape, millions of women everywhere hate you. Just kidding! You're one of the lucky ones who can pull off almost any design of gown. Whether you opt for a fitted mermaid gown, a loose sheath, or a gathered skirt, you'll likely look fabulous without even trying.

- If you have a thicker waist, an empire or A-line silhouette can conceal your pudge while showing off your shoulders and bust. Steer clear of any gown with a tightly fitted waistline and instead opt for dresses with flowing fabrics and eye-catching embellished necklines, which draw the gaze upward toward your beautiful face. Matte fabrics, like some satins, won't cast shadows and can deemphasize curves, while long veils and trains may make you look wider than you actually are.

- If you have what my grandma would call good birthing hips, try a gown with a square, off-the-shoulder, or horizontal neckline, as your décolletage will balance out your bottom half. Say no to butt bows, no matter how pretty they are, because they scream out for attention, and keep in mind that heavy, layered, yet still fitted fabrics can add the illusion of extra bulk. Look for ball gown silhouettes with plain skirts and embellished bodices, and pair that with a chapel-length veil to create smooth lines.

- If you're tall and slender, make the most of a long torso with a brilliantly colored sash or elaborate bodice embellishments. While you are lucky enough to be able to wear tiered skirts, ruffles, and bustles unapologetically, you may feel compelled to deemphasize your height with raglan or butterfly sleeves and flowing fabrics. Avoid straight or clingy dresses, which may make you look ungainly or skeletal, and keep your proportions in mind while buying veils and other accessories.

- If you're tiny, a sheath silhouette can add length to your figure, while a princess-cut gown can make you appear taller. Frills and excessive embellishments can shorten your figure unless they come together to create vertical lines, like seams or long lace appliqués. Opt for smaller cuffs, collars, and sleeves, as larger ones can look as if they're swallowing you whole. Any gown that draws the eye upward (think A-line, empire, or tea length) will help you stand a little bit taller as you walk down the aisle. You, too, will need to remember your proportions when making accessory purchases.

Ultimately, these are only recommendations. You may find a gown that, according to the standard rules, should make you look like a disproportionate blancmange yet is actually breathtakingly stunning when draped over your curves (or lack thereof). The choice is yours and yours alone. Your wedding dress should reflect your personality, your tastes, and your personal comfort levels. Even if strapless is all the rage this year (or this decade), don't hesitate to opt for cap, three-quarter, or long sleeves if you'd rather not bare your shoulders. The same goes for necklines. Regardless of what's in, there is no reason you absolutely need to show off your décolletage—or cover it up completely. And let's not forget length—tea-length dresses can be a lovely choice, especially in the summertime.

The people behind Weddings.pirate-king.com have created a comprehensive gown glossary filled with all the keywords you need to know (accompanied by illustrations) before you shop. But if you'd rather just quickly peruse a variety of sleeve lengths, necklines, and hemlines, visit Dressbydesign.com's custom dress app and see how your favorite styles come together in a single customized dress. There's no need to actually buy your creation, but you may just end up loving it. Naturally, there is also a checklist that can help you decide what you love and what you hate. Find it at Theelegantbride.net/wedgownlistpfv.html.

Your next step should be to give a little thought to fabrics. Unless you're a seamstress by trade or enjoy sewing as a hobby, you may have never considered the way different fabrics look, act, and feel on your skin. Today's wedding gowns are made out of everything from silk shantung to French taffeta to charmeuse satin. Sites like Fabrics.net and Housefabric.com can help you decide which fabric or fabrics you might like to wear as you hoof it down the aisle, and the guide at Bridalfabric.com/images/fabric.htm comes complete with photos, so there are no surprises. Whether you want a gown that is clingy and sleek or something so stiff and regal it will stand up on its own when you take it off, there is a fabric out there that will meet your needs. Remember to take your wedding season and your comfort into consideration. A weighty velvet gown can suffocate you in the summer and may turn out to be a drag in any season after hours of making chitchat with distant relatives. Likewise, wintertime may not be the best season to don a flimsy chiffon sheath.

Now consider color. That's right, color. The stereotypical white wedding gown is not the end-all and be-all of wedding fashion. More and more modern brides are tying the knot decked out in jewel blues, deep reds, and vivid greens, not to mention pinks, browns, and even black. If you're not ready to make a splash in living color but feel washed-out in white, gold, rum pink, and champagne can all stand in beautifully. And, frankly, even white means way more than white when you're talking about gowns. Among other hues, brides-to-be can choose between:

- Diamond, natural, or silk white, a subtle white that works well with a wide range of skin tones, from fair to dark.

- Stark white, the whitest white, which is extremely crisp and bright. It looks great on brides with dark skin and deep tans, but can also flatter those whose paler skin has yellow or olive undertones.

• Ivory white, also called eggshell, which is sometimes described as the creamiest shade of white. It works best on brides with fair skin and pink undertones.

Now it's time to window-shop the designers' own sites. Even if you plan on buying a no-name gown or having your gown custom-made for you, the designer sites can be a wonderful source of inspiration and help you get a feel for fabrics, colors, silhouettes, necklines, train lengths, sleeves, and more. Expect to come across a lot of embedded music (which can't be turned off a lot of the time) and Flash animation (which makes for a smooth interface but means you can't save pictures for later reference without taking a screenshot). Each time you come across a gown you absolutely adore, bookmark the page so you can come back to it later, or take a screenshot. You'll have easy access to the designer, model name or number, and image whenever you feel like comparing two or more gowns. Or, instead of searching individually for designer websites, check out Onewed .com's dress section. There you'll find information about more than one hundred designers and manufacturers, along with links to their sites.

Once the research portion of your gown search is over, it's finally time to shop. If you do try on a few gowns before hitting the online bridal shops—something you should do if you're a hard-to-fit size—bring a friend. And not just any friend. Bring a very good friend who is confident enough of your continuing esteem to give you her (or his) honest opinions. A friend who tells you over and over again that you look gorgeous can be a real self-esteem booster but won't be much help when you're trying to choose between a strapless and a halter neckline. When you finally fire up your browser, remember your keywords. Whatever search engine you use, don't just type in the words "wedding" and "gown" and hope for the best, because if you do, you're going to find yourself confronted with more than five million results. Try "wedding gown" followed by "online" and then "wedding dress," again followed by "online." Try "white gown" if that's what you're looking for, or even "red gown," "green gown," or "blue gown." A general search for gowns will lead you to a number of formal-wear sites that also offer gowns in wedding-ready colors like white, silver, and gold. Try expanding your criteria, as many bridesmaid, prom, and quinceañera dresses come in shades of white and can stand in beautifully for traditional wedding gowns. Or just hit up the sites in the resource boxes at the end of the chapter—most stock thousands of gorgeous gowns.

It's natural to feel a little nervous about buying your gown on-line when so many designers, salon owners, and salesclerks are ready to jump at the chance to put down web-based retailers. The fact of the matter is that retailers who rely exclusively on real-world store-fronts for business know that women who set foot in a physical retail space are more likely to buy in a physical retail space. There are only so many future brides to go around, and every web-savvy bride is one less bride who's scouting out gowns in salons. Again, the bottom line is this: If you feel uncomfortable buying from a particular online store or the store you're considering has earned itself some really harsh reviews, stay away. In fact, run away. Your wedding gown probably represents the most expensive dress you'll ever buy, so do it right by doing your research and buying from a reputable source.

Before your gown arrives in the mail, be sure you've arranged suitable storage measures, as it will likely come pressure-packed in plastic and stuffed into a cardboard box. Look for archival-quality garment bags, which are perfect for storing gowns pre- and postwedding. Under no circumstances should you leave your dress in its original plastic packaging, as over time, certain types of plastic will give off acidic fumes that can cause fabric to turn yellow (learn more at Weddinggownspecialists.com). Once your gown actually does arrive, wait until your SO is not nearby, make sure your hands are clean, and then unpack your gown. This first in-person glimpse of your dress can be a moment of great awe or a moment of great remorse. Don't worry if you feel disappointed by what you see—what you're feeling is quite common. The dress of your dreams you initially viewed online was perfectly pressed, fit to a regally made-up model, and bathed in lighting calculated to capture your attention. The dress in front of you has been squished up in a box for the past few days and may seem overwhelmingly huge and wrinkled in a normal-sized room.

Prior to packing it away, inspect your gown for loose threading, beading, or lace; hard-to-manage zippers; missing hooks or eyes; and other minor imperfections. Write these down so you can pass them along to your seamstress when it's time to start your fittings (look for more on fittings later in the chapter). Finally, carefully roll those parts of your dress that don't hang flat in your garment bag, gently put it into said bag, and find a place for it that will be safe from your future spouse's prying eyes. Now, pat yourself on the back and cross "Buy the gown" off your wedding checklist!

If, however, you're worried you won't find anything, take comfort in the fact that online gown shopping is going mainstream. Target.com now features an online-only bridal salon, and David's Bridal—the megacorp that always insisted that its gowns could *only* be purchased at David's locations—now has a growing online collection that can be accessed at Davidsbridal.com/dbonline1.jsp. David's is even making the most of online functionality, with easy-to-access videos of models walking and turning in the featured gowns and a fun virtual wedding party app, Davidsbridal.com/dress_your _wedding.jsp.

The Accessories

Your bridal accessories—both those your guests will see and those they won't—are the embellishments on the gourmet confection that is your gown. Just as you probably wouldn't sit down and eat a bowl full of icing, you probably have no intention of icing yourself out with an overabundance of pearls, rhinestones, swaths of satin, and so forth. But you may find that your intentions go right out the window when you see all of the magnificent and eye-catching accessories out there. If you keep moderation in mind as you browse (make Perfectdetails.com one of your first stops), you won't end up looking like you just stepped off the set of a hip-hop video.

Your (and your bridesmaids') undergarments form the foundation of your whole look. Though many brides-to-be envision themselves wearing flimsy corsets, thigh-high stockings, and frilly panties on the day they finally become Mrs. So-and-so, it's important to realize that you're going to be on your feet wearing a weighty gown for hours and hours. And the inside of that gown will not necessarily be so comfortable that you'll want it rubbing against your bare skin until well into the afternoon or evening.

When considering your undie options, look for fabrics that won't cause you to perspire or itch. Don't layer anything bulky or dark under your gown, lest it show through or cause the fabric of your gown to pucker. And, if your preferred undergarments have boning or underwire, make sure that they aren't so tight as to cause you discomfort. It's hard enough to get a wedding dress on and off once. You don't want to have to sneak out halfway through the reception to covertly divest yourself of a bunching bra or panties that won't stay put.

Your main focus in choosing your wedding day underwear should be finding a bra, corset, panty, body shaper, or slip that makes you feel cool, comfortable, and confident that no part of your anatomy will pop out during the ceremony or reception. The style of bra you choose will also need to conform to the neck, shoulder, and back lines of your dress. Consider going to a high-end bra shop to have yourself sized by a professional. Though you may not notice that your everyday bras are a size too big or too small, you should endeavor to find a perfect fit for your wedding day undergarments.

Here's an unbeatable tip: You can't go wrong with the underthings you'll find at Spanx.com or Seamlessbody.com. But if you're not sure what type of lingerie look you want, browse thousands of bras, panties, bustiers, and shapewear pieces at Figleaves.com, Barenecessities.com, or Herroom.com.

If you want to look super sexy for your new spouse at your, er, private wedding after-party, you can always change into something lacy, elaborate, uncomfortable, and complicated just before settling in for the night. Something from Corsetconnection.com might just do the trick.

Before you buy your wedding footwear, remind yourself two or three times that you'll most likely be on your feet all day long. Try to keep this oh-so-easy-to-forget fact in the forefront of your mind every time you encounter a shoe store. Remember, too, that the right wedding footwear can come from anywhere and be anything. When you find the ultimate bridal shoe—a shoe that is as elegant as it is stunning—walk in it for a while. If the thought of wearing it not only down the aisle but also during a lengthy reception makes you cringe inwardly, go for a second choice. The right shoe will be as comfortable as it is awesome. That doesn't mean you have to dance the night away in boring ballet flats, especially if you practically live in three-inch heels. Stick to a lower heel, however, if you're already being plagued by nightmares in which you stumble your way to the altar.

One of the most comprehensive bridal shoe sites (i.e., sites that sell nothing but shoes for brides) is Bellissimabridalshoes.com, but before you buy from them, shop around. Zappos.com and Shoebuy.com both have a wide selection of wedding-specific shoes and formal footwear. And if you're in the market for dyeable flats, pumps, or sandals, but don't know what you want, Dyeableshoestore.com will give you a good idea of what's out there. No matter what style of shoe you eventually choose, don't forget that they'll need to be broken in. You'll want to get used to your footwear a few weeks before the wedding so they aren't cutting into or otherwise hurting your feet on the big day. If you're worried about dust and dirt, don your wedding shoes and then put on a clean pair of men's tube socks over them. You'll look silly, but your shoes will stay pristine.

Even if you're totally comfortable putting your hair into elaborate updos at a moment's notice, consider leaving that duty to a pro on the day of your nuptials—preferably a pro who also does makeup and works well at a hummingbird's pace. You'll have plenty to think about on the morning of your wedding without having to worry about frizz, curls that won't set, or runaway bobby pins. As competent stylists fill their appointment books quickly, reserve this service as early as you possibly can. To browse thousands of hairstyles quickly, search for "wedding hair," "wedding hairstyle," or "updo" at Images.google.com. Or check out Hairfinder.com, which allows users to upload pictures of themselves and virtually try on different hairstyles for a small subscription fee. As for locating a stylist, there are stylist search engines—like Stylist911.com—but they're really crappy. The best way to find a hair and makeup expert still involves asking around. Once you find a style that suits you, talk it over with your stylist and schedule a test run (a few weeks before the wedding) to see how your chosen style will look in the real world.

Though your headpiece will ultimately complete your look, it may also be one of the first pieces of your ensemble that your guests notice. While veils are the headgear of choice for many brides, don't immediately rule out stand-alone tiaras, wreaths, headbands, bun wraps, combs, and barrettes adorned with rhinestones, crystals, pearls, and more. If you're married to the idea (*rimshot*) of wearing a veil, almost any type of headpiece can be paired with a simple veil or customized with an attached veil. For a great explanation of veil lengths and styles, visit Veilshop.com, which sells made-to-order veils, or Bridalveilcreations.com. Don't like what you see? You can design your own veil at Budget-bride.com or have a Swarovski tiara crafted to your specs at Weddingshowergifts.com. Adventurous? Thrifty? Consider making your own veil using the step-by-step directions at Brilliantweddingpages.com.

Then again, if you're planning on wearing a particularly elaborate hairstyle or one to which your stylist will add embellishments such as pearls or flowers, you may not want to wear any headpiece at all.

When you combine a show-stopping gown and a luxurious headpiece with dazzling hair and makeup, think about keeping your jewelry as simple as possible. The world of wedding jewelry is unfortunately overrun with examples of gaudy fake pearls and big shiny rhinestones that end up clashing miserably with embellished dresses and otherwise lovely tiaras. Steer clear of most bridal jewelry shops online, and don't fall into the trap of thinking you need to deck yourself out in bling or walk down the aisle dripping with pearly embellishments. In wedding fashion choreography, jewelry should play nothing more than a supporting role. Think simple legit-pearl earrings and a matching pendant necklace, or an understated choker. Never limit yourself to jewelry that others have deemed appropriate for weddings. Like your gown, your hair, your headpiece, your manicure, and everything else, your necklace and earrings should reflect your personal style. You may already have something in your jewelry box that will look stunning when paired with your matrimonial ensemble. And your wedding can be the perfect excuse to have a piece of jewelry custom-made by a skilled jewelry artisan like Katherine DeJarnette of Dejarnettenola.com.

The Maids

The days of the ugly, outlandish, and tacky bridesmaid monstrosity are almost over, because today's bride tends to be far more thoughtful than her foremothers when choosing her attendants' uniforms. And thank goodness. Pop over to Uglydress.com and you won't doubt for a moment that some brides picked dresses out of pure spite. You are probably a thoughtful and compassionate bride who wants nothing more than for her maids to look their best. Great! To make that happen, you're going to need to take your bridesmaids' sizes, body types, comfort levels, and financial health into account when picking out their dresses. The good news is that ordering attendants' dresses online is often far less stressful than ordering a wedding gown online, and some major retailers are even hip enough to take orders online, though most still prefer to accept orders by phone or fax. The bad news is that while you can please some of the people all of the time, you won't be able to please all of your bridesmaids all of the time.

This means that the dress your sister loves will likely be hideous in the eyes of your best friend. And the dress that looks so fabulous on your SO's sister makes your favorite cousin look like a sallow scarecrow. No matter what, consider your preferences before consulting your attendants. Why? Because there is nothing more harrowing than trying to deal with the disparate ideas of three, six, or twelve vocal women who all have very strong notions of what constitutes a classy dress. One may hate sleeved dresses while another hates her arms. Two may band together in their love of empire waistlines. Three may bicker over hem lengths. The larger your bridal party, the larger the potential for differences of opinion. Of course, there may be no bad blood whatsoever. One of your bridesmaids may simply be pregnant, of a different age than the rest, or unable, for whatever reason, to wear your preferred style of dress.

All of the information that helped you find the perfect wedding gown can help you pick out great bridesmaids' dresses that the friends and relatives standing up with you on your wedding day will love. The fabrics, hem lengths, and bodice styles worn by your bridesmaids will help you reinforce the established atmosphere of your wedding. An easy rule of thumb states that the formality of the bridesmaids' dresses should match the formality of the wedding gown. In semiformal or formal weddings, attendants typically wear floor-length or tea-length dresses. In informal, daytime, or destination weddings, bridesmaids usually wear cocktail-length dresses. Whatever your preferences, don't forget to consider the depth of your bridesmaids' pockets, because that absolutely amazing $600 dress you have your eye on can be an undue financial burden on your closest friends.

Before anyone buys anything, be sure to have a look at the popular designers' websites to get an idea of the sort of dress you're looking for. Many, like Barijay.com, Watters.com, Dessy.com, Siriinc .com, and Impressionbridal.com, feature virtual salons that let you see how a dress will look in another color, fabric, or hem length. Or, if you'd prefer to peruse without any pressure, just drop the word "bridesmaid" or "bridesmaids" into Images.google.com to see thousands of pictures of bridesmaids' dresses in every conceivable shape, cut, and color.

There are only a few foolproof ways to get around the challenge of creating a great-looking wedding party without alienating your loved ones. You can choose a designer, choose a fabric, choose a color, and let your bridesmaids pick out their own cut. This is becoming a very popular option among brides-to-be who find themselves with friends who range in height from a petite five feet to a whopping six feet tall, with some being zaftig and others skinny. Most of the dresses at Ariadress.com can be ordered in any of their selection of fabrics, colors, and hem lengths, allowing brides and their attendants to work together to create a cohesive look. And at Threaddesign.com, brides can specify a fabric from their wide selection of luxurious choices (think silk wool, layered organza, and bengaline) and a color, giving their bridesmaids an opportunity to choose a dress they will feel comfortable wearing and perhaps even wear again.

Or you can buy a fabric in a color you love from one of the many wonderful online fabric retailers and have a qualified seamstress custom-make individual dresses according to your and your attendants' preferences. When price is an issue, consider that you needn't buy dresses specifically earmarked for bridesmaids. Online formalwear shops (like Cybergown.com) and clothing stores (like the wedding shop at Jcrew.com) often have a tolerable selection of dresses and carry each in a wide range of sizes. Many prom and quinceañera dresses can stand in easily for traditional bridesmaid dresses. And look for bridesmaids' dresses at the shop where you bought your wedding gown, because sites like Bridalonlinestore .com and Weddingdressonline.com also carry bridesmaid dresses. A retailer may even be able to give you a bulk discount or special order a dress you love in a different color. Remember, there is no harm in asking for what you want—the worst a retailer can say is no.

Some sites function just like the big-name chain salons in that they carry dresses from a wide range of labels. Thebridalshop .com and Thebridalworld.com both sell dresses from Mori Lee, Impressions Bridal, Alexia Bridesmaids, and more, as well as bridal and bridal party accessories you can buy with a quick click of your mouse. Perfect-bridesmaid-dresses.com carries a large selection of dresses from Watters and Watters, Essence of Australia, and Venus Bridal, among others. The benefit here is that you can drool over dress after dress after dress without ever leaving your desk chair.

How else can you keep your sisters and girlfriends happy?

- Take your bridesmaids' budgets, personalities, shapes, sizes, and opinions into account. Then choose a cost-effective, attractive dress in a color and cut that your attendants can wear again. Never try to turn your bridesmaids into fashion victims in an attempt to make sure all eyes are on you. It won't work. You can practically guarantee good wedding pictures if you allow your attendants to wear dresses that are timeless, elegant, and flattering. The special women in your life will thank you for your kindness in this area.

- Choose dresses that are similar to your gown but don't match exactly. If your gown is strapless, your attendants don't necessarily have to wear shoulder-baring dresses. As long as your outfits are similar in formality and don't have contrasting fabrics, you'll look great as a group. Simpler designs (nix the embellishments) will look great on your attendants and highlight the intricacy of your gown.

- Consider your bridesmaids' complexions and hair colors when choosing the color of their dresses. Even if you have your heart set on orange, blue, green, or purple, there are many hue variants of every color in the rainbow, and some will naturally be more suitable than others. Traditional pastel wedding party attire will look best on ladies with light complexions or blond locks. If there is no one color that will be universally flattering on your attendants, consider allowing them to wear different shades of a single color. Keep in mind that your attendants' attire should complement the color of your gown if you've decided to eschew white.

- If you have no clue what your maids ought to wear, have your attendants look at Theknot.com's bridesmaid search and e-mail you examples of dresses they think are beautiful and flattering. While you don't have to use any of their suggestions, the examples they send you can help you get a feel for each bridesmaid's personal style.

- Some brides choose to set their MOHs apart from the other members of their wedding party by having them wear a dress of a slightly different style, cut, or color, or a headpiece of some sort, but whether you choose to do so is entirely up to you. You can also honor your MOH by having her carry a larger or more elaborate bouquet than her fellow attendants.

Wherever you buy your bridesmaids' dresses, place your order (or have your bridesmaids place their orders) as early as possible—preferably at least five months before the wedding. If you're a stickler for color, order most or all of your attendant attire at the same time to ensure that they all come from the same dye lot. Don't forget that your bridesmaids will most likely have to have their dresses fitted. Here's a solid fitting tip: Have seamstresses measure from the floor. A hemline that falls four inches below the knee on one gal may turn out to fall far lower than midcalf on another. When the hems are measured from the floor up, the bottoms of your bridesmaids' dresses will make a nice straight line in your wedding photos.

The Flower Girl

Outfitting the FG online will likely be the easiest part of your foray into the world of wedding fashion. For one thing, children's clothing retailers seldom have the same qualms about putting their goods online that big-name wedding-wear manufacturers do. And now that you've done your gown research and put it to use buying your attendant uniforms, you know all you need to know about fabrics, silhouettes, necklines, and so on. Unfortunately, little kids tend to shoot up like weeds, so you'll likely want to buy your FG's gown a size or two up and have it altered down as necessary. Seriously. A five-year-old girl can grow a lot in a month or two.

There are three schools of thought where FG dresses are concerned. Some brides like to dress up the FG as if she were a miniature bride. There are plenty of poufy white dresses out there that look like scaled-down versions of traditional wedding gowns. Other brides prefer to send their FGs down the aisle in dresses that match their attendants' dresses. A third subset of brides chooses dresses that represent a happy medium—they don't match the bride's gown or the attendants' attire, but rather take cues from both where color and style are concerned. If your goal is to have guests saying "awww" when the FG makes her debut, go for something girlish and innocent rather than a dress like a scaled-down ball gown.

Consider asking your FG to help you choose her dress. She'll probably enjoy sitting with you in front of the computer reviewing sites like Pegeen.com, Foxnlily.com, and Boutique4kids.com, all of which feature good selections of pretty pint-sized wedding wear. Besides making her feel very grown up, this will help you get a firm idea of the sorts of dresses she likes to wear. The better and more confident your FG feels in her dress, the more likely it is that she will stroll down the aisle with her head held high (and a minimum of fuss).

Traditionally, FGs wear dresses with semifitted bodices and full or ruffle skirts. Many feature floral embellishments, and most are crafted of smooth fabrics that won't irritate delicate skin. Whatever your personal preference, the color and style of an FG dress can set the tone for the ceremony and serve as a sneak preview of your own wedding wear. A darker-colored dress made of velvet or shimmering satin will hint to guests that your gown is going to be formal and quite elegant. A flowery pastel dress will suggest that your gown will be light and feminine. Dresses that are a shade or two lighter or darker than those being worn by the wedding party will ensure that your FG stands out while still staying true to your basic color scheme. Just make sure that the dress you ultimately decide on isn't too long so your FG isn't left tripping her way down the aisle or walking around the reception with a soiled, frayed hem.

In the end, don't tear your hair out if you can't find the perfect FG dress. Most little girls can melt hearts without even trying. If the dress you (and your FG) like best doesn't match your wedding colors perfectly or doesn't quite mesh with the overall theme of your nuptials, it probably won't matter, as your wedding guests will no doubt be too busy oohing and ahhing at the concentrated cuteness of the FG herself to look too closely at what she's wearing.

The Moms

Throughout history, MOBs have borne the indignity of wearing shapeless pastel frocks that make them look twenty pounds heavier and ten years older so as not to outshine the bride. The main traits of the traditional MOB dress are twofold. The dress typically matches the wedding colors to some extent (to make everything nice and tidy in pictures) and is appropriate for the formality level of the wedding. That's it. There is, unfortunately, no magic formula for choosing MOB and MOG outfits. Some brides will leave the choice up to the respective moms. Others, especially those whose mothers can be frequently seen strutting about town in hot pants and tube tops, will diplomatically steer their moms toward dresses they consider stylish and appropriate. Either way, the buying of the moms' dresses can be very emotional for MOBs and MOGs, as moms typically want nothing more than to find dresses that please their offspring, look elegant, and feel comfortable. This can be tough when it's hard enough as it is to find dresses that fit well.

It is technically the responsibility of the MOG to contact the MOB in order to find out what she will be wearing to avoid embarrassing mishaps such as the two moms showing up in the same dress or, worse, showing up in vastly different styles of dress. Think about it. If you show up to a party in a ball gown only to realize that your fellow guests are wearing conservative suits, you're going to feel pretty dang stupid. At your wedding, the MOB and MOG basically share a role. If one shows up in said gown and the other shows up in said suit, they will likely both be utterly horrified—unless they dislike each other, in which case the discrepancy will further fuel their feuding for years to come. To avoid any potential misunderstandings, set both moms up with Flickr accounts and create a Flickr group so each can post pictures of the outfits she likes. They'll be on the same page and out of your hair!

Though numerous manufacturers and designers are quick to label certain dresses as being the sole domain of MOBs, the truth is that any dressy, semiconservative frock will do. After all, this isn't 1955 and women old enough to have marriageable daughters are no longer considered sexless or over the hill. Your mom (not to mention your SO's mom) is likely a vibrant, stunning, and dynamic woman. So why not suggest she wear something that reflects that? If your mom is looking at boxy, boring, matronly dresses, consider that she may be doing it to please you. This can be the perfect time to arrange a mother-daughter online shopping afternoon where you sit down together in front of a computer (or e-mail back and forth) to discuss your respective expectations. If your mom isn't a frills-and-frippery type, pass on your newfound knowledge of formalwear fabrics and cuts.

Have a look at the MOB dresses on Weddingchannel.com and then head over to Audreysmotherofthebride.com or Motherofthebride.com to browse or shop. But, as always, don't limit yourself to lines specifically designed for the MOB or floor-length dresses with matching coats. Why not suggest a tea-length dress, a long gown, a fitted cocktail suit, or a dressy, flowing pantsuit? There are hundreds of classy MOB-appropriate special occasion dresses at Nordstrom.com, Chadwicks.com, Spiegel.com, and other online stores with formalwear sections. A simple search for "formalwear" will net you plenty of viable—and beautiful—options.

Tell your mom (and your SO's mom) to start shopping for her wedding day apparel six months or so before your wedding if she plans to buy online. This way, she'll have more time to savor the shopping process and more time to spend helping you iron out nuptial details. If your mom is a hard-to-fit size, you may want to suggest she get her dress tailored to fit. If she takes her dress to the seamstress altering your gown and schedules her appointment on the same day as one of yours, fittings can become a great chance to work in a little mother-daughter time together before the wedding.

It's common knowledge, but it bears repeating: MOBs and MOGs should not wear white, ivory, champagne, or other hues usually reserved for brides, or don dresses flashier than that worn by the bride herself. In this modern age, fashion etiquette rules have been greatly relaxed, but guests may still cluck their tongues at moms who seem to be making an effort to steal attention away from the bride and groom or show too much skin. Black is another big no-no. And brides? Never try to convince your mom to wear something she dislikes. After all, your wedding represents one of the most important days of her life. Do you really want her to spend the whole day in an outfit that makes her feel ugly and old?

Finding That Perfect Fit

Because every woman has a unique shape, you and your attendants will likely need to have your dresses altered to fit your bodies perfectly—in other words, to avoid puckers and unsightly folds, as well as untimely and embarrassing rips. If you're miffed that you have to lug your gown across town to the nearest seamstress who does bridal alterations, try to think of this unique errand as your penance for saving so much time and money while shopping for your gown online. You may already have a relationship with a seamstress you trust. If not, look for one who makes you feel comfortable and inspires your confidence. Check PACCprofessionals.org for tips on finding a sewing pro and lists of Professional Association of Custom Clothiers members by state. Feel free to ask how long your seamstress has been working with wedding attire—she may even have a portfolio of brides she outfitted in the past for your perusal. Once you've found your seamstress, you'll want to schedule two or more fittings, the first about six weeks before your wedding day, and the last no later than two weeks before.

It's a good idea to buy your actual bridal shoes, undergarments (including your petticoat, hoops, or slip), and accessories before going to your first fitting so you can bring them along. Knowing what sort of headpiece you'll be wearing, the length of your veil, if you'll have gloves, and the type of jewelry you plan to wear can help you and your seamstress create a game plan of alterations that will ensure you look your best. Having your shoes and underthings on hand helps your seamstress find the hem and fit that will flatter your figure. Also, during at least one of your fittings, take a moment to ask whether she has the equipment to press your gown, veil, and slip so you can effectively kill two birds with one stone.

At the first fitting, your seamstress will have you put on your gown so that she can determine where it fits and where it doesn't. Try to stand tall and keep your back straight while she looks you over, as this is no doubt how you'll be carrying yourself on the day of your wedding. Then she'll pin the hem and seams and plot the bustle, if necessary. This is the time to point out any loose threading or beading on your dress and to bring up any concerns regarding its care. Be sure to discuss bustling options if your gown has a train—visit Leanna.com (a super-informative website created by an experienced seamstress) to see some examples of the different ways gowns can be bustled for the reception. At the last fitting, your seamstress will make any minor corrections necessary to ensure that your gown fits you like the proverbial glove. Don't forget to bring your mother, father, MOH, man of honor, sister, or brother to this fitting so she (or he) can learn to work the bustling on your gown, because bustling is one of those things a gal just can't do on her own.

Do Your Research

- Dressking.com/search/fabrics.htm

- Fabric.com/sitepages/glossary.aspx

- Fabriclink.com/Dictionaries/PerformanceGlossary.cfm

- Marysbridal.com/dictionary.htm

- Onewed.com/dresses

- Weddings.pirate-king.com/bride-glossary-head.htm

- Weddings.pirate-king.com/bride-glossary-neck.htm

- Weddings.pirate-king.com/bride-glossary-train.htm

Find the Perfect Dress

- Bridalchalet.com

- Bridalonlinestore.com

- Bridecouture.com

- Bridepower.com

- Chryscrossbridal.com

- Elegantgowns.com

- Gownsales.com

- Houseofbrides.com

- Lynettes.com

- Momsnightout.com

- Preownedweddingdresses.com

- Thebridalshop.com

- Thebridalworld.com

- Usedweddingdresses.com

- Vintagegown.com

- Vintagewedding.com

- Weddingo.net

Buy for Your Bridesmaids

- Ariadress.com

- Bestbridalprices.com

- Bridesmaidexpress.com

- Bridesmaidtailor.com

- Charsa.com

- Lynnlugobridal.com/dressmaker

- Magicmomentscollections.com

- Modernbridalshop.com

- Nowand4-ever.com

- Perfect-bridesmaid-dresses.com

- Simpledress.com

- Vintageous.com/dressy.htm

- Weddingdressonline.com

Build a Strong Foundation

- Barenecessities.com

- Bristols6.com

- Corsetconnection.com

- Freshpair.com

- Herroom.com

- Seamlessbody.com

- Spanx.com

Embellish, Embellish, Embellish

- Adornbrides.com

- Ameliarosedesign.com

- Bellaumbrella.com

- Bellissimabridalshoes.com

- Chloescrown.com

- Designsbykristen.com

- Dyeableshoestore.com

- Etsy.com

- Haircomesthebride.com

- Hairfinder.com

- Headdressdesigns.com

- Io-mareas.com

- Juliettewear.com

- Makeoversolutions.com

- Pearlstruck.com

- Perfectdetails.com

- Princessbridetiaras.com

- Tejanibridaljewelry.com

- Veilsalamode.com

- Veilshop.com

Outfit Your Littlest Lady

- Boutique4kids.com
- Dressygirls.com
- Flowergirldressforless.com
- Foxnlily.com
- Mygirldress.com
- Pegeen.com
- Petalsbyxavi.com
- Winniemini.com

Shop for the Moms

- Audreysmotherofthebride.com
- Chadwicks.com
- Motherofthebride.com
- Nordstrom.com
- Spiegel.com

Alter or Preserve Your Dress

- Bridalgownpreservation.com
- Gown.com
- Gownsremembered.com
- Heritagegown.com

- Jscheer.com

- Leanna.com

- PACCprofessionals.org

- Wedclean.net

- Weddinggownspecialists.com

Chapter II
Suited Up and Ready to Go

Sexism is still alive and well in the world of weddings. It is still widely assumed that the bride-to-be is going to call all of the shots because the groom-to-be isn't going to care one way or the other. Clueless grooms and dopey best men are still a fixture in romantic comedies. Faced with both a man and a woman, vendors will make a beeline for the female because they assume that she's got the money, and therefore, the power. And there is nothing more annoying than that helpful male relative who takes the future groom aside to pass on the advice that his father gave him.

"Son," he says, "your job is to show up. When the little woman gets to plannin', you just stand back and shut up. If she asks your opinion, you just tell her that you like whatever she likes. Trust me on this one."

No wonder groom's checklists like the one at Evahforsyth.com/groomschecklist.ivnu have so little on them; almost all of the items on the checklists for grooms-to-be appear on the much longer checklists you can find on websites specifically geared toward brides-to-be. Sites like Thegroomguide.com are entertaining but operate on the assumption that men are all cretins incapable of getting a good haircut without help. Groom411.com is the notable exception—even with its tongue-in-cheek thank-you note generator and other wacky apps, it manages to pass on plenty of pertinent planning advice.

While it's true that most grooms-to-be probably don't care that much about chair covers or pew bows, it's much easier to get interested in something you're paying for. More couples footing some or all of the matrimonial bills means more men taking an active interest in the wedding planning process. It's not surprising if you think about it. If two people manage to do the impossible and save $15,000, what are the chances that one half of that couple is then going to step back, put up his hands, and say, "Good-bye, honey. I'll see you when our bank balance hits zero."

Even so, ladies do handle most of the planning duties when the engaged couple is heterosexual. When it comes to homosexual couples, people can still fall into established historical patterns, with one half of the pair shouldering 90 percent of the prenuptial burden while the other half gets off almost scot-free. This chapter does not, however, deal with the methods frustrated brides-to-be can use to coerce layabout fiancés into choosing china patterns, because this book does not buy into the usual wedding-related stereotypes. Presumably, you and your intended are both ready to involve yourself in every part of the wedding planning process regardless of what's in your pants.

This chapter does deal with clothes, accessories, and information traditionally associated with the male half of the wedding party. You may have noticed that the previous chapter was fairly woman-centric. This is because traditionally, women wore the wedding dresses. You'll find this chapter fairly man-centric because suits and tuxedos have generally been a part of men's formalwear lines. If you and your intended plan to wear the same matrimonial uniform or

Leah's Engaged Groom

"My groom had a Weddingchannel.com login that linked to my own account so he could check out all the things I was looking at. I was basically in charge of everything related to etiquette, but Will handled both the honeymoon and everything relating to the groomsmen. Overall, he didn't think a lot about etiquette—I know he was reading at least one blog for grooms, though I didn't pay attention to it at the time. In general, I let him do his own research, and he picked out these great frock coats."

you're thinking of spicing things up by switching roles, feel free to refer to whatever chapter best fits your needs. Just ignore any erroneous pronouns and move forward as directed.

There was a time when menswear was as opulent and uncomfortable as any dress-and-corset combo, and everyone who could afford to was flaunting their inner peacock. Coats and vests made the scene in the 1600s, as did the basic prototype of the three-piece suit, though none of these were designed to be utilitarian in nature. It wasn't until the latter part of the eighteenth century, when upper-crust Englishmen were romping about on their country estates, that the modern suit was born.

For a broader history, you could do worse than to read the article at Wikipedia.org/wiki/Suit_(clothing), which discusses everything from leisure suits to zoot suits to sack suits. If you absolutely cannot get enough of historical attitudes toward men's fashions, have a glance at the essay on menswear at Bartleby.com/95/34.html. Written by the late, great Emily Post, it is a rather definitive guide to what should be worn where and when . . . provided you've decided to model your wardrobe after the fashions hot in 1922. There are plenty of updated menswear guides on the web, and if you've been secretly hiding the fact that you're just not a scrubbed-and-shined kind of guy, all you need to do is search for "buying your first suit." Better yet, pore over the tutorial here: Men.style.com/gq/fashion/landing?id=content_4800.

In general, dudes have it much easier than chicks where wedding fashions are concerned. It's likely that no one will notice if the men's attire doesn't match exactly. The FOB is supposed to wear what the groom's half of the wedding party is wearing, but you can buck tradition there. The RB can wear almost anything and people will just gush over how adorable he is. Basically, you've got a lot of options open to you.

Overall, you're also going to spend a lot less than your fiancée, your alterations will not be anywhere near as complicated, and if you're renting, you won't even have to worry about having your for-malwear dry-cleaned after you've said your I dos. That's no reason to throw caution to the wind, however. Order the menswear as early as possible—though RBs shouldn't be fitted any earlier than six weeks before the wedding, because kids *grow.* And no matter what kind of suit or tux you do end up wearing, try it on as soon as it arrives on your doorstep. Don't let it sit in its garment bag until the morning of your wedding day, lest you find out that you'll be getting married in pants that are five sizes too big.

The Standard Suit

Wedding day attire for men is typically serious and somber, which means you'll likely be looking at darker-colored fabrics and conserva-tive cuts. Some grooms-to-be gravitate automatically to tuxedos because they're the easy choice, but there is no reason you shouldn't consider opting for a distinguished two- or three-piece suit that will be useful to you for as long as your metabolism holds out. This is not, as you might imagine, the less expensive option. It will cost you about $100 to rent a standard tuxedo, whereas a quality well-cut suit can cost anywhere from $500 to $1,000. Suits aren't even really the less formal option—a strik-ing pinstriped suit can be every bit as refined as a tuxedo.

You'll inevitably look sharp in a suit made to your measure-ments, whether you're tall and skinny or a little on the rotund side.

If you're nervous about buying online because you don't want to have to deal with a painful returns process if your suit doesn't fit, remember this axiom: Measure twice, buy once. For best results, you should see a tailor who has experience working with menswear, because it's damn hard to measure oneself. Alternately, look up a thorough measurements guide online—try Colemanstuxedos.com/ measure.htm—and have a someone whose touch you can abide take the measurements for you. Once you've got a lengthy list of numbers at the ready, it's time to start browsing.

When you're wearing a suit rather than a tux, there's no reason to limit yourself to basic black. Browns, blues, and grays are all appropriate, provided they gel with the overall wedding color scheme and the formality of the event. Dress for your size and for the season. Thick wool isn't going to be at all comfortable in the summertime, and it may very well look incredibly "off." If you're tall and stout, go for clean lines without a lot of frippery, and steer clear of double-breasted jackets. Tall and thin fellows are the lucky ones who can pull off just about any style of suit. Short and slim men should watch out for suits that engulf them—jackets with two or three buttons that sit low will give your height a boost in the eye of the beholder. If you're both short and broad, single-breasted jackets with a natural shoulder contour are the way to go.

Finding a suit online is as easy as searching for "men's suits" on Google. You can choose between established stores like Mens wearhouse.com and discount shops like Mensusa.com. Department stores like JCpenney.com stock suits, as do clothing shops like Jcrew .com. Or you can custom-build a suit created to measure at sites like Execstyle.com/Build_Custom_Suit.asp and Ravistailor.com. Being that you're buying sight-unseen, stick with styles, colors, and brands you're comfortable with, and don't buy from stores that strike you as shady. If you find the perfect suit in a shop that doesn't seem to be on the up-and-up, do a Google search for that suit or style of suit to find it in a more reputable store.

Jeanette and the Online/Offline Experience

"I think we spent more time shopping for tuxes than most couples. I mean, we browsed *a lot,* mostly at Men's Wearhouse. We needed the versatility offered by a national chain that also has an online component so everyone in our wedding party could get the same thing with a minimum of inconvenience. It was great—the Men's Wearhouse people were some of the nicest and most knowledgeable individuals I've ever encountered in a retail setting. I was so happy with the phenomenal service that we and our groomsmen received that I actually wrote up a glowing e-review."

You can even let your groomsmen wear suits they already own, provided each of them has a suit in the appropriate color or you don't actually care whether or not they match. This is as good a time as any to mention that some grooms want their BM to stand out from the crowd, much like the hypothetical bride in the previous chapter who has her MOH wear or carry something that sets her apart from the other bridesmaids. This isn't commonly done, and if anyone is set apart by their clothing, it's usually the groom. But there's no reason you can't outfit the BM and the groom in something that is slightly different (think color, cut, or vest style) than what the rest of the groomsmen are wearing. If nothing else, you can always pimp out his boutonniere.

The Upgrades

Black tie? White tie? Morning dress? The lingo associated with men's formalwear can be painfully obscure. "Black tie" traditionally alludes to an evening outfit comprised of a short black coat with shiny lapels, matching trousers with a shiny stripe, a black waistcoat or cummerbund, a white shirt, a bow tie, and some shiny black shoes. This getup is your basic tuxedo. White tie takes black tie to the next level, with a black tailcoat and trousers, a white waistcoat, a white shirt with an unbearably stiff collar, a white bow tie, and shiny black shoes. Morning dress is all about the jacket. Historically, sporting chaps would wear cutaway-front single-breasted coats (as opposed to longer and more formal frock coats) while out on their morning rides, but those cutaway coats eventually overtook frock coats in the formality department.

The classic penguin suit can look good or it can look ridiculous. Take it too far and you'll end up looking like a part of the waitstaff you've hired to work the reception. Cummerbunds and pleated shirts look great on symphony orchestras and at New Year's Eve parties, but are no longer de rigueur for weddings. In this informal world, tuxedos are considered formalwear when they are in fact semiformal. The tux originated as a simple, short dinner jacket that made its American debut at the Tuxedo Club in Tuxedo Park, New York, and guys who were bored to death of white tie and tails suddenly had an alternative. If you're thinking of wearing a tux but want to know more, there are plenty of online guides to black tie out there. However, the most comprehensive decade-by-decade look at this iconic piece of menswear can be found at Blacktieguide.com/History/01.htm/.

Many men struggle with the "rent or buy" question. Luckily, both can be accomplished online without ever setting foot inside a shop. You will, of course, need your measurements, just like you would if you were ordering an off-the-rack or custom suit. Renting is the budget option, but do you really want to share your wedding day garb with last year's homecoming king? Know that renting online from places such as Awesometuxedo.com/rentals is a dicey proposition for the hard-to-fit fellow because alterations are not an option. Men who've successfully bought suits off the rack in the past will have the best luck when renting online. Buying is the better option, and there is no shortage of online tuxedo shops. All in all, tuxes aren't that much more expensive than suits, even after you factor in the price of alterations. Do, however, consider how often you've donned a tuxedo in the past before you decide to become a proud tux owner.

Head over to Classictuxedo.com/cybertux/cybertuxpg1.htm to "try on" different lapel and vest options to see how they'll look next to the bridal gown (if you've seen it) or the bridesmaids' dresses. Matching the groomsmens' waistcoats to the bridesmaids' dresses will make your men look as if they're off to the senior prom, so you're better off sticking with basic black peripherals. That's just a recommendation, however. If you're not down with black or silver, there are always the novelty vest-and-tie sets like those sold at Formalonline.com. It takes a certain kind of man to rock the camo on his wedding day, and you may just be that kind. At Menswear house.com, you can create your own tuxedo with the site's build-a-tux app or shop by theme, season, and formality level.

Finding all the gear you need to outfit yourself in high white-tie or morning-dress style is fairly easy, as most shops with tuxes will have some white-tie and morning-dress options. Try searching for "morning coat" or "cutaway coat." You may be surprised to discover that formal trousers are pretty much uniformly embellished with side stripes, but that's what makes them formal. Well, that and the fact that they don't have belt loops. Formal trousers are meant to be worn with suspenders, though some trousers are adjustable. And in case you happen to be having a wintertime wedding, the proper coat to wear over men's formalwear is a chesterfield topcoat. You can order a custom one at Worldofelegance.com/Topcoats/topcoats.htm.

A. J. Gave Her Groom Free Rein

"My groom didn't use the Internet at all when coordinating the menswear. I did a lot of online research on Matt's behalf because I'd come across things relevant to the guy's side when looking up other stuff for the wedding. Basically, I left it up to him—I handed over the info I found, and he ended up going to his favorite suit shop. Knowing him like I do, I was confident that he'd choose something great."

Collars, Cuts, and So On

The etiquette of proper matrimonial menswear is just as complicated as the etiquette surrounding bridal gowns and bridesmaid garb, but you may as well wear whatever you like best, as it's highly unlikely that your guests will be all that familiar with the relevant rules. In a nutshell, those rules are as follows. For a relatively informal daytime wedding, a dark suit or a traditional blue-blazer-and-khakis combo will suffice. Top it all off with a tie done up in your standard four-in-hand knot. You can go with the same suit for an informal evening wedding, unless it's summertime and you feel like wearing something both lightweight and lighter in color.

Wear a stroller suit—a longish black or gray jacket with matching trousers worn with a trusty four-in-hand—for a semiformal daytime wedding. For a semiformal evening affair, go with a tux or a black business suit. As tempting as it might be to try the whole Casablanca white jacket look, you will end up looking like a waiter. Formal affairs demand formality, of course. A formal daytime ensemble should consist of a morning coat, black striped trousers, a lighter-colored waistcoat, and a spiffy starched shirt. You can even break out the old ascot! For a formal evening wedding, you can't go wrong with the white-tie-and-tails look.

Suits are thought by many to be indistinguishable from one another—after all, that's why corporate culture worshippers are called suits, right? Not quite. The suits and tuxedos pictured at Sarnotux .com/choosing-your-formalwear.asp are all quite different. Some jackets have tails while others don't, and some are quite long while others are much shorter. You've got your single-breasted coat (one to three buttons arranged in a vertical line), your double-breasted coat (two to six buttons arranged in two parallel vertical lines), your single-button cutaway, and your buttonless tailcoat. Then there are the different cuts—the roomy full-cut suit, the classic American-cut suit, and the slim-fitting, tailored European-cut suit. If this all sounds like gobbledygook, get thee to Images.google.com.

As if that weren't enough information to digest, you also have to think about lapels. The three basic styles are the downward-pointing notched lapel, the upward-pointing peak lapel, and the smoothly rounded shawl lapel. The notched lapel is usually regarded as being the least formal of the three, though this will only matter to you if you're really into splitting hairs. The peak lapel is partly responsible for having fomented the tuxedo revolution in the late nineteenth century; people loved it. The somewhat outdated shawl lapel is most commonly seen on white dinner jackets—if you favor this sort of lapel, be prepared to be mistaken for James Bond.

It's likely that you'll gravitate toward the cuts and styles in which you feel most comfortable, and this is as it should be. Unless you're reasonably confident that you'll feel like a million bucks in a type of suit or tux you've never worn before, go with the familiar. Experiment only if you have plenty of time between now and the wedding plus plenty of money to burn. If you get the urge to try something kooky and new at the last minute—like a zoot suit or one of those really tight numbers—imagine a big pocket of sweaty air trapped in your jacket or picture yourself splitting your pants on the dance floor. Sometimes conventionality really is the more comfortable option.

The Other Stuff

When it comes time to buy a dress shirt, the first question you should ask yourself is whether you want to spring for a custom job. A good custom shirt from a shop like Garytailor.com/catalog/OrderShirts.php will look as good uncovered as it does under a jacket, but that doesn't mean you should drop a lot of dough to get yourself a made-to-order shirt. There are plenty of fine mass-produced shirts out there in the world. The second question you should ask is what sort of suit or tux you'll be wearing, because your answer will influence your shirt selection. Take a look at Wikipedia .org/wiki/Dress_shirt, and you'll see that there are all sorts of collar and cuff options to choose from. Too many, really.

Visit Mens-fashion-tips.com/mens-dress-shirts-collars.html, but know that the most common standard collars are the straight-point collar and the spread collar. Both can accommodate your typical tie but look all right without one. If you're planning on wearing a tux, hit up Tuxedoshirts.net, which explains the differences between pique and pinwale shirts. Tuxedo shirt collars come in two basic varieties: lay-down collars, which are basically spread collars; and wing or tabbed collars, which are starched bands with two little tabs at the front. If you're not a tie guy, you might want to see how you look in a Mandarin collar or the rather unusual crosswick collar, both of which are meant to be worn sans tie.

Those cuff links that so many grooms like to give their grooms-men work only with shirts with French cuffs, convertible cuffs, or single cuffs, i.e., cuffs that don't have the buttons already built in. Cuff links are big business, as you can easily see when browsing shops like Cufflinks.com and Cuffart.com. Once you have a pair, you can either wear them in the overlapping barrel style—meaning your cuffs will look like they do on a standard dress shirt—or the "kissing style," where the cuff's corners are pressed together.

A nice shirt is nothing without a tie, though you can't just slap on any old tie unless you're having a very informal wedding. There are entire online shops devoted to neckties and cravats, which means that there is a multitude of buying and style guides out there. Academia-cravatica.hr/etiquette is one of the more interesting tie guides on the web. For a quicker rundown of the types of ties you're likely to encounter, visit Tiewarehouse.co.uk/buy-ties.php. Of course, a tie's flair usually has everything to do with how it's tied, so consult the sidebar. There are technically eighty-five distinct ways

Lots and Lots of Knots

- The Four-in-Hand: Tieguide.com/four-in-hand.htm

- The Double-simple: Tieknot.com/en/double-simple.html

- The Prince Albert: Brooksbrothers.com/TieKnots/prince-albert.tem

- The Half-Windsor: Tieguide.com/half-windsor.htm

- The Windsor: Brooksbrothers.com/TieKnots/windsor.tem

- The Small knot: Tieknot.com/en/small-knot.html

- The Pratt-Shelby: Tieguide.com/pratt-shelby.htm

- The Cross knot: Tieknot.com/en/cross-knot.html

- The Cocolupa (or Ruche) knot: Thecravatcompany.co.uk/howtotie.htm

- The Bow tie: Blacktieguide.com/Supplemental/05_Tying_a_bowtie.htm

- Knotting a plastron: Meutejagd.de/plastron_2.html

- Knotting an ascot: Bensilver.com/style04/knots_ascot.htm

If you're looking for the St. Andrew, the Plattsburgh, the Onassis, the Persian, the Oriental, the Turkish, the Half-English, or the Diagonal knot, visit: Krawattenknoten.info/krawatten/Krawattenknoten/tieknot.html.

one can tie a tie, though most men are familiar only with the standard four-in-hand knot.

Have you considered the classic bow tie? They're not just for waiters, magicians, and nerds! Bow ties come in two varieties, the bat wing and the thistle. The former model has parallel edges, while the latter bulges twice at the ends, but the dissimilarities end there. You can use the same set of instructions to tie both varieties unless you happen to be tying the more unusual single-ended variety of bow tie. There is only a handful of online shops that sell single-ended bow ties, and there are no tying tutorials whatsoever. Should you accidentally buy this sort of bow tie, you may be able to solicit help from an older relative who remembers what to do with it. If your rented tux happens to come with a clip-on bow tie, do yourself a favor and spring for a standard bow tie of your very own. Few people are capable of tying a bow tie these days, and your wedding day getup will be regarded as all the more impressive because you decided to put so much thought and effort into your attire.

Finally, have a look in your closet. Do you have a serviceable pair of dressy shoes in a complementary color? If the answer is yes and you're wearing a suit, you can breathe a sigh of relief, because you are done dressing. If your nuptials are shaping up quite formally, you'll be needing some sort of reflective patent-leather shoe. A simple shiny oxford or lace-up shoe from somewhere like Tuxedosdirect.com or even Zappos.com will suffice, but if you feel a pressing need to overwhelm people with your knowledge of fashion, traditional opera pumps are the way to go. Brooksbrothers.com is one of the few places they're sold.

This Is Your Chance to Pontificate

Let's say you've got your tux or suit all picked out, your accessories are in the bag, and you've made an appointment to have your hair trimmed. Maybe you're even planning to get your first-ever manicure or spruce up your own nails using directions you found in an online guide like www.Lindarose.com/art-manicure-men.asp. As much as it seems like you're all ready to go, there is one last detail you should be thinking about: your speech. You do not have to make a speech if you don't want to—some people dread speaking in public, while others are antispeech on principle. If, however, you're cool and collected in a crowd, eloquent, and more than able to make yourself understood, why not spend a couple of minutes regaling the crowd with your wit?

The groom's speech is your opportunity to thank your guests for honoring you with their presence, to thank your new spouse for all their hard work, and to give a shout-out to all the people who helped you foot the bills. This speech usually happens after the FOB has had his say but before the BM grabs the mic. You can wing it if you have a talent for freestyling, but your speech will be way more impressive if you prepare ahead of time by making a mental list of all the people you should be thanking. Who deserves an honorable mention? Consider paying your respects to the moms and the dads; your attendants, including the littlest ones; your officiant; extended family you're close to; guests who traveled very far; and all those who were unable to make it due to circumstances outside of their control, but try to avoid reciting a laundry list of thank-yous.

If you want to do more than express your gratitude, you should really prep your speech ahead of time and memorize it. There's nothing wrong with reading off a crumpled-up slip of paper, but connecting with a crowd means making eye contact. Even though Easyweddingtoasts.com/grooms-speech-at-the-wedding.html suggests opening with a snappy one-liner, what you're aiming for here is sincerity and originality. Don't get too funny or too sentimental—your family may think your reenactment of your first date is hilarious, but your spouse's family may not be used to your brand of humor. Personal anecdotes are good, and you can win major brownie points with your new in-laws by telling everyone how lucky you are to be married to your new mate.

You could pay someone to write the ultimate groom's speech for you; the Internet is overflowing with automatic speech generators like Speeches.com and professional speechwriters looking to make a buck. Your guests probably won't care, however, whether you recite a good canned speech or give an okay speech that comes from the heart. They're there to support you, not to judge you. You shouldn't talk on and on in the interest of making your speech a certain length—a minute or two of chatter is sufficient if you've gotten your point across. End with a one-sentence toast, like "To my beautiful bride!" or "To the families that were joined today!" and pass the mic on.

One last thing: Before you assume that you are responsible for thanking everyone on your better half's behalf, you should consult with your intended. Yes, it is traditional for the groom to make a speech while the bride looks on in silent and loving awe of his rapier wit. Nevertheless, wipe that assumption from your mind. This is the age of equality, and your new spouse may just want to say a few words before the mic is handed over to the BM.

Dress the Men

- Alsformalwear.com

- Awesometuxedo.com/rentals

- Buy4lesstuxedo.com

- Discounttuxedos.com

- Etuxedo.com

- Finetuxedos.com

- Jerrystuxshop.com

- Josbank.com

- Smarttuxedo.com

- Suavecito.com

- Tuxedo-rental.com

- Tuxedosdirect.com

- Tuxrentalonline.com

Clothe the Little Gentleman

- Dapperlads.com

- Dressmeupcute.com

- Oneofakindkid.com/ring-bearer-outfits.html

- Perfectsuit.com

- Snipsnsnails.com

- Tinytux.com

Learn Something

- Bachelor2groom.com

- Blacktieguide.com

- Groom411.com

- Groomadvisor.com

- Groomgroove.com

- Groomsmagazine.com

- Groomsonline.com

- Necktieaficionado.com

- Thegroomguide.com

- Theknot.com/grooms
- Tuxedo-shirts.net
- Twogrooms.com

Chapter 12
The Sweetest Thing

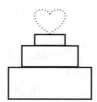

The first wedding "cakes" were nothing more than loaves of barley bread. Roman grooms would nosh on a loaf for a minute or two, then break the remainder of that loaf over the new bride's head. Using the bridal coif as a crumb-catcher may have been a symbolic deflowering or a tribute to male dominance, but that's no reason to look askance at modern wedding cakes. The loaves of barley bread broken over the bride's head became small oat cakes that were still broken over her head, though some accounts do allude to the use of courtesy napkins. Guests grabbed for the crumbs in the hopes that they would share in the newlyweds' good fortune.

In medieval England, the oat cakes became small sweet buns brought by guests to the celebration. These were placed in as tall a pile as possible, and the happy couple was expected to rise up on tiptoe to kiss over the topmost bun. If they smooched without knocking over the pile, they were guaranteed a lifetime of prosperity. If they knocked the stack over, all bets were off. As was mentioned briefly in chapter 2, the modern tiered and frosted wedding cake appeared in France in the 1600s. That doesn't mean, however, that there weren't other options. In the sixteenth and seventeenth centuries, English wedding guests would occasionally enjoy bride's pie, a sweet or savory pie traditionally dished out by the groom himself. The baker would hide a glass ring somewhere in the pie, and whoever found it would be blessed with lots of luck.

The stacked cakes now traditionally associated with weddings can be found everywhere in the world touched by the hand of British, French, and American colonialism. The cake flavors and types may differ and the icings may change from locale to locale, but the general configuration remains pretty much the same. Wedding trends move slowly, which means that many of the wedding cakes you see today are not all that different from the wedding cakes of yesteryear. What has changed is the ease with which brides- and grooms-to-be can find a baker who will make them a cake that is more artful than the standard white-on-white basketweave buttercream tower.

Toppers are still around, but the crazy props you'll see in older wedding snapshots have mostly been confined to the annals of history. When was the last time you saw a wedding cake with pillars, fountains, or staircases anywhere outside of a bakery window display? Today's tiers are typically stacked one on top of the other with no room in between, and a system of hidden dowels keeps the whole works from collapsing in taller cakes. Little brides and grooms are still a popular topper option, but that doesn't mean there aren't alternatives to be had. The topmost tier may be adorned with a jeweled monogram from Topperswithglitz.com, a seriously personalized picture-perfect topper from Thumbprint kids.com, fresh flowers, a set of Matchbox cars, or a sculptural keepsake. The tradition of the "humorous" topper featuring a determined plastic bride dragging an unwilling plastic groom to the altar is unfortunately alive and well.

Don't forget groom's cakes. Whether or not you plan on having a second, manlier cake is entirely up to you, but consider it if you're a chocolate fan, as most groom's cakes are chocolate. The tradition was born in the southern United States—remember the bloody ar-

Leah Surprised Her Groom

"The groom's cake tradition started in the South, and I've always been familiar with it. Will, on the other hand, had no idea what kind of awesomeness he was in for. Once he found out he was going to get his own cake, he was pretty thrilled. Our groom's cake was a big original Nintendo controller, and we actually got an e-mail from a guy in the UK who had seen the pictures on Flickr and wanted to use it in his gaming magazine.

"I didn't spend very much time browsing cakes online—I found a picture of one I liked on some site and just brought it to a meeting with the caterer. I did sketch a version of the cake I wanted, scan it, and e-mail it to the caterer. I also considered the idea of a small cake for us, with tons of cupcakes on tiers, because I'm a big fan of cupcakes and easy finger-foods for dressed-up guests. But the cake wasn't a very big deal to me. In fact, the topper that the caterer made broke right before the reception, and one of her assistants ran up nearly in tears to tell me. I told her that it was perfectly fine and that no one would notice.

"The caterer did our cake, and she was remarkably good at figuring how much we'd need. She also knew which cakes would freeze best, but I'll be honest with you. Will and I got out our top layer on our first anniversary, and we agreed that we loved each other enough not to force one another to eat year-old cake. We then ceremoniously dumped it in the trash."

madillo cake from *Steel Magnolias*?—but has made its way northward. Nowadays, the groom's cake tends to reflect the groom's own interests, so you'll see a smaller video game console cake or car cake next to the main wedding cake. When it comes to desserts, you can never really please everyone, but your chances of making almost everyone happy certainly go up when you have two or three flavors of wedding cake with a groom's cake on the side!

Now, this may be one of the few times in your entire life that you'll be spending a ton of money on dessert, so you may as well make the expenditure count. Wedding cakes come in all shapes, colors, and configurations, and there is no shortage of seriously droolworthy cake porn on the web. The best time to look up "wedding cake" on Images.google.com is right after you've eaten a nice big meal. Search on an empty stomach and you're liable to go nuts. The results you get will help you find photo galleries filled with luscious-looking cakes created by master bakers, and you may very well find all the inspiration you need there. But there are also sweet,

sweet blogs for you to browse, like Thecakeblog.livejournal.com and Blog.pinkcakebox.com. Pink Cake Box posts its photos to Flickr at Flickr.com/photos/pinkcakebox.

Want to browse nothing but square cakes? Then check out Squarecakes.blogspot.com. For everything you've ever wanted to know about cupcakes, look no further than Cupcakestakethecake .blogspot.com and Cupcakeblog.com. Cupcakes are an awesome option because they give you a chance to feature multiple cake flavors and colors in a unique and whimsical way. Plus, a tiered stack of cupcakes on a specially designed stand like the one at Cupcaketree .com looks chic, modern, and impressive when done right.

Once you've explored all of your aesthetic options and hit on one that speaks to you, it's time to locate a baker who can replicate your vision in reality. Before you talk to anyone in your area about cake, print out, save, or bookmark pictures of your favorite cakes. If you're looking for someone who can replicate a particular cake in a different color, bookmark that cake in addition to pics of cakes that are the colors you want. Ideally, you should start looking for your baker four to six months before your wedding date; you'll have plenty of time to iron out the details later, but you need to make sure that the baker you like best isn't already booked.

Bakers are underrepresented in wedding vendor searches for some reason. Weddingwire.com—a site highlighted in chapter 7 for its venue and caterer reviews—has a searchable directory of bakeries and cake artisans, complete with reviews. You can also hit up Maps .google.com and search for "wedding cake near ?????" or "wedding bakery near ?????," substituting your zip code for all those question marks. Some of the resultant listings will have pics and reviews, but not many. The other problem with the Google method is that links are sometimes missing for bakeries with web pages. When it strikes you that a bakery or cake artisan you just found in Google's listings really ought to have a web presence, search for that place, because there's a good chance that it does. Weddingcakecreations.com has

Cake Porn Didn't Do Much for A. J.

"I didn't spend as much time online looking at cakes as I did, say, flowers. I *loved* looking at flowers. Cakes just did not strike me as that interesting. I mean, you've got your square cakes and your round cakes, and there are some funky shapes to choose from. I found my baker through my MIL, and I knew they'd be willing to work with any design I brought in. I looked at a lot of cakes online when I was figuring out what kind of design I wanted. I went in knowing that I did not want fondant or anything too showy. I also knew that I definitely wanted a floral theme, but that was the extent of my preferences. In the end, I found a design I liked at the cake shop, so that was all set. I never considered making my own cake, and the only good cake maker I know is my MIL. I couldn't ask her to bake our wedding cake!"

no reviews, but it has a fair number of listings and you can contact bakers directly through the site.

After you poke around in a cake artisan's online gallery, get in touch via e-mail and ask to see their larger portfolio if they have one. It's important that you know if they create distinctive custom cakes, because some bakers charge extra for design work and others offer only a limited number of set designs. If you're planning to talk to a lot of different bakeries, it may be helpful to bring a list of questions, including but not limited to the following:

- Can you create a custom-designed cake? Are you willing to replicate a cake from a photograph?

- What is the base per-serving charge? Will increasing or decreasing the number of tiers affect this price?

- How much do you charge for your various flavor, filling, icing, and decor options?

- Can each tier of our cake be a different flavor?

- Are you willing to match icing and decor colors to a dress swatch, type of flower, or other decorative items?

- Can you recommend cake styles and flavors that will help us stick to our budget?

- Do you deliver and set up the cake? Is this service included in the price?

- Will you provide cake stands and any other necessary accessories? Will we need to return these to you?

- How far in advance will you prepare our cake? Do you use any preservatives?

- Can you accommodate dietary restrictions such as veganism and gluten allergies?

- Do you offer fresh flower decorations? Are any of these edible?

- Can you provide references?

- How large of a deposit do you require? When will you require that the balance be paid?

- Can we see a copy of your standard contract?

Interviewing bakers is matchlessly awesome because of the cake tastings. If you're doing this all online because you're getting married out of state, you're out of luck unless you're willing to make a tasting trip. At the tasting, bakers will let you sample some or all of their usual flavors, discuss your budgetary needs, and listen to your design ideas. This is why you should print out pictures of the cakes you really like—a quality cake designer will make you the cake that you want, provided you can adequately convey your desires. Their job becomes that much easier when you can hand them a couple of pics and say, "I want something like this in these colors." Of course, if you have something specific in mind that is entirely original, they'll work with you to create it.

When you're shopping around for cakes, you should know how to talk the talk. Spend some time studying up on cake terminology if your previous experiences with baked goods have revolved around box mixes and canned icings. Baker's glossaries like the one at Shop.pattycakes.com/Guides/glossary_of_cake_decorating_terms.asp will help you understand just what prospective bakers are talking about when they suggest you think about decorating your cake with lambeth fondant and gum paste flowers.

Buttercream is a whipped mixture of butter, milk, and sugar that can be spread over cake and piped into shapes. Some bakeries cut corners by adding shortening to the mix, but really good bakeries never will because buttery buttercreams taste best. Cream cheese icings are basically buttercream with cream cheese mixed in—a combo that is really tasty when paired with the right cake. Fondant is a stiff and some say flavorless icing that can be rolled into sheets, molded into 3-D decorations, and turned into beading. It looks smooth and polished when applied over a thin layer of buttercream, but its core ingredients—sugar or corn syrup, gelatin or glycerin, and water—don't add much in the way of taste. Royal icing is basically meringue, which means that it dries out and hardens over time. More often than not it's used to make edible embellishments. You may also encounter ganache, which is a glaze made of chocolate melted into heavy cream, and flat icing, which is simply a pairing of confectioner's sugar and some liquid.

Every baker will have their signature flavors. Many cake artisans will allow you to choose between a set list of proven flavor combos like moist vanilla cake layered with lemon curd and raspberries or red velvet cake layered with rich white chocolate mousse. Others have lengthy lists of fillings and flavors that can be combined any which way. There are still others that have basic flavors and fillings and premium flavors and fillings, each with different price points. You may have to pay extra for something like caramelized peaches or a brandied chocolate torte.

And what's that sitting on the cake? Maybe it's marzipan, a paste made of sugar and almonds that can be molded into flowers, fruits, and lots of other stuff. It could be gum paste, which can also be molded but tastes so bad some bakers label it as "inedible." Boiled pulled sugar is used to make edible ribbons and bows, while modeling chocolate (a mix of chocolate and corn syrup) is used to make things like baskets. Those shiny silver and gold balls you'll sometimes see on cakes and cookies are known as dragées. There's a lot to absorb, though the cake artisan you ultimately choose will probably know what you're talking about even if your terminology's a little off.

Your cake contract should list your name and your intended's name, your wedding venue address, your wedding date and the time your cake will be dropped off, the name of your bakery or baker, a thorough description of your cake that includes all of the options you've chosen, an estimated head count, deposit amounts and due dates, the date on which the full balance is due, and the baker's re-fund and cancellation policies. You can check out a sample contract

Good to Look At, Good to Eat

Here's a short list of the most common floral cake embellishments.

- Roses
- Violets
- Pansies
- Lilacs
- Johnny-jump-ups
- Scented geraniums
- Daisies
- Daylilies
- Cornflowers
- Lavender

Don't run the risk of decorating your mouthwatering cake with blooms that'll put your guests in the ER. Some flowers look good enough to eat but are actually deadly. Others have been grown with harsh pesticides and should not be consumed. Your florist and your baker should know which blossoms fall into the edible category, but you can stay on the right side of safe by doing your own research. Whatscookingamerica.net/EdibleFlowers/EdibleFlowersMain.htm has a long list of good-to-eat flowers.

at Augustinesbakery.com/weddingcakecontract.pdf. Be aware that your bakery contract may include fewer specific details than some of your other vendor contracts because many cake designers allow you to change your flavor and decor options as often as you like until two weeks before the wedding.

Things to Think About

If you've put down a deposit on a reception space that has a dedicated caterer, you may also find you're obligated to obtain a cake from a bakery with which the space has affiliated itself. This would be a good time to check on that. Should you discover that you're contractually bound to use their baker—how did you miss that?—you may want to opt for the smallest, cheapest cake they offer and then source your actual wedding sweets elsewhere. You can also employ this technique if you don't particularly care for cake or didn't plan to have one in the first place. Have some other more memorable dessert on display and set your unwanted cake down somewhere off to the side. Don't even concern yourself with it—people generally like a nice slice of cake, so you can take comfort in the fact that someone will dig into it before the night is over.

You'll come across two bodies of opinion when looking into how much cake to order. One camp will suggest ordering at least one serving per person, lest someone who wants cake end up without their dedicated slice. The other camp will tell you to underestimate your cake needs because there will always be some people who don't eat cake. The first method of cake quantification is the safest, though you may feel justified in underordering cake if you're also serving other desserts like chocolate-covered strawberries or candy. Then again, your baker may allow you to adjust your slice count as late as one week before the wedding so you don't have to overestimate your figures too broadly. As tempting as it is to lowball your numbers to save money, few things are sadder than a guest who's been denied their dessert.

One of the sneakiest ways to stick to your budget involves foam. Cakerental.com will create a beautiful custom-designed foam cake that you can rent or buy. Because all of the cakes are covered in fondant and decorated with gum paste embellishments, they look just like the real thing. Your guests will ooh and ahh over your pricey-looking confection, never knowing that they'll actually be eating slices of a matching sheet cake you acquired quite inexpensively from the local bakery. The best part? You can still do the whole cake-cutting ritual because there is a notch cut into the foam where you can stow a bit of genuine cake!

Just so you know, buying cake online is easy, while buying wedding cake online is all but impossible. There are a few ways to get around this. You can buy an assortment of ten-inch cakes from shops like Blackhoundny.com/cakes.cfm and Oldstyledesserts.com, then stack them on graduated pedestal plates. You can have fresh pies airmailed right to your doorstep, and fruit pies can even be bought ahead of time and frozen. Cheesecakes are also readily available on the web from shops like Elegantcheesecakes.com.

Speaking of doing things ahead of time, don't assume that you can whip up a great wedding cake because you're a crack birthday baker. Putting together a wedding cake is a serious and time-consuming business that requires a rather thorough knowledge of different sorts of sweets and how they perform under pressure. That isn't to say, however, that you can't study up and produce a stunning cake in the days leading up to your nuptials. Test runs are *such* an important part of DIY baking. Some cakes are too light and fluffy to survive the weight of more than one tier. Some icings are just not viscous enough to keep dripping down, down, down the cake. Some fillings will seep into cake, making it all mushy.

If you're a committed DIYer, you'll be glad to know that there is no shortage of baking info on the Internet. A good portion of that information specifically concerns wedding cakes and their construction. The chart at www.Wilton.com/wedding/cakeinfo/cakedata.cfm can help you determine how much cake you're going to need when baking tiered cakes for large groups. The site also has guides that explain how to bake, level, tort, fill, ice, assemble, transport, and slice a wedding cake. Baking911.com/decorating/101_intro.htm is a great decorating resource, and look no further than YouTube for visual baking instructionals.

But I Don't Like Cake!

Assuming that you're absolutely sure that cake is not your thing, feel free to ditch the dang cake. It may, however, be "wedding cake" rather than just plain cake that puts a frown on your face. The days of bland white cake filled with blah chocolate pudding and topped with flavorless sugared-up shortening are mostly over. The right baker can create a wedding cake made of almost anything, from carrot cake to lemon poppy-seed cake to a torte. There are cheesecakes and fruitcakes. You shouldn't feel obligated to have a cake if you're just super-anticake, but don't discount cake because you've had bad experiences with wedding cake in the past. Wedding cake can actually be really, really tasty.

That said, there are all sorts of yummy things you can serve your guests in place of cake once the remains of lunch or dinner have been cleared away. Before you settle on one, you should ask yourself whether you and your intended want to participate in the cake-cutting ritual that's a standard part of so many postnuptial parties. Take away the cake, and you're left with the cutting. You can cut pie, sticky cream-puff towers known as pièce montée or croquembouche, a fruit tart, a tower of doughnuts, tiramisu, or an ice cream bombe. Or you could also cut out the cutting and skip right to the feeding each other part, no knives necessary.

Christa Terry

Jeanette and the Elusive Pie Stands

"Chris doesn't know it, but I spent quite a bit of time looking at cakes online. We didn't talk about pies at first, which is one of the reasons I was looking at cakes. Once we did decide on pies, I still spent time looking at cakes because I wanted to get some display ideas. The pies themselves came from the caterer—it's actually one of their specialties. They have a huge bakery business that is just too awesome. But, ugh, pie stands! I searched every website I could think of. We really wanted the pies to be arranged to look like a cake, but we never did find anything that met our needs. I found a lot of neat ideas, but they just weren't right."

If cutting the whatever is just not that important to you, let everyone involved in the matrimonial choreography know that. You'll run less risk of having sweets shoved into your maw by an overzealous spouse. Your photog will be happy to know that they don't have to elbow aside relatives with disposable cameras while you and your spouse are backed into a corner slicing chunks from a mammoth confection. Your catering or facility manager won't have to wait until the photo ops are over to start doling out dessert. Furthermore, your family won't be left wondering when exactly you're going to announce that dessert and coffee are being served. People really look forward to dessert and coffee.

Know that almost anything can be set into tiers on the proper stand. You can enjoy the whole wedding aesthetic without having to settle for some dessert you don't like just because it's easily stacked. Chilled mousse can be served in glasses that are then artfully set one on top of another in a mimicry of the traditional champagne fountain. Sundae bars can be set up on multilevel table displays with the ice cream at the bottom and the cherries at the top. There are also lovely tiered serving dishes and stands that are sized just right for pastries, cookies, chocolate-dipped fruits, and truffles. Your caterer may be able to provide you with these, but there's no shortage of online shops selling them if you feel comfortable budgeting for them. Simply search for "tiered serving tray" or "tier serving tray."

Alternative wedding desserts are typically less expensive and

{226}

more convenient. Many sweets—like cookies and candies—can be made ahead of time, and some can even be purchased on the Internet, well in advance of the wedding. A candy bar or candy buffet is one of the most wallet-friendly dessert options out there. Search eBay for cool apothecary jars or grab discount vases from Save-on-crafts.com/vases.html, and fill the containers you buy with personalized M&Ms from MMs.com/us, a custom mix of jelly beans from Jellybelly.com, and Jordan almonds from (duh) Jordanalmonds.com. No-name candies bought in bulk work just as well, and Candywarehouse.com and Candyfavorites.com both let you shop for candy by color. Your bar can double as a favor station if you set out to-go boxes or bags for guests to fill.

What else can you buy online? Plenty of shops sell chocolate-dipped fruits by the pound, personalized wedding cookies, gourmet brownies, flaky pies, and elegant chocolates. You can even get empty slice-shaped favor boxes that come together to form a beautiful and unusual two-tiered wedding cake from Orefelici.com/wedding.html. If you're worried that your guests will be disappointed when they realize that they're not going to be able to chow down on cake, relax. Your older loved ones have probably eaten lots of second-rate wedding cake, meaning they'll appreciate the change of pace, and younger friends and relatives will think it's cool that you didn't buy into the WIC hype.

When buying foodstuff online, go with a company that has been doing volume business online for at least a couple of years. Plenty of shops list their establishment dates somewhere on their website, but those that don't will no doubt be more than happy to give you some company background via e-mail. To ensure that larger orders won't come as a shock, drop the store a line ahead of time to let them know that you're planning on placing a bulk order on such and such a date. You're basically giving the store a chance to either prepare themselves to fulfill your order or to back out gracefully because it's not equipped at this time to make your dreams happen. Additionally, let whomever you speak with know that the cakes or pies or whatever are for your wedding so that that person knows it's really super-important the company gets your order out on time.

A Frostbitten Tribute to Love

When you have a tall multilevel cake with an itty-bitty top tier, you may very well be tempted to leave that uppermost tier untouched so you can enjoy it on your first wedding anniversary. It is tradition, after all. The problem is that the tradition began ages ago in England, when wedding cakes were made of dense liquor-infused fruitcake. The tier was served to guests when the newlyweds' first child was christened. A fruitcake, as you probably know, can sit around for up to twenty-five years if stored properly; it is that indestructible. Sponge cakes—iced or not—keep their flavor for about two months if wrapped up nice and tight and kept in the freezer.

How tight is tight? Really tight. This would be a good time to bust out that vacuum sealer someone bought off your registry. Your cake will look nothing like it did on your wedding day, but it may actually be edible after twelve months. Steer clear of the specialty cake preservation boxes like the one at Bridestreasures.com/Shop Site/CakeSupplies.html unless you fancy paying twenty bucks for a silver cardboard box that will let air circulate around your cake, effectively destroying it. Freezer burn occurs when air causes ice crystals to form in frozen food and the ice evaporates in a process called sublimation. Go on, look it up—it's interesting.

While freezer-burned cake is safe to eat, it tastes incredibly nasty. Putting your top tier on ice is a risky proposition—think about how disappointing it will be to unwrap a crumbly hunk of dried-out cake on your first anniversary. Feel like gambling? At your reception, ask a server or a relative to stash the top tier of your cake in the fridge. This will temporarily keep it fresh and safe from prying hands. The cold will also firm up the icing, making it easier to seal up later on. When you're ready to preserve your cake, wrap the whole thing in a heck of a lot of plastic wrap. Make sure there are no bubbles or air pockets, because that's where freezer burn starts. Then put your sealed lump of cake into a freezer-safe container and wrap the whole thing as tightly as you can with aluminum foil. For added protection, put the whole shebang in a freezer bag, push out the air, seal it, and wrap a few rubber bands around it for good measure.

It sounds like overkill, but it's really not. Ever found an unopened bag of year-old frozen peas in the back of your freezer? They probably weren't very nice even though those peas were originally flash-frozen in a factory. A really hardy yellow cake that didn't have a lot of flavor to begin with may stand up well to the perils of freezer life, but fancier, more delicate cakes will probably be blah a year later. What it comes down to is this: Your wedding cake was designed to be savored on the day you said "I do," not months after the fact.

If you're absolutely hell-bent on having a nibble of wedding cake on your first anniversary, ask your baker whether they take orders for replica tiers. Some will gladly whip you up a little cake made to look like the confection you and your spouse enjoyed when you were the newest of newlyweds. To ensure authenticity, keep a snapshot of your cake along with a list of flavor and icing options handy so you won't be stymied when your forgetful baker asks you to describe your cake. These records will also prove helpful if your wedding day baker has moved or gone out of business, because you'll be equipped to shop around until you can find a new baker capable of replicating your top tier. Just don't be surprised when you're charged an arm and a leg for a cake that barely feeds two people—most bakers will hear the word "wedding" and charge you accordingly.

So what should you do with your leftover cake? Arm yourself with cake-slice boxes from Lcipaper.com/accessories/cakeboxes .shtml and send your guests home with something sweet they can eat. As early as the seventeenth century, happily married couples sent their single female relatives and friends home with boxed cake, usually slices of the groom's cake. A lovelorn lady was supposed to sleep with her slice stuffed underneath her pillow so she could see the face of her future spouse in her dreams that very night. This tradition likely fell out of favor as gal after gal dreamed of that annoying guy in accounting and woke up with icing in her hair. Let your guests know that they're better off noshing on cake while daydreaming about Mr. (or Ms.) Right.

Get Cake Envy

- Blog.pinkcakebox.com
- Brides.com/weddingstyle/cakes
- Cakeamerica.com/weddingcakes.aspx
- Cakechannel.com
- Celebratecakes.com/mysite/photo_gallery.htm
- Cupcakestakethecake.blogspot.com
- Eweddingcake.com
- Mcneillmanor.com/gallery.cfm
- Photos.ivillage.com/weddings/inspirations/cake
- Projectwedding.com/photo/browse?tag=cake
- Thecakeblog.livejournal.com

Bake Your Own Cake

- Allinonebakeshop.com/documents/armadillocake instructionsheet.pdf
- Allrecipes.com/recipe/grooms-cake/detail.aspx

- Allrecipes.com/recipes/holidays-and-events/events-and
  -gatherings/weddings/main.aspx

- Baking911.com/cakes/wedding.htm

- Epicurious.com/articlesguides/holidays/weddings/cake

- Intotheoven.com

- Joyofbaking.com/cakes.html

- Kitchenlink.com/ch/2002/december/joc6.html

- NYcake.com

- Pastrychef.com

- Pastrywiz.com

- Recipes.howstuffworks.com/how-to-make-a-wedding
  -cake.htm

- Recipezaar.com/recipes.php?q=wedding+cake

- Weddings.about.com/od/weddingcakesfoodmenus/a/
  weddingcakedeco.htm

- Wilton.com

Edible Alternatives

- Bakemeawish.com

- Berries.com

- Burdickchocolate.com

- Candyfavorites.com

- Cheesecake.com

- Ediblearrangements.com
- Elegantcheesecakes.com
- Gtpie.com
- Orefelici.com/wedding.html
- Othos.com
- Parkavepastries.com
- Rollingpinproductions.com/Wedding.htm
- Romanicoschocolate.com

Top It Off

- Applebride.com/pages/Make_your_own_cake_topper
- Caketoppers.com
- Fancyflours.com/site/vintage-wedding-cake-toppers.html
- Klaykabobs.com/caketoppers.shtml
- Magicalday.com/wedding-cake-toppers-main.html
- Porcelainroses.com/cake.htm
- Sculpturedglass.com
- Thumbprintkids.com
- Tobyrosenberg.com/weddingcaketoppe.html
- Topperswithglitz.com

Chapter 13
Picture This!

After the last crumb of cake has been eaten, the guests have all gone home, and the leftover favors have been stashed away in a box in the attic never to be seen again, you'll still have your memories and your wedding photographs. You may also have a wedding video that will get taken off the DVD shelf approximately once a year on your anniversary until your kids (or someone else's kids) use it as a makeshift Frisbee for an entire summer. Some people care deeply about these images of what should be a once-in-a-lifetime event, stowing photo albums and vids in their fire safes, while others crack these visual mementos open once or twice before losing them.

Your attitude toward snapshots and home videos will have a huge impact on how much money you end up dropping on your wedding photographer and videographer. If pictures mean the world to you and you regularly browse through your well-organized photo collection, don't scrimp here. Hire the best shutterbug you can afford—cut back on the hors d'oeuvres if that's what it takes. On the other hand, if you can't think of photographs without glumly picturing the disordered box of snapshots lurking somewhere in your storage closet, you may want to consider stocking your reception tables with disposables and calling it a day.

Before you decide that professional matrimonial documentation isn't really worth it, wipe the images of dull poses and grainy video from your mind. Wedding photographs can indeed be among the most boring pics in an album, but that's a product of historical precedent more than anything else. When the art of photography was still in its infancy—say, around 1850 or so—photo shoots were studio affairs. Ever wonder why people in old daguerreotype portraits are never really smiling? It's partly because the exposure times were fairly long and partly because having your picture taken was a sober, serious event in one's life. If you had the money, you went into a photographer's studio and sat for a single portrait.

As the years passed, photography became both faster and cheaper, but in-studio, rigidly posed shots were pretty much all you were going to get. That changed after World War II, when photographers with portable cameras saw money in the growing wedding industry. These plucky guys would show up uninvited to weddings in the hopes they could sell their candid snapshots to brides and grooms after the event, which forced the studio photogs to come out of their studios. The equipment was still bulky and unwieldy, meaning that more often than not, all of the seemingly candid shots in a wedding album were actually posed shots taken between the ceremony and the reception.

Sound familiar? That's because most wedding photographers still take scads of posed shots between the vows and the eats. These posed shots look smashing framed and hung on a wall, but an album full of them is pretty boring to look through. When you're standing stock still, surrounded by the bodies of your attendants with a big-ass grin plastered on your face while your guests are enjoying the cocktail hour, you can thank the evolution of camera technology for the crick in your neck. For a little context, read up on the history of photography in general at Wikipedia.org/wiki/history_of _photography.

Videography is obviously the younger of the two forms of nuptial documentation, with roots going back only as far as the 8 mm cameras of yore. Silent footage was still footage, and amateur filmmakers were happy to have a chance to shoot their loved ones' weddings. In the eighties, Sony started selling that clunky personal home video recording device known as the camcorder, and the aforementioned amateurs dumped their Super 8s and never looked back. In fact, it was those very same hobby videographers who went on to become the first professional videographers, shooting the first grainy, tinny, oversaturated wedding videos for delighted brides and grooms.

Were those videos ugly? Yes, but what could you do when there wasn't much out there for the home-based video editor? The originals degraded over time, and the copies were inevitably inferior to the originals. Were the videographers themselves obtrusive? Sure, but you just couldn't shoot in low light with the technology out there, so bright spotlights were a necessary evil. Did people happily overlook these little issues and hire videographers anyway? Oh yes, they did.

The problem is that people still remember watching their relatives' dim and gritty videos and are afraid that their own will turn out similarly unimpressive. But have no fear! If you've always dreamed of having a perfect wedding video to watch wistfully in the years following your nuptials, know that most of the videographers of today have lost the spotlights, shoot clear footage using digital cameras, and know how to edit that footage using the affordable video editing software that's out there.

Costs vary *a lot* for both of these services, which is why it's so important to ask yourself whether you're going to regret nixing the videographer or going with a budget photog. You can save money by asking talented relatives or friends to fill these roles, but they may not appreciate having to work when they ought to be celebrating. Some brides- and grooms-to-be are lucky enough to find cheap labor in the form of fledgling photogs and videographers looking to build their portfolios, but this doesn't happen all that often. If you're really in a budget bind in this area of your nuptials, try calling the art departments of local colleges or putting an ad up on Craigslist.org. The very easiest way to save money without sacrificing quality involves cutting a pro's hours; after all, do you really need to capture the last two hours of the reception?

Still-Life Magic

It was once customary for photogs to hold on to newlyweds' negatives for years. This was a great racket—they could charge a "lookup fee" whenever couples or their loved ones asked for prints, and then they charged them again for those reprints. And when these same photographers made the switch to digital, they held onto the JPGs, GIFs, TIFs, or PNGs and sold the prints one by one through sites like Photoreflect.com and Shutterfly.com. This is all on the up-and-up because photogs own the rights to your photos as soon as they take the shot. They don't even have to apply for copyright, which means that scanning your prints for the purposes of reproducing them could earn you a big fat lawsuit.

Paying $3,000 for a photographer's time and a handful of prints sounds like a real bummer, and that sum gets you only a midrange photog according to Costhelper.com/cost/wedding/wedding-phographer.html. One of the first questions you should ask any prospective photog is whether they will hook you up with a reproduction release form that says you can reproduce and use the pictures as long as you don't sell them or let others use them for profit. Without that release, it is technically illegal for you to scan or otherwise make copies of your wedding pics and to put them up on MySpace, Facebook, Flickr, or your very own website. Many photographers have strong opinions about copyright, as you can see in blog posts like Acellisblog.com/2007/03/copyright-vs-reproduction-rights.html. If you discuss rights with your photog before ever signing a contract, you can be sure that you're getting what you think you're getting.

Now, if you and your intended happen to look like catalog models and your wedding venue has perfect lighting, you can confidently choose your photog based on their sample sets. If, however, you're a couple of regular folks who don't know jack about light levels, you should ask to see as many photographs as possible from the past few weddings a prospective photographer shot. Those stunning sample sets most photogs post on their websites are the twenty best snaps culled from the thousands of photos the photographer has taken. What you want to know is how that photographer will perform when their "models" are old, grumpy, over- or underweight, awkward, shy, and generally imperfect, and the lighting is low or unpredictable.

If you want to have an edge when interviewing photogs, read through the FAQ at Wedfog.com/faq.html and the articles at Wedpix.com. Knowledge is power when you're dealing with vendors who know they can charge insane amounts of money for their services. Back in the days when film was king, photographers had

A. J. Discovered the Pros and Cons of Online Proofs

"Our photographer used Collages.net to display the proofs, which was nice because people could buy prints right off the website about a month after the wedding. The only problem was that some of our attendees received multiple e-mails from the site that said something along the lines of "Matt and A. J. photos make great holiday gifts," and I know it got on at least one person's nerves.

"We made up our own list of must-have shots instead of relying on any one list we found online. Unfortunately, the photographer pretty much disregarded the whole thing. As we were leaving at the end of the night, people were asking us whether we'd gotten this or that photo. We were pretty well occupied throughout the reception, so it never struck us that we hadn't been photographed with certain people or in certain poses. Afterward, I really regretted not having given my MOH a copy of a shot list so she could make sure we got what we wanted. It wasn't anyone's fault—except the photographer's—but I felt like someone, somewhere along the line messed up, and I'm still pretty mad about it."

to pay for that film, for the darkroom space where they developed their prints, the processing materials they used, and album components like matting, so the high cost of wedding photography was justifiable. Photogs who favor digital—which is most of 'em, because digital is way more versatile than film—do not have the same overhead, so you're paying for skill and style—two assets that are pretty hard to quantify.

Being that you can't exactly haggle for more style for your money, be sure you're getting what you want from the very beginning. Ask photographers to show you everything from their latest wedding samples to the albums they create. If they show you nothing but eight-by-tens, ask to see their biggest enlargements and their smallest reductions so you can see how good (or bad) their photo printer is. Are you looking for traditional wedding shots, with plenty of portraiture and poses, or artistic photographs that tell the story of your wedding in a creative and abstract way? Some brides- and grooms-to-be lean toward the photojournalistic style of wedding photography, which captures candid shots of the wedding party and guests being themselves.

Find traditional photogs at Wedding & Portrait Photographers International (WPPIonline.com/directory) and Professional Photographers of America (PPA.com), and photojournalists at the Wedding Photojournalist Association (WPJA.com). PPA.com is a particularly good resource for brides- and grooms-to-be because you can view member photographers' portfolios right on the website. Pictage.com also highlights photogs' best samples. Once you've found a couple of photographers whose samples look pretty good, you'll need to quiz them on things like their background, professional associations, and equipment. Common queries include:

· Will you be shooting our wedding? Can you guarantee that ours will be the only shoot you schedule that day?

- How long have you been photographing weddings? Can we get one or more referrals?

- Do you specialize in any one style, e.g., formal, photojournalistic, artistic, relaxed, or candid?

- What do your packages include? How can we order extra prints? Will you grant us a reproduction release or transfer the copyright to us?

- Do you shoot digital? If so, can we buy CDs of the image files from you? If not, can we buy the negatives?

- What type of equipment will you bring with you? Do you typically travel with any backup equipment?

- Will you follow a shot list (like the one found at Frugalbride.com/photochecklist.html)? Will you get our must-have shots?

- Do you work with an assistant? Can we meet him or her?

- Roughly how many photos will you shoot during the ceremony and reception?

- Is photo editing included as part of your package prices? What are your per-print charges?

- What will you wear during the wedding? Have you worked at our venue before?

- Do you have liability insurance?

- How long does it typically take you to send proofs? To send prints? To create a complete album?

This is the short list, because just about anything else you're going to want to know will be a product of your personal preferences. You may want to know how a photog handles large or blended families. Maybe you want to know how the standard packages can be expanded to ensure that stepparents, grandparents, and friends can also get in on the photographic action. If you feel the need to throw some extra questions out there but you're not sure what to ask, check out Chicagoweddingservices.com/planning/articles/questions _photography.htm for a longer list, or search for "questions to ask your wedding photographer" to find even more lists of queries.

When every detail has been nailed down, it's contract time. Check out a bunch of sample wedding photography contracts at Wedfog.com/contracts.html to be sure you understand the basics, but make sure the contract you eventually sign includes the photog's name and contact info; the date, time, and location of your wedding; the names of any assistants; the number of hours the photog will work and the minimum number of shots they will take; all of the items included in your chosen package plus any extras; the total cost and overtime fees; the deposit and payment schedule; and the photog's refund and cancellation policies.

Remember that photographers, like all wedding vendors, get booked up well in advance, so don't be surprised if your first choice isn't available on your wedding date. Keep second, third, and even fourth choices in mind while you're browsing. No matter who you

Leah Modified the Must-Have Shot Lists

"I looked up lists of must-have shots online, and then my mother and I looked through her wedding pictures and compiled a second list of must-have shots from those. That was actually one of the more personal and memorable parts of planning the wedding. I'll never forget sitting down with my mom to figure out what the family tradition shots are. We have some specific ones, like the 'Maid of Honor telling Bride-to-be the Secret' photo. There were some must-haves that I saw online that I initially rejected, but once we were actually taking photos, the photographer suggested that we try them anyway. I went along with it, just in case they turned out to be awesome, but most of them did end up being as cheesy as I thought they'd be."

ultimately choose, just be sure that your photog is someone you're comfortable with, because you're going to be spending the entire day with them snapping away at your elbow. And if you're planning to pose in some high-profile public place, make sure you don't need to secure any permits; this goes for video, too.

Movie Magic

On a regular day, six or seven hours feel like six or seven hours, give or take a few minutes. On your wedding day, those same hours will fly by in what seems like seconds, leaving you gasping for breath and wondering just where all that time went. This is where your videographer comes in. You may only ever watch your wedding video once, but it will be during that sole viewing that you'll finally get to see how your dad's face lit up when you said "I do" and the look on your great-aunt's face when you started serving guests at the buffet. Of course, that also means hearing how weird your voice sounds on TV and seeing all of the funny faces you made while speaking your vows. It's up to you whether seeing the smiles of loved ones is worth that kind of indignity.

Videography is very much like photography in that you get what you pay for. If all you really want is to be able to watch the ceremony again and again, $500 will get you about an hour of single-camera coverage with some supplementary lighting and a little bit of video editing. Conversely, $5,000 will buy you a professionally edited documentary-style movie with all sorts of neat effects, on-screen menus, photo montages, and interviews with loved ones. No matter what your budget is, there's probably a videography package that will fit into it nicely. You can learn more about the services offered at different price points by asking for samples from the most expensive and least expensive videographers in your area. You may not be able to afford the former and the latter's work may be complete crap, but you'll have a good idea of what's out there.

Back in the olden days—you know, twenty years ago—having a videographer meant that your ceremony and reception spaces would be cluttered up by wires, lights, and tripods. The cameras well-equipped videographers use nowadays tend to be small, wireless, and able to take passable footage in low lighting conditions. Right now, you should be asking yourself what you hope to get out of your video. If you're not sure what you want, take a look at some videographers' blogs (try Blog .elysiumproductions.com or Dvideography.com/blog) to see what the different styles of videography actually look like on a screen.

Documentary-style vids are a record of your wedding as it happened, with minimal editing. You'll see your wedding play out from start to finish—your videographer won't miss any key details and you can enjoy all of the candid moments you missed while table hopping. The cinematic style of videography is all about sweet special effects, good music, and creative editing. You're going to pay more and wait longer for this style because videographers spend a lot more time futzing with the footage before proclaiming it ready to go. You can create a shot checklist like the one found at Desktopvideo .about.com/od/homevideoprojects/a/wedvideocheck.htm regardless of which style you prefer, but be sure to give it to your videographer well in advance of your wedding.

You want specific music piped over everything except for the important talky bits of the ceremony and reception? It can be done. You want everything cut together in a very specific way? All you have to do is find a videographer flexible enough to make your vision happen. You will pay more for a completely customized vid, but don't imagine that you have to settle for something like the cookie-cutter samples most videographers will send you. Ask for what you want up front so that the videographers you're interviewing have a chance to say "Yes, I can do that" or "No, I don't work that way" before you start delving into the nitty-gritty.

What do you absolutely, positively need to know? Read up on wedding videography at Wikipedia.org/wiki/wedding_videography, then brush up on your lingo so you know what videographers mean when they say something like, "I shoot in DV and use live switching." DV is digital video, and live switching is a technique that allows a videographer to edit your wedding video as the action is happening using multiple cameras feeding information onto one tape. DV rocks, live switching doesn't. The best editing happens when the editor doesn't have to make split-second decisions. Have a look at some online videography glossaries like 4evergroup.org/misc%20 page%20files/Wedding_Video_Terms.html to make sure nothing goes over your head.

Chances are that you know a lot more about photography than you do about videography, so ask all prospective videographers to clarify anything that's unclear. The last thing they want is for you to get pissed later on because they were talking straight shop talk and you didn't grasp a word of it. There are the usual "_ questions to ask your _" online guides (Weddinggazette.com/content/002486.shtml, for example), but you should commit the following list of questions to memory:

- How long have you been in the wedding videography business? What's your primary shooting style?

- Can we see a range of samples and get some referrals?

- Will ours be the only wedding you're shooting that day?

- What sort of packages do you offer? Can you modify those based on the services we need?

- Will you be shooting alone? If you'll have colleagues or assistants working with you, can we meet them?

- What kind of cameras, mics, and lighting will you use? Will we have to wear microphones?

- Do you bring backup equipment?

- How many cameras will you set up? Will all but one be stationary?

- Can you interview our loved ones? Or add a photo montage to our video? Can we choose our own music?

- What editing services do you offer? How long does the editing typically take?

- Do you offer extras like title menus and chapter stops on your DVDs? How much do extra DVDs cost?

- Who owns the rights to the finished video?

And naturally there is the ubiquitous contract. You can check out a sample contract at Mediacollege.com/video/wedding/business/contract.html, but make sure your videography contract includes the videographer's name and contact info; the date, time, and location of your wedding; the names of any colleagues or assistants; a list of your must-have scenes; all of the items included in your chosen package plus any extras; the total cost and overtime fees; the deposit and payment schedule; and the videographer's refund and cancellation policies. More info is always better than less.

Before you book, check with your ceremony space to make sure that videotaping (and photography) is actually allowed. Some religious institutions have fairly strict rules about where and when cameras can be filming. Once that's out of the way, make sure your videographer will be attending your rehearsal so they'll know exactly what to expect. If you're making up an order-of-events sheet for your reception, print out an extra copy for your videographer for the same reasons. The last thing you're going to want is a videographer who's consistently on the wrong side of the room during the pivotal moments of your matrimonial celebration.

Your Alternatives and Options

It's fairly tough to personify the DIY spirit in this area of wedding planning. You can't exactly spend a lot of time behind a camera when you're supposed to be making a commitment to spend the rest of your life with someone you love. Sure, you can set up a video camera on a tripod and hope for the best, or snap a few pics during the reception when you're not schmoozing with your uber-crazy uncles. Budget photography and videography is more often than not a matter of finding someone who can do it on the cheap. Sometimes that'll mean having someone you know step up to the plate, but that only works if you happen to be lucky enough to know a really fabulous amateur photog or filmmaker.

What you can do is DIY wedding portraiture. The ultimate online guide has to be Diyweddingphotos.com, a site created by two enterprising newlyweds named Rain and Peter Kwan. They'll teach you everything you need to know about being your own stylists and portrait photographers, from the basics of composition, lighting, and exposure times to the fine art of posing. If you're nervous about doing your own wedding portraiture or editing your photos, you'll definitely feel a lot more comfortable after reading through this site. There are other DIY photography tutorials out there, but none are as thorough or easy to use.

There's also the dreaded disposable camera option. The main problem with letting your guests stand in for a pro photographer is that you run the risk of ending up with twenty-six exposures of Cousin Edna's cleavage taken by your sister's date. Only opt for this alternative if you like photos but they don't mean that much to you in the grand scheme of things. The good news is that disposables are sold all over the web at bargain-basement prices. Try Camerasforall.com or grab 'em directly from Kodak.com. The bad news? Even the priciest disposables take shoddy snapshots,

Christa Terry

Jeanette Got Her Disposables on the Cheap

"I looked everywhere offline for plain-ish cameras, but they were all at least $3 each. Finally, I found plain Kodak disposables on eBay, and I paid $25 for twenty-five cameras. For a buck each, I got cameras with better-quality film than anything I could have found at the drugstore. The best part is that I still have eight of them—hey, free film!

"The disposables were only our backup. We were lucky enough to have three photographers, so we ended up with all kinds of different shots without having to make a specific shot list. One of my favorite pictures was completely candid and was probably shot by accident. The photo at the end of our wedding album is of me and Chris playing Pooh sticks on the bridge in the park across the street from the reception venue. We were just messing around, waiting for something to get fixed, and Chris's stepmom just happened to take a picture at just the right moment. My advice is this: You can print out all the shot lists you like, but make sure there's time for breathing room, because the best photographs just kind of happen on their own."

standard photo developing isn't exactly cheap, and as widespread as the practice of leaving cameras scattered around for guests to use and abuse is, some attendees may not understand that they're not just more free swag.

Then there's Youshoot.com, the natural next step. This company rents out entire boxes of digital cameras to brides- and grooms-to-be so that guests can snap away all night long and you can avoid grainy photographs that may or may not be of your MOH's butt. When you send the cameras back, the company uploads them to some web space set aside just for you so you can delete any humdingers before opening your site to the general public. Guests can upload any pics they took with their own cameras, or you can provide prepaid mailers and CDs to those guests so they can send their pics into YouShoot directly. The company does sell prints, but you can download the full-size image files for free if you'd rather just save the pics to your computer.

Once you have your photos in hand and you're absolutely sure you have the right to do more than just look at them, it's time to share and play. Get yourself a Flickr account if you don't already

have one, or try Photobucket.com, Picasa.google.com, or Web-a
-photo.com. What else can you do with your wedding photos? You
can turn them into an iPod advert at Podapic.com or Ipopmyphoto
.com. You can mess around with them using the Gimp, a free
image-editing program downloadable at Gimp.org, before making
them into a professional-looking coffee-table book at Blurb.com
or Picaboo.com. Sites like Photoworks.com let you put your pics on
cards and other gifty-type items that your more sentimental relatives
are just going to die for next holiday season.

And here's one last unique idea, via a comment left on Manolo
brides.com: Set up a laptop with the appropriate memory card
readers on a table at the reception, and let your guests know that
they should feel free to upload their pics before they call it a night.
This does require computer-savvy guests, but it can really cut down
on broken promises from people who say again and again that they'll
send you a link to their photos sometime real soon. Because, yeah,
that's really gonna happen.

Find a Photographer . . .

- Bellapictures.com

- Photoreflect.com/PhotographerSearch.aspx

- Pictage.com

- PPA.com/files/public/portfolio_frame.htm

- Weddingbureau.com

- Weddingphotographydirectory.com

- Weddingphotousa.com

- WPJA.com

. . . Or a Videographer

- Gatheringguide.com/ec/videographers.html
- Visualbride.com
- Weddingvideo.com/search.cfm
- WEVA.com

Sexy Up and Share Your Media

- Blurb.com
- Dyowa.com
- Gimp.org
- Mypublisher.com
- Ourweddingcast.com
- Photoblog.com
- Photoworks.com
- Picaboo.com
- Propicsexpress.com
- Shinyphotos.com
- Storybookpages.com
- Viddia.com
- Wedding-album-maker.com
- Youshoot.com

Check Out Photogs' Blogs

- Aperturaphoto.com/blog

- Blog.photographybychristos.com

- Dallasweddingfilms.net

- Godinavideo.com/blog

- Harvardphoto.com/blog

- Homepage.mac.com/rvantuyl/blog/index.html

- Jameschristianson.typepad.com

- Jessicaclaire.net

- Makelovereal.net

- Nashvillewedvideos.com/blog

- Sibblog.com

- Trashthedress.com

- Weddingphotographyblog.com

- Xanga.com/stagi

Chapter 14
Play That Funky Music

Memorable reception music? Sounds like an oxymoron. You may remember that you danced your ass off at the last wedding you attended, but it's not often that the actual tunes make an impression. Everyone loves to hate on the "Electric Slide" and "YMCA," but those are the types of songs that inevitably draw people out onto the floor like some kind of musical magnet. Most brides- and grooms-to-be don't regard this as a problem—they've enjoyed getting footloose and walking like an Egyptian at plenty of receptions, so they see no reason to break with tradition. If, however, gettin' jiggy with it isn't your thing and the twist makes you dizzy, you may be wondering what the alternatives are.

Take a quick look at the list of the top two hundred most-requested wedding songs at DJs-unlimited.net/top200.htm. Go to enough weddings and you'll eventually hear all of them, even though a bunch of them are pretty naughty and some are thematically inappropriate. There's just no getting around the fact that these are the songs that will get people dancing, which means that one of the first decisions you'll need to make with regard to your wedding music is whether or not you want people to dance. If you think empty dance floors make for uncomfortable affairs, there is a good chance you'll be slipping "Electric Slide" into your playlist. It is possible to have a reception that doesn't include any dancing whatsoever—especially if your venue doesn't come equipped with a dance floor—but it's not at all common.

There's no denying that music is another one of those details that can influence the tone of a wedding from beginning to end. When guests walk into a ceremony space and are greeted by the sound of a live quartet playing classical favorites, they'll guess that the vows they're about to hear will be fairly traditional. Some religious institutions have strict rules about what sorts of music can and cannot be played. Hearing a whole lot of hymns can clue guests into the fact that the upcoming ceremony will be pretty religious. If they hear something else—like folk, rock, or jazz music—they'll infer that they're about to witness a ritual that may not include the whole "Love is patient, love is kind" shtick.

At a reception, the music serves as a kind of guest herder. When friends and relatives start hearing songs that you just can't dance to, they can be pretty sure that it's time to chow down or listen to speeches or do something equally sit-downish. As soon as the band or DJ or laptop plays any of the two hundred wedding favorites previously mentioned, guests know that it's time to party down. Music acts like a shepherd precisely because people who have been to their fair share of weddings have heard the same songs over and over again and know what they signify. Play "Hot, Hot, Hot," "Who Let the Dogs Out?," or "It's Raining Men" and guests will respond like they've been conditioned to respond.

It's all right to use nontraditional music in both your ceremony and your reception, but don't be surprised if your guests get a little confused and aren't quite sure when to stand up or sit down. As romantic as it is to order a custom wedding song from someplace like Customweddingsong.com, none of your guests will know that you paid beaucoup bucks for it unless you include a note about it in your program. Swing bands are fun, but you can probably tally up the number of people you know who can swing on one hand. You may be thinking about having an orchestra instead of a DJ, but can anyone in your clique actually waltz? When you rely on your own tastes rather than the musical zeitgeist, you simply cannot guarantee that there will be rump-shaking going on.

All of this is moot advice if you plan to book a DJ or band with a fairly standard repertoire. Even if you do decide to hand them a Do Not Play list, they'll be taking the reins where music is concerned and it will be their job to entertain your guests. Some brides- and grooms-to-be just feel better delegating the event's entertainment to professionals who have worked enough weddings to know what will make guests happy. Another benefit to hiring pros is that they'll know how to maximize the acoustic properties of your reception space, they'll know how to work with any audio equipment provided by your venue, and it will be their responsibility to conform to whatever licensing and insurance regulations apply.

Just so you know, there are four organizations that handle music rights licensing in the United States: ASCAP, BMI, SESAC, and Sound Exchange. Mobile DJs, and, by extension, your brother with the stocked MP3 player, are not required to pay the fees these organizations levy. It's the responsibility of the venue to obtain the proper licenses for live performances and the playback of prerecorded music. As long as your wedding is a private, not-for-profit event (and etiquette demands that it is), you have nothing to worry about. All four organizations have websites, so if you're interested in this rather dry topic, there's no shortage of info online.

Been shouldering most of the prenuptial burden? This is one of the best times to delegate. There's a good chance that either you or your intended is disproportionately into music. Pass the buck now by handing off all the music selection duties to your SO or foisting

Your Premade Do Not Play List

Even though the following song titles *sound* romantic, they're not the best choices for your wedding. If you can't figure out why you probably shouldn't play these songs, look 'em up at Lyricsmania.com. Remember, folks, lyrics matter.

- "I Will Always Love You"—Dolly Parton/Whitney Houston
- "White Wedding"—Billy Idol
- "Every Breath You Take"—Sting
- "I Touch Myself"—The Divinyls
- "My Heart Will Go On"—Celine Dion
- "I Will Survive"—Gloria Gaynor
- "Paradise by the Dashboard Light"—Meatloaf
- "One"—U2
- "Billie Jean"—Michael Jackson
- "The Dance"—Garth Brooks
- "Blister in the Sun"—Violent Femmes
- "Crash"—Dave Matthews Band
- "If Loving You Is Wrong, I Don't Want to Be Right"—Luther Ingram
- "Total Eclipse of the Heart"—Bonnie Tyler
- "When a Man Loves a Woman"—Percy Sledge
- "The One I Love"—REM
- "Crazy"—Pasty Cline
- "Saving All My Love for You"—Whitney Houston
- "The Thong Song"—Sisqo
- "More Than Words"—Extreme
- "Follow Me"—Uncle Kracker

- "In Another's Eyes"—Garth Brooks and Trisha Yearwood

- "Like a Virgin"—Madonna

- "If I Could Turn Back Time"—Cher

- "I (Never Promised You a) Rose Garden"—Lynn Anderson

Every one of these songs was culled from message board posts and blog posts written by people who'd just attended weddings and were appalled by what they heard at the reception. Then again, if you want to shock grandpa or have a little fun at the expense of people who don't normally listen to lyrics, don't hold back. Forget songs with veiled references to infidelity—go all out and put King Missile's "Detachable Penis" on your playlist.

some other duties on them so you can concentrate on choosing the best-ever tunes. If your musical tastes are radically different, you can meet somewhere in the middle by contributing your individual choices to a shared playlist or choosing from the list of songs offered by your DJ or band.

Have a look at your CD collection, your hard drive full of MP3s, and the old party playlists you never bothered to delete from iTunes. It's time to think about your aural priorities. Would you rather see your guests cutting a rug to the same old songs or listen to a lot of great music that just doesn't have the same inspirational effects? There are no right or wrong answers here, because it's your wedding. Maybe there is certain less-than-popular music that is really important to you and your intended. Or perhaps you're vehemently opposed to the thought of ever doing the locomotion ever again. To paraphrase another song you'll occasionally hear at wedding receptions, that's your prerogative.

Musical Milestones

Before you feel compelled to worship at the altar of originality for originality's sake, remember that your wedding will be creative and unique because it's yours. There's no reason you should go out of your way to be different if you really do enjoy the standard wedding favorites, just like there's no reason to resign yourself to playing Canon in D because that's what everyone else is doing. That said, it's highly likely that your matrimonial music selections—whatever they are—will end up grouped into a fairly standard set of categories, because it's just plain easier to incorporate them into your day that way. Maybe you're skipping the whole aisle-walking ritual and seating your guests in a big-ass oval. Could be that you and your SO have decided to dish out little liquor-infused bonbons instead of cake. Maybe the bride's wearing the tux and the groom will be donning a dress. Fantastic, but that doesn't change the fact that certain music will be associated with certain rites.

Traditionally, you've got your prelude music, processional music, and recessional music. There is also cake-cutting music, bouquet-toss music, and garter-removal music. You may or may not have a first dance song, a father-daughter dance song, and a mother-son dance song. Some brides and grooms designate specific introduction music, dinner music, and dancing music. The Internet will serve you well in this area if you're planning to serenade your guests with the usual favorites. DJs have gotten into the habit of posting song lists on their website so future husbands and wives have some idea of what guests will expect to hear. At Wedalert.com/songs and a handful of other sites, you can take the most popular ceremony and reception songs for an auditory test drive. You'll need either RealOne Player (download here: Forms.real.com/service/download_player) or Real Alternative (download here: Free-codecs.com/download/Real_Alternative.htm) to listen to the samples.

You know the song commonly referred to as "Here Comes the Bride"? It's the Bridal March from Wagner's opera *Lohengrin,* which is actually a rather tragic tale. But when wedding attendees hear it, they know it's time to stand up, turn around, and watch the bride make her entrance. That's not to say that your organist needs to bust

Jeanette Abused Amazon

"We did quite a bit of online research on popular songs and made up a whole Do Not Play list based on what we found. One of the things we struggled with was finding music for the ceremony. I refused to use "Here Comes the Bride," but I couldn't think of a replacement song off the top of my head. Finding music that didn't make me want to puke was important, and we totally abused Amazon for music samples. It helped! We picked out a few classical pieces and finally settled on Pachelbel's Canon for the processional. We wound up using the wedding march for the recessional even though I wasn't really into it because my brother already had it.

"Figuring out the parent dances wasn't easy, either. I went through list after list after list before we came up with a Sinatra song that my dad and I could dance to and an instrumental piece for Chris and his mom to dance to. I spent a lot of time looking up popular father-daughter and mother-son dance songs because it's not something you really think about until you have to. All in all, it was pretty discouraging, because we just didn't really like the suggestions we found."

out the Bach before the vows or your band has to cover Sinatra while you cut the cake. Any guest that doesn't already know when it's time to sit down and hush up isn't going to be influenced by your evocative music choices. Remember that you can process and recess in any order you please. BMs and GMs can walk out together or separately. Whereas some grooms wait at the altar, others are escorted in by mothers and fathers. A bride can walk alone, with her pop, with both parents, or with her groom. Sometimes, the MOB and the MOG are even seated by ushers to the tune of a preprocessional.

Choose your ceremony music well and choose it wisely. You may hear a few snickers as you tromp down the aisle to the tune of the Imperial Death March from *Star Wars,* but if it's meaningful to you, go for it. Make sure you're not breaking any rules first—some religious institutions frown upon the use of secular music during sacred ceremonies. Canticanova.com suggests that any music not fit for use during Mass should be considered off-limits. Find out if your chosen house of worship agrees before you go falling in love with the idea of playing something seriously punk as your maids and men make their way toward the altar. Never forget that today's most popular preludes, processionals, and recessionals are doomed to become tomorrow's clichés.

As far as the dedicated dances go, don't think you have to play a bunch of sappy songs because it's expected of you. If you've got mad dance skillz because you and your intended have been taking classes for years, now's your chance to show off. Dance lessons are a good idea, period. It's way more fun watching two people who know how to boogie strut their stuff than it is to sit quietly while two people wobble from side to side in a tight circle. Keep it brief—even ballroom pros leave the floor after just a couple of minutes. How do you ensure a perfect first dance? The same way you get to Carnegie Hall: practice, practice, practice—preferably in the shoes you plan to wear on your wedding day. Creative first dances are awesome when done right. Search YouTube for "first dance" to see how other people sexied up their first dance routines.

Parent dances take many forms, and you can skip this tradition entirely if it doesn't gel with your particular familial circumstances. Dancing with the parent of the opposite sex is a nice way to get a minute or two of uninterrupted conversation in. Sure, everyone's looking at you, but it's just about all the private time you're going to get during your reception. Most dads and moms love this part of the wedding. If you appreciate brevity above all, you can always combine the father-daughter and mother-son dances into one event with a song like "I Am Your Child" by Barry Manilow. This can, however, be a touchy subject for some parents, so be considerate and ask your parents if they are looking forward to sharing a dance with you and you alone before making the decision to combine or cut out certain dances.

Who else gets to dance? You can make your attendants dance with each other during the latter half of your first dance song if you want to, but there's really no good reason to force unattached men and women to shuffle around the dance floor. Some brides and grooms get a kick out of inviting all of the married couples to dance a special dance. They may even play an elimination game in which the couple that's been married the longest wins a small prize, like a bottle of wine, and this can be a very touching way to honor older relatives who may not have had a role in the wedding itself.

When it comes to postmeal dancing, keep things up-tempo. Sharing a romantic dance is great and all, but most people slow-dance once or twice a year at most. Generally, the only partner-dancing most people do is at weddings, and it's frequently of the rocking-side-to-side-while-turning-in-a-circle variety. If you play a handful of slow songs just after the dedicated dances and just before the cutting of the cake, you can rest assured that your guests will get their fill of slow dancing. The dancers you know may be kind of disappointed, but even they realize that regular folks are more interested in visiting the Love Shack than trying to remember how to fox trot.

For every wedding rite, there is a song list somewhere out there on the net. Start thinking about the music you want as soon as you start planning the wedding so you don't end up dancing to a bunch of tired old songs because you felt too rushed to be creative. In all likelihood, you've already got a pretty good idea of the songs that mean the most to you. Now it's simply a matter of brainstorming with your SO, making a list of possibilities, and presenting that list to your DJ, discussing it with your band, or downloading the music you want.

Here's a tip: Do not rely on your band, DJ, or memory to help you filter out songs with patently objectionable themes or lots of cussin'. Songs that seem totally appropriate when you're listening to them on your morning commute may not actually be as family-friendly or romantic as you think. "Paradise by the Dashboard Light," for example, is so not wedding appropriate, and yet it gets played at receptions all the damn time. Brides and grooms even go so far as to act out the parts! Profanity is also really easy to miss. Listen to the lyrics of any songs that you're unsure about, even if it takes you an entire afternoon, lest you become forever known as the F-bomb bride.

DJ or Band? Band or DJ?

Forget the cheesy DJs you've seen at other people's weddings. Experienced DJs who count professionalism among their virtues will not play the songs you've asked them not to play or hand out giant novelty sunglasses when that's not something you've specifically requested. The person you hire to spin the tunes is a vendor like any other, meaning he or she should provide the services you're paying for. If you want to micromanage the playlist, that's fine, but consider letting your DJ have some control over the order of songs. A really good DJ will keep an eye on attendees' reactions and choose the music accordingly, almost guaranteeing that all guests at your reception gets to hear at least one song they like.

You can find DJs through sites like Discjockeys.com and Free djamerica.com, but if it's reviews you're after, look no further than Weddingwire.com. A lot of DJs post their schedules and song lists on their websites, so have a gander at those before calling around so you can rule out anyone who seems overly partial to the Chicken Dance. As you search, you'll come across all kinds of rates, and the prices you're eventually quoted will likely be based on your needs, the time of year, the distance the DJ has to travel, and the DJ's ability, equipment, and musical expertise. Most DJs charge between $100 and $300 per hour, plus a 20 percent tip; in return they'll listen to your music preferences, set up all sorts of neat professional-grade sound equipment, act as MC, and keep your party flowing smoothly. Getting a discount is usually a matter of having your wedding in the off season on an unpopular day.

Before you hire a DJ, meet them for a consultation. A face-to-face meeting gives you a chance to decide whether a DJ's personality will be compatible with your particular event. Johnny Longhair may clean up really well, but the fact that he came to your consultation looking like he just rolled out of bed might mean something. Searching for "questions to ask your wedding DJ" will pull up the usual lists of questions, like the one at Mydeejay.com/advice_40questions.html, but you should never neglect to ask the following:

- Can you give us a breakdown of your career experience? Can you offer references?

- What kinds of packages do you offer, and what do you charge for each?

- Are you able to provide music for the ceremony if the whole wedding is taking place in one location? Does this cost extra?

- How large is your music library? Will you obtain any songs we request that you don't already have?

- What equipment will you bring with you? Do you travel with backup equipment? What about lighting?

- Do you use CDs or MP3s?

- Will you respect our Do Not Play list and also play the songs we specifically ask for?

- When do you arrive at the venue and begin setup procedures?

- What will you be wearing?

- Are you familiar with our chosen venue? If not, will you tour it beforehand?

- What do you charge for overtime? Will we have to pay that in cash?

When you're interviewing DJs, get as much info as you can in writing. DJs with blogs and websites will sometimes post prices—take screenshots! E-mail interviews are great because you can save them and then refer back to them later if you suspect something has changed. If you decide to go with a DJ, it's time once again to think about contracts. You can see a sample contract at Northtexasdj.com/contract.html, but remember that the contract you're given may look a little different. DJ contracts should always include your name and the time, date, and location of your event; the name of your DJ and DJ company; the package price you've agreed upon and services included in that package; overtime charges; the deposit amount and the date it is due; the date the balance is due; and the DJ's refund and cancellation policies.

Another entertainment option is live music in the form of a band, jazz ensemble, or classical group. Having a quartet or orchestra playing softly in the background during your reception is romantic and classy, but it won't get people out onto the dance floor unless your performers are playing something people can shake a leg to. Keep this option in mind if you're dreaming of an elegant reception where cocktails and conversation—not dancing—are the diversion of the day. On the other hand, a charming bandleader backed by a talented band can be everything a DJ is and more, adapting to the flow of the party and keeping the dance floor packed all party long. If you want a rowdier reception, a rock and roll band might be just the thing.

Live music at weddings is relatively rare because it's so freakin' expensive. Three thousand bucks can get you a five-man group for four hours, but expect to pay more because that is pretty cheap. There are bands out there that charge $10,000 a gig! Overtime fees can run you as much as $800 an hour, in cash. The fact is that many brides- and grooms-to-be reject the band option not because they don't love live music, but rather because they just can't afford it. This may be one of those instances in which prioritization is an absolute must. If you're a swing aficionado and you really, really, really want to celebrate your newlywed status with an authentic big band, budget accordingly.

Want to save money on your live music? Search online for the colleges in your area and call their respective music departments, because you may be able to land a pretty cool band that's just looking for some extra cash. Going this route requires that you put your faith in college students, but if you talk directly with the chair of the music department, you shouldn't end up with any bad apples. This is also a great way to find classical musicians to play at your ceremony, as there are many young performers hoping to make it big who are looking for any opportunity to play for pay.

There are two main sites dedicated to connecting live musicians with clients, Weddingmusicusa.com and Gigmasters.com/weddings. The cool thing about the latter site is that there are listings for all types of performers, from soloists to groups, and those listings include MP3s, video samples, and the occasional review. The downside is that you'll pay a 5 percent fee if you book through the site, though you could try getting around this by contacting any bands you're interested in directly. If you come up empty, try Wedalert .com/local_wedding_services (look under Entertainment Bands) or try searching Google for "wedding bands" along with your city or state. Are you looking for a "variety band" that plays all different kinds of music? Add that—or "reggae," "swing," "rock," "country," etc.—to your search parameters.

The band you choose should not only play music you like but also appeal to you on a personal level. Some people, for whatever reasons, find professional musicians intimidating. Don't book a band whose members give you the heebies, because there's a good chance that they'll make your guests as uncomfortable as they make you. The right band will energize you and make you feel like dancing. When you've found a few groups that seem interesting, try to interview with more than one member and print out a list of questions before you meet up with them. The basic need-to-knows are as follows:

- Can you give us a breakdown of each band member's experience? How long have you played together?

- Will you provide references? Can I see a video of one or more recent performances?

- Do you have a demo CD that we can listen to on our own time?

- How many people are in your band, and what does each member do?

- Will a member of the band serve as MC?

- Do you provide your own sound equipment? Do you travel with backup instruments or amps?

- Can you provide us with a song list? Will you learn songs that are not in your repertoire?

- If a band member is sick, will you find a suitable replacement? What if a member quits?

- When do you arrive at the venue and begin setup procedures?

- How much room do you need to play comfortably? Will you require a private space to change or store your gear?

- What will the band members be wearing?

- Are you familiar with our chosen venue? If not, will you tour it beforehand? What are your parking needs?

- What do you charge for overtime? Will we have to pay that in cash?

As always, you should get everything in writing whenever possible so no one tries to pull any kind of bait-and-switch crap on you. Get the contract as soon as possible after making your reservation! There are bands out there that will delay writing up a contract for as long as possible because they want to dump your booking in favor of a corporate client booking that pays more. You absolutely do not want to work with a band that does that to its clients. The basic wedding ensemble contract should look a lot like the basic DJ contract. Because wedding bands change members now and then, it's unusual for a contract to list all of the members of a given band. A good bandleader will always have a list of talented backups they can turn to if one of their guys decides he'd rather be in some other band.

When you ask yourself the question that brides- and grooms-to-be all over the world must ask themselves at this stage of the game—band or DJ?—consider the pros and cons.

DJ pros: They're less expensive than bands and easier to book. Many of them will search for and obtain the music you want, meaning you'll end up with a lot more musical variety at the reception. Your DJ knows how to get people onto the dance floor and how to calm 'em down when it's time for the serious stuff. Originals versus covers—nuff said. DJs take up less space, but they can fill rooms of all sizes with the right amount of sound.

DJ cons: If your DJ takes requests, you may end up listening to music you don't particularly like. Your DJ's personality and musical preferences can shape your event in unexpected ways. Wedding DJs aren't typically club DJs, so you can't assume they'll beatmatch or do any actual mixing. The stereotypical cheesy DJ does in fact exist.

Band pros: Live music is way impressive and can be extremely sophisticated. People tend to get up and groove when there's a band because live music is somewhat of a nuptial novelty. Bands are visually appealing and give guests something to focus on while the newlyweds are circulating. If you love a specific genre, you'll probably be able to find a band that rocks the socks off that genre. Live music can sound amazing.

Band cons: You're going to pay a lot more for a band. Many bands operate from a set preplanned playlist and don't take requests. Unexpected drum solos in the middle of your favorite songs—nuff said. Your band may specialize only in a single genre, which means you might not get to hear some of the songs you like best. A band that sounds good in one space may not sound so hot in another space. Band members will typically take a ten-minute break every hour or so, and their absence can affect the party atmosphere. Cheesy eighties hair bands aren't just a myth.

No matter what kind of music moves you, aim to hire your entertainment as far in advance as possible. Good DJs and musicians, like all other vendors, book up quickly. Bandleaders and DJs can both serve as MCs, but you should discuss that with them ahead of time so they know what your expectations are. To make things easier on your MC, provide a list of VIP names with the necessary pronunciation guides, a list of reception events and how you'd like them introduced, and a list of anything you'd rather they not say. If at all possible, find a way to see your preferred DJs or bands in action before booking them. They may have actual clips from recent weddings posted on their website, or their clips may only be available upon request. Make sure that the people you see in the videos are the same ones who will be working your wedding so you don't have to contend with any unpleasant surprises. Lastly, don't forget to feed your entertainment—a satiated entertainer is a good entertainer.

Canned Music Done Right

There is another entertainment option out there, though it hasn't yet made the mainstream scene. Some enterprising brides- and grooms-to-be decide that they're not too keen on paying the high prices DJs and bands charge, and they retaliate by defiantly busting out their MP3 players and laptops. Being a part of the DIY action is a matter of getting your hands on the right equipment and learning a little something about sound equipment and manipulating moods with music.

Search for "iPod wedding" and you'll come across hundreds of DJs on the warpath. Have a look around some of those forums mentioned in chapter 2—the moment a bride-to-be brings up her choice to ditch the traditional disc jockey in favor of some digital alternative, pro DJs start weighing in. It's a bad idea, they say. You can't anticipate what people will want to listen to or read the energy of the room like a real live DJ. Guests will mess around with your playlist when you're not looking, and the rented sound system will fall over and injure someone who will then slap you with a hefty lawsuit. Your reception will be a colossal failure!

At Mydeejay.com/advice_ipoddjwedding.html, you can browse some of the most common objections raised by pro DJs and decide for yourself whether you think you are ready to give DIY wedding tunage a try. It's not as heinously difficult as the objectors make it sound, but there is research and hard work involved. There's really no reason for professional entertainers to get so defensive, because no one is trying to permanently replace DJs and bands with iTunes playlists. The fact is that some people can't afford either, some people have tastes that are way too eclectic, and some people just don't care overmuch for the two standard options.

If you want to explore the DIY music angle, don't let anyone make you feel guilty, because DIY DJing isn't exactly a cakewalk! Read some how-tos and learn the basics of live sound so you understand what the challenges are before you rush out to buy or rent anything. Search for "sound reinforcement" or "sound system basics" to find plain-English tutorials that will give you a handle on the equipment you're going to need.

Angry message board DJs are right about one thing. You've probably made a party playlist or two in your day, but being your own wedding DJ is a lot more complicated. You can't just hook your computer speakers up to some music source and call it a day. First, you need to find out what kind of sound system (including mixer, amp, crossover, EQ, speakers, mics, and cables) your reception venue has. You need to be sure you can go from a headphone jack to whatever kind of sound system is available. Some venues may not even have a PA. If you need to source everything, have a look at Meetingtomorrow.com/category/sound-system-rental for all-inclusive sound system rentals. And do not neglect to go over your setup with the venue manager ahead of time to make sure the equip-

Leah's DIY Groom

"I had Will look this stuff up because he's the one with the larger music collection. We've both had iPods for a couple of years, and we fixed up our home sound system so we could have music throughout the house coming from a single source. Basically, I let him handle the technical details of the reception music.

"We did meet a couple of the local DJs at the bridal festival our reception venue held, but none of them really gelled with our musical taste and wedding style. I did end up buying a few new songs off of iTunes for the reception—including "More" by Bobby Darin and "My Girl" by the Temptations—but other than the few classics that I have on vinyl and not on CD, almost all of the music we played was stuff we already owned."

ment you're planning to use will work in your reception space so you don't end up having to send the BM to the local music store for cables on your wedding day.

When your MP3 or your laptop will be standing in for a disc jockey, it helps to have hundreds of CDs in every possible genre, from acid rock to hip-hop to new country to reggaeton to zydeco. Those CDs—or folders full of MP3s—will be the raw materials with which you will build your ultimate wedding playlist from the ground up. You may need to borrow some music from friends, hit up the iTunes music store, and download some fresh albums (legally, of course). Speaking of the iTunes store, a search for "wedding collection" will net you albums and individual tracks that will definitely help you round out your matrimonial playlist.

You can play the most obscure music in the world if you don't mind seeing an empty dance floor. By all means, play your favorites, but give your guests something to latch on to. Your chances of seeing some serious rump-shaking will increase exponentially when you play a mix of pop, oldies, ethnic stuff, and straight-up dance music. If you're worried about the dead space between songs, the latest versions of iTunes offer gapless playback and crossfade options so one song will blend into the next. To keep it seamless, try to match tempos so you have slow songs grouped together and fast songs grouped together.

It's easy to do this using iTunes because you can set up multiple playlists and give them names that will help your music coordinator do their job. What's that? You don't have a music coordinator? This'll probably be your MC—you're going to have to designate someone to introduce people and announce things like the first dance. The BM is often the most natural choice for this job as he'll be up on the mic anyway, but your mileage may vary. Give your MC plenty of advance warning as well as the opportunity to back out if they're not sure they want to shoulder that kind of responsibility. E-mail them a link to Wednet.com/articles/HowToPrepareAs

MasterOfCeremonies.aspx (or any other site that lists MC duties) and ask them if they're equal to the task.

The beauty of the iTunes organizational system is that the music coordinator only really has to mess with the music just before or just after they make announcements. Musical categories can include Cocktail Hour, First Dance, Father-Daughter Dance, Mother-Son Dance, Meal Music, Pre-Cake Slow Songs, Cake-Cutting Song, and Post-Cake Party Songs. Your MC will already be on the mic—and thus close to the sound system—while letting guests know that it's time to eat or dance or whatever. They can click over to the appropriate playlist while they're close to the laptop without missing too much of the action. Just make sure to pad the playlists so that you have more than enough music in each category and don't accidentally run out of sweet tunes just when guests are starting to boogie. That would be a tragedy of epic proportions.

Find a DJ . . .

- Adja.org
- Discjockeys.com
- Freedjamerica.com
- Weddingwire.com
- Wedj.com

. . . Or Live Music

- Gigmasters.com/weddings
- Weddingmusicusa.com

Listen to Some Tunes

- NYcityweddings.com/planning/wedding_songs

- Topweddingsites.com/wedding-music.html

- Wedalert.com/songs

- Weddingmuseum.com/tools/wedding-music-samples .htm

- Weddingsongs.weddingwire.com

Do Your Own Thing

- Apple.com/itunes

- Byreconly.com/magazine/weddingtopics/ipodMusic.htm

- Ehow.com/how_2108877_throw-ipod-wedding.html

- Kvetch.indiebride.com/index.php?t=msg&th=11419& start=0&rid=1393&

- Meetingtomorrow.com/category/sound-system-rental

- Thesingingtutor.com/pasetup.htm

- Wpi.edu/Academics/Depts/HUA/TT/TTHandbook/ sound/setup.html

- Youdjit.com

Chapter 15
Petal Appeal

Weddings and flowers go together like love and marriage, chocolate and peanut butter, and all those other cultural icons that get grouped together in the collective consciousness. The association is so ingrained in the minds of most brides- and grooms-to-be that few ever ask themselves what the alternatives are. You can absolutely plan a wedding that involves no florals whatsoever, but few people end up going that route. It's hard not to like flowers! Flowers are attractive because they have to be—fruits, honey, and the next generation of blooms are all products of floral sex appeal. The fact that they smell good doesn't hurt, either. Humankind figured out the relationship between flowers and fertility pretty early on, and it wasn't long before blooms came to be associated with bountiful marriages.

Herbs and florals have found their way into rites of all kinds ever since the first human being had the wherewithal to take notice of nature's beauty, which means that flora has been a customary part of nuptial celebrations for thousands of years. The very first wedding "bouquets" were more than likely bundles of strong-smelling greenstuff meant to ward off those ever-present evil spirits. In ancient Greece, brides wore wreaths made of flowers symbolizing love and fidelity, and herbal garlands were hung to commemorate the union being formed.

Nowadays, very few brides-to-be consider walking down the aisle with a string of garlic in one hand and a bunch of sage in the other, yet the tradition lives on in the form of the bouquet, the boutonniere, pew ends, and centerpieces. Flowers pop up in other places, too. Brides and grooms who love their moms and grandmas give these honored guests corsages to wear during the ceremony and reception to distinguish them from the hoi polloi. Some brides incorporate real or faux blooms into their hairstyles, though this works best on those lucky ladies who are not prone to picking at their updos. Edible petals like those mentioned in chapter 12 appear on classically elegant cakes, and flowers can even take center stage in ceremony and reception decor.

For floral ideas, look no further than Images.google.com. You may be sick of reading the URL, but there really is no one website that will show you as many pictures of flowers (or favors, or cake, or whatever) in their many forms as Google will. A search for "wedding flowers" grabs over one million shots of bouquets, bouton-

A. J. Loved Browsing for Blooms

"I loved looking at flowers online! There are so many beautiful arrangements. I found some great information about what's in season and how different flowers hold up. Gardenias, for example, bruise very easily. I considered ordering flowers from an organic place and having my maids help arrange them the night before, but ultimately scrapped that idea. I eventually met with a wonderful florist my MIL recommended. She listened, confirmed that she understood what I was asking for, and offered her advice. Overall, I was totally impressed with what I got!

"I didn't intentionally dry my bouquet. I just hung it upside-down to keep it out of the way and away from the cats! A few days later I was already amazed at how well it had dried, and now it's on a bookshelf where the cats still can't reach it. I never considered sending it out to be preserved, though I did think about buying preservatives to keep them looking fresh. But there would have been a lot of prep involved with that, so I decided not to worry about it. In case you were wondering, it was hard to keep track of the bouquet all night, but I'm glad I did."

nieres, accessories, and decor. There are, of course, other sources of inspiration floating around on the net, like Marthastewart.com/wedding-bouquets-and-flowers and Myweddingflowerideas.co.uk. Plenty of florists now have blogs where you can scope out arrangements they've made for other couples and learn a little about how flowers can be incorporated into weddings. Bloomeryweddings .com/blog stands out as one of the best, because it's more than just an ad for the Bloomery Florist and it's updated regularly.

Whether you lust after lavish bouquets of brilliant red roses or modern earth-tone centerpieces embellished with lots of greenery will have a lot to do with what kind of wedding you're planning. That said, you'll want to wait until you know what you and your wedding party will be wearing before choosing flowers—or choosing to forgo them. Bouquets and boutonnieres spend a lot of time against a backdrop of dresses and suits, so they need to be somewhat complementary. The color theory websites mentioned in chapter 5 can help you nail down a floral color scheme that isn't too matchy-matchy. If the bridesmaid dresses are a lovely shade of periwinkle, the periwinkles you love so much are going to get lost in your photographs.

Some floral guides would have you believe that you need to choose informal flowers for informal events and formal flowers for formal events. What's an "informal" flower, you may very well ask? There really isn't any such thing. The relative formality of a bouquet or a centerpiece has a lot to do with how its component florals are arranged and the color scheme you choose. Carnations—a flower often found in bargain prom corsages—can look stunningly chic in the right arrangement. Roses, which are considered by many to be a most formal flower, can look happy-go-lucky when gathered loosely into a hand-tied bouquet.

If you're still concerned that your floral choices won't reflect the solemnity of your event, do a study of Victorian flower meanings before you make any decisions. Don't you want fair warning that your lovely centerpieces of yellow carnations, saffron, and larkspur

Christa Terry

It's All in the Bloom

Your favorite flowers may not mean what you think they mean! In the interest of being proper—if you're interested in this sort of old-school etiquette—consider the meanings of your favorite flowers before you decide to incorporate them into the men's boutonnieres. The handful of definitions that follows represents only the tip of the stamen. Where there's a flower, there's a meaning, even if it is far too obscure to matter much.

Camellia—*Gratitude*

Carnation—*Fascination and love*

Daffodil—*Regard*

Daisy—*Innocence*

Delphinium—*Boldness*

Hibiscus—*Delicate beauty*

Hydrangea—*Boastfulness*

Iris—*Warmth*

Ivy—*Eternal fidelity*

Jasmine—*Grace*

Lily—*Majesty*

Passionflower—*Piety*

Ranunculus—*Dazzled*

Sweet pea—*Bliss*

Tulip—*Love*

Violet—*Faithfulness*

White chrysanthemum—*Truth*

White rose—*Innocence and worthiness*

Learn more about Victorian flower meanings at Grasmeretheshop.com/flower_meanings.htm or any of the other hundreds of sites obsessed with Victoriana.

are conveying a message of disdain, dangerous excesses, and infidelity? Have a gander at what your floral preferences mean at Todays-weddings.com/planning/flowers/flower_meanings.html, but don't worry if you adore the way autumn leaves look when scattered about on ivory tablecloths. It's pretty unlikely that any of your guests will know they signify melancholy!

As you peruse petals, think about what form you'd like your wedding florals to take. Floral centerpieces can be as simple as groups of stems stuck in water-filled mason jars or as ornate as towering architectural arrangements that incorporate live trees. If your ceremony space allows the use of outside decor, you can deck it out with standing floral arrangements, topiaries, and floral pew cones.

Don't forget the petals for the FG! Reception venues can be outfitted with garlands, table bouquets, archways, and floral cake decor. You may feel that boutonnieres are a nonnegotiable must-have. Will the honored ladies in your life be wearing artful wrist corsages? Do you envision your maids carrying lavish cascading waterfall bouquets or dainty pomanders?

That's right—the bridal bouquet is a species made up of many different breeds. Whereas men's blooms may be composed of all sorts of florals, they're still just boutonnieres. Bouquets, on the other hand, are classified by shape, composition, and the manner in which they are held. Round bouquets are circular in shape (duh) and tend to be rather dense. Nosegays and posies are also round bouquets, but the former has more greenery than a traditional round bouquet, and the latter is a lot smaller. The Strauss bouquet is like a larger and looser posy with longer, natural stems, and the Biedermeier is just a round bouquet with even rings that are each made up of a different type of flower.

The bouquet taxonomy does not stop there, however. There are cascade bouquets, arm sheaves, pomanders, hand-tieds, crescents, composites, wristlets, trails, teardrops, tussie-mussies, ballerina bouquets, and floral scepters. Some brides and bridesmaids carry their blooms in little totes, and there are specialty fortune bouquets designed to break apart into multiple minibouquets when tossed. The easiest way to get a feel for each of these types of portable floral arrangements is to Google 'em because a picture really is worth a thousand words. If, however, you'd really prefer textual definitions, there are plenty of bouquet glossaries on the web—Something spectacular.com/article3.htm, for instance—though none are particularly comprehensive, so you should have a look at lots of them.

Should you or your intended decide that you'll be carrying a bouquet, you may want to take your bodily dimensions into account when picking one out. Generally, bouquets that are smaller than the bride's head look best, though that shouldn't stop you from sizing up if you fancy big bouquets. Short brides should consider smaller bouquets, while bigger brides should choose bigger bouquets. It's all about scale. Your flowers should neither look as if they're about to eat your arms nor appear dinky when framed against your person. When it comes time to carry your flowers, don't hoist them up too high because you'll look unnatural and stiff. Carry them comfortably—whether that means your blooms are resting at boob height, crotch height, or anywhere in between. If you don't want to cover up your pretty bodice, carry your flowers low, but don't risk pulling a tendon just because you want people to see your beading. They'll have plenty of time to admire your middle at the reception.

Remember that it doesn't have to be all about the blooms. All of the accessories and decorations traditionally made of fresh or faux flowers can also be crafted using branches, wood, tulle, lace, greens, fruits and vegetables, wire, feathers, and just about anything else that looks good gathered. Don't limit yourself because you haven't come across anything more interesting than the usual bowls full of roses in your searches. Sometimes looking at floral galleries can be a little limiting—expand your knowledge of decor by searching for "????? centerpieces," where the question marks represent whatever sort of centerpiece you're looking for.

Now if you simply can't stomach the idea of buying your blooms online, it's time to find a florist. The easiest way to do this involves looking for florists in your area on Maps.google.com or Yp.yahoo .com, then calling around to see who does wedding flowers and is available when you need them. That isn't to say that you should just hire the first person who meets both of these criteria. Treat florists like you've treated all your other vendors so far, and hit them with a thorough interview. But don't tarry too long when you're trying to decide between florist A and florist B—some floral designers are booked up more than a year in advance. Be sure that the initial consultation is free before you schedule your meeting lest you be caught without your checkbook.

Appear at each interview armed with a list of questions like those you can find all over the net by searching for "questions to ask your florist" or "questions to ask your floral designer." Some lists have a sum total of five questions, while others have twenty or more. No matter what, you should always ask the following questions:

- How long have you been making wedding arrangements? Can we see a portfolio of your previous work?

- Can we get some references?

- What packages do you offer? Is there a written list of à la carte prices we can take with us?

- Will you provide us with an itemized quote based on our needs?

- Do you create the arrangements yourself, or does another florist actually arrange the flowers?

- Will you work with us to create a unique design based on our wedding colors or theme?

- Can you provide us with a floral design based on pictures we provide?

- Will you provide sketches or models of our florals for our approval before asking us to sign a contract?

- Can you provide us with a list of flowers that will be in season around our wedding date?

- If you work with faux florals, can we see samples of the blooms and greenery you use?

- What are your setup, breakdown, and delivery fees? Are there additional rental charges for vases, or will we be buying them outright?

- When do we need to finalize our order? How often can we change it without penalty?

- What time will you deliver and set up our flowers?

- Are you familiar with our ceremony and reception venues? If not, will you visit them beforehand?

Make sure that your chosen florist is willing to write up a contract for you. Be wary of any floral designer who is unwilling to put together a simple contract—they may be dithering because they're hoping to land a pricier deal. If your wedding is taking place on or around a holiday, your floral contract will be even more important, as florists do a brisk business around that time and may not devote as much time or effort to your order. See a sample contract at Floralshops.net/ideas/weddingcontract.html, but keep in mind that your contract should include your name and your wedding date; the date, time, and location of your nuptials; your floral designer's name and contact info; the exact specs of your order, including package elements, flower types, colors, and delivery times; a breakdown of charges; deposit amounts and due dates; the date upon which the balance is due; and the florist's refund and cancellation policies.

Had enough of the serious stuff yet? If you're ready to take a break, head over to Links2love.com/weddings/build_your_bouquet .htm. On the site you'll find a fun little app that lets you drag and drop all sorts of flowers and greens into different arrangements. Getting the hang of this toy takes a couple of trial runs, but it's a neat way to take your mind off of the more annoying elements of the wedding planning process.

Fresh, Not Faux

Flowers are expensive not because they're beautiful, but because they're shipped all over creation in special climate-controlled containers. The existence of planes, trains, and trucks means that there are no limits to the types of florals you can obtain. You want pristine springtime ranunculus blooms in the dead of winter? It can be done, but you may have to pay a premium to get them because they were grown in a hothouse or overnighted to your locality from some warmer clime. If, however, you're planning an eco-friendly matrimonial celebration or want to save a few bucks on your florals, seasonal is the way to go. Your locale may be fairly hot all year long or on the cooler side no matter what the month, but growing patterns will still be affected by the earth's revolution.

You can maximize your chances of getting the blossoms you want by taking the time to find out what's in season before visiting with florists or placing an online order for fresh flowers. The guides you'll find on the Internet won't be all that helpful unless they specifically pertain to your geographical area, but you can use the list of common wedding flowers at Weddings.about.com/od/weddingflowers/a/Season.htm as a jumping-off point. Some sites seem to use "summer," "autumn," "winter," and "spring" as euphemisms for "toasty warm," "getting cooler," "chilly," and "things are warming up," so check with a florist to be sure that the guide you're looking at works in your particular locale. Alternately, sign up for gardening enthusiast message boards or the Marthastewart.com forums to get advice from people who spend a lot of time thinking about plants and flowers.

There are flowers that are readily available year round, which means that the prices you'll pay for them won't change much from season to season. Roses, calla lilies, stargazer lilies, orchids, daisies, carnations, and tropical flowers are always in stock at florists' shops. Likewise, you'll seldom have any trouble finding ivy, ferns, baby's breath, or heather. There's really no standard pricing in the world of floral design, and you may pay anywhere from $500 to $2,000 for a complete floral package, regardless of what each component of that package is made out of. The final costs levied by your supplier or florist will depend not only on the type of flowers ordered but also on the sorts of arrangements requested and the complexity of those arrangements. The one thing you can count on is this: The price of flowers ordered around Valentine's Day will be jacked up significantly.

Some brides- and grooms-to-be have favorite flowers and base their wedding colors off of those blooms. Others start with a theme or color scheme and choose florals that match. At Blissweddings .com/weddingfloral you can search for flowers using color, season, region, or the color of your bridesmaids' dresses as your criteria. If cost is one of your concerns and you're working with a florist, they can help you stay true to your budget by finding the most cost-effective flowers in your colors. Give your florist a list of your wedding colors and tell them what kind of arrangements you'd prefer, then let them create your bouquets, centerpieces, and whatever else you've ordered using the flowers and greens that happen to be inexpensive due to their abundance.

Whether you want premade arrangements or you plan to DIY, you can order your florals from the comfort of your desk chair if you're fine with the idea of sourcing your blooms sight unseen.

Leah Searched, but Was Inspired by Tradition

"I did spend time looking up bouquets online because I wanted to find flowers that weren't fragile. After looking at a lot of different kinds of flowers, I realized red roses weren't too delicate and matched my color scheme. Most of the resources I found had a lot of information about what kinds of flowers were in season and the meanings behind them. I also came across sites that explained how and why some flowers keep their color when dried."

Organicbouquet.com carries a selection of sustainably grown stems in a variety of colors, but you'll have to find your greenery elsewhere. Fiftyflowers.com sells roses and other fresh flowers in bulk quantities along with prefab centerpieces and DIY wedding deals. Some sellers, like Growersbox.com, have wedding-in-a-box packages that include everything you'll need to make bouquets, boutonnieres, corsages, and centerpieces—er, everything except florist supplies, that is.

It's ridiculously easy to find fresh flowers and greens online, and you'll save plenty of money by doing it. It's nowhere near as easy to find fresh flower bouquets in Internet shops, because a search for "bridal bouquets" will return results that are predominantly local florist websites and silk bouquet retailers. ProFlowers is one of the few wedding flower specialists on the web—at Proflowersweddings .com, you can order all-inclusive packages containing all of the florals you need. There aren't many opportunities for customization on the site, but the site does offer free consultations so you can speak to someone about the individual packages offered. Surprisingly, you can buy a number of wedding flower packages at Costco.com, and you don't even have to be a member to do it. Then again, maybe it's not so surprising considering that Costco.com also sells caskets and $10,000 children's playhouses with real hardwood floors.

Most fresh-flower retailers who sell roses and other blooms in bulk know that customers need them for specific events, so you'll be asked to provide a delivery date along with your order. Flowers, being the delicate creatures they are, need time to recover after being packed in boxes and trucked around. Try to arrange to have your order arrive three days before the wedding, and make sure you buy a bunch of extra blossoms to account for any oopsies that occur when you're putting them together. Don't forget to grab some petals for the FG while you're at it!

When your flowers arrive, open them immediately, inspect them, and then put them in buckets of water plus floral conditioner so they can drink up and their petals have a chance to relax. Recut

Brittle or Beautiful: Keeping Your Bouquet Forever Fresh

If you want to keep your blooms looking display-worthy postwedding, think about preserving them. A search for "flower preservation" can help you find out what your preservation options are. You can indeed DIY with the right supplies, but there are dozens of people out there who've made it their business to desiccate your florals using sublimation or silica gel. Before you ship your browning bouquet to a preservation service, make sure that it will be taken completely apart prior to drying and then reassembled once it's ready to go. Freeze-drying is the most expensive method of preserving flowers because the equipment is pricey and the process takes weeks, but the results are generally the most aesthetically pleasing. The colors stay truer, and the flowers themselves are way less brittle than air-dried blossoms.

Some companies will dry and then artfully flatten your flowers so they can be mounted in a frame, preserving the original silhouette of the bouquet. There is even one woman out there who will turn your blooms into beads—find out more at Fromblossomtobead.com. If you do decide to DIY, you can disassemble your bouquet and hang-dry the individual blooms. Reassemble the whole works once everything is good and crunchy. You can achieve slightly nicer results by taking your bouquet apart and covering each component in silica gel, sand, or borax. Make sure no one flower is touching another! Your blooms should be ready to roll in about a week, at which time you can reassemble them using floral wire, pins, and the original ribbon. Be careful, though, because home-dried flowers are kind of delicate.

each stem underwater using a really sharp knife, and strip away any leaves that are hanging in the water. Until you're ready to use your blooms, keep them away from sunlight, drafts, hot or cold surfaces, and fruits or veggies. A cool, dark place like a pantry is the kind of storage space you're looking for. Do not put your flowers in the fridge for any length of time—a florist's refrigerator is very different from a home refrigerator.

Faux, Not Fresh

Of course, if the idea of dealing with finicky flowers leaves you feeling flat, faux is the way to go. Faux blooms can sit around for weeks or months without fading, wilting, or losing their shape. You don't have to worry about whether your house is too hot or too cold when storing them. They're hardy, and they come in colors that Mother Nature hasn't gotten around to making. You'll see the term "silk flowers" bandied about willy-nilly when you look for stems and prefab arrangements, but know that only flowers with 100 percent silk petals are technically silks. Most faux flowers have petals made of polyester, though some are made of fabric, latex, or plastic. Have your heart set on real silk flowers? Expect to pay as much as if not more than you'd pay for real stems.

You will have zero trouble finding suppliers of polyester silks online, whether you're in the market for stems, bouquets, garlands, centerpieces, or accessories. The problem is that there are so many sellers out there, meaning you're going to have one hell of a time separating the wheat from the chaff. If your only experiences with silk flowers have involved cheap-looking, brightly colored blossoms with fake water droplets on the petals, you may be dismayed to find that there is no shortage of retailers who market exactly that toward brides- and grooms-to-be. A search for "silk wedding flowers" will reveal more cheap-ass arrangements than you can shake a stick at. You may be tempted to buy these because you don't care much about flowers, but be warned that they look absolutely awful in photographs.

It's possible to stay on budget and have good-looking faux flowers in your arms as you walk down the aisle, but you won't save quite as much money as you might want to. A nine-inch $30 bridal bouquet will look as if it cost thirty bucks, whereas an $80 bouquet can look as good as a fresh bouquet if you source it from a good designer. Beware of cheap greenery—the fastest way to ruin a perfectly good faux floral arrangement is to add crappy plastic leaves and buds. If you want your faux flowers to mimic live ones, in person and in pictures, spend a little more and put together your arrangement yourself. Choose natural-looking stems from high-end sellers like Pyob.com, or browse sites like Afloral.com, which has a huge selection, so you're bound to find something you like.

Jeanette's Unexpected Florals

"I shopped for flowers online, but it was kind of hard because of my budget constraints. I hadn't intended to spend more than $100 total on flowers. I looked and looked, and eventually I found supplies that would have brought that total up to about $125. What I found was obviously limited but sufficient. Then we got the tartan samples, which messed up our intended color scheme! At that point we gave up on flowers. We pretty much decided that the attendants would carry candles.

"We still wound up with flowers, though, because my mother insisted we have them *and* got them for free from one of her coworkers whose daughter had recently gotten married. Mom rearranged them all using the supplies I'd bought to do the whole candle thing. All of a sudden, I had flowers, my girls had flowers, the guys had boutonnieres, and the tables had decorations. Looking back on it, everything turned out all right. But it wasn't at all how I'd originally intended it to be, and that upset me."

Do you keep stumbling upon the same group of sellers? That means it's time to adjust your search parameters. Look for "artificial flowers," "faux flowers," "silk bouquets," and even "fake flowers." Add the word "wedding" to your search if you want to browse arrangements made by other people. It's tough to gauge the quality of silks from photographs, so buy a few stems before you place a bulk order, or ask potential bouquet designers whether they'll send you a few sample blossoms so you can see what kind of stems they use.

Many people think faux florals are tacky no matter how good they look. If this sounds like you, why not go for something ultra fake, like wood flowers, paper flowers, feather flowers, or porcelain flowers? You can carry these blooms without wondering if they look real enough to fool your guests because they aren't supposed to look real. Porcelain blossoms like those at Porcelainroses.com are the most wedding-y, though you may want to forgo these if you're prone to fits of klutziness. Few things are worse than hearing the crunch that means your bouquet has become a mass of shards.

You need heed no such dramatic warning with the other ultra-fakes. Wood roses are an interesting choice—the whole concept may sound hokey, but they're actually rather stunning. Search for these and you'll find a variety of distributors selling budding, half-open, and fully open wooden roses in colors ranging from natural to not. Look for shaved, dyed blossoms on flexible stems, like those sold at Flowersofwood.com, so you can be sure each petal will be uniformly beautiful. Feather flowers are somewhat difficult to source when you're not buying wholesale, and if you do manage to find them in quantity you'll still be paying about four bucks per stem. Ouch!

Paper flowers have a long history that you'll likely find fascinating if you're into craft evolution. Skilled Chinese artisans began making these unique blooms around the time that paper was invented, some two millennia ago, and a couple thousand years later Victorian ladies of leisure coopted the practice so they could enjoy out-of-season blossoms all year round. For stylized blooms, look no further than Paperblooms.com, a store selling uniquely wrapped thick paper flowers. You can find a more realistic selection of paper flowers at Mommymakesroses.com, and search for "tissue paper roses" to find yet another ultra-fake floral option. Then there's origami flowers, like those you'll find at Lisashea.com/japan/origami/sales. A Google image search for "origami bouquet" will show you just how striking folded flowers can look.

The upside of all faux florals is that they last forever. While the fresh-flower set is rushing to get bouquets preserved—a process that involves packing and shipping an already wilty arrangement—you can just set your wedding day blooms in the nearest vase and hit it with the spray-can duster every few weeks.

There Are Alternatives

Your allergies leave you in agony whenever you get within two feet of a fresh flower, but you think most silks look hella cheap. Freeze-dried flowers make fine postnuptial keepsakes, but dead blooms don't strike you as an appropriate bridal accessory. And twenty-four-karat-gold-dipped roses are a tad too expensive to buy by the bunch. What's a gal to do? While you know that it's perfectly all right to hightail it down the aisle empty handed, you wouldn't mind having a little something bracing to hold on to when you take those first tentative steps on that hand-painted aisle runner you bought in a fit of matrimonial fervor.

The bride and her maids can walk bathed in candlelight . . . if the ceremony venue allows open flames, which many don't. Visit Candlemagic.net/bridesmaid.htm to see what bridesmaids look like when they're holding luminaries instead of bouquets. Don't waste your time looking for special wedding party candles if you go this route, because you'll end up searching a lot of sites that want to sell you candles in jars reading "To my bridesmaid" and things like that. The easiest way to make the whole candle thing happen is to buy some cool candlesticks (try eBay) and the candles that fit in them. Or you can get around the no-flame rule by using flameless tea lights in small lanterns or glass goblets. Obviously, your illuminating options will always look best in dim light.

How about a flower-free bouquet made out of something sparkly? Crystal bouquets are an edgy choice, and they are everywhere. It doesn't matter that you've never seen one at a wedding—someone somewhere decided these babies were trendy, and hundreds of on-line shops opened up to sell 'em. Austrian-crystal.net will custom-make you a bouquet using your choice of more than thirty colors of Swarovski crystals. Keep two things in mind. The first thing is that the largest crystal bouquets out there are still kind of small, so if you're worried you'll overpower a teeny tiny bouquet, consider that this may not be the floral alternative for you. The second thing is that Swarovski crystals are just faceted bits of lead glass, so don't go setting them down in your drink.

Ultimately, the bridal party can carry anything it damn well pleases. Give everyone a peacock feather if your colors are blue and green. For religious services, give your maids *and* your men prayer books to carry. Anything portable can stand in for flowers—Christmas ornaments, bowls of fruit, bundles of sticks, folding fans, little purses, sparklers, chalices, parasols rented from Vintage.bella umbrella.com, or even little potted plants. Seriously, you and your attendants can carry anything.

Can I Do It Myself?

Only the very calmest, with-it brides- and grooms-to-be should attempt to delve into the world of DIY wedding florals using live flowers. Cakes can be made ahead and frozen. Invitations, as you'll find out in the next chapter, can be whipped up whenever. The same goes for favors and all of the day-of decor. But flowers? They are alive and thus subject to all of the inconsistencies of living matter, which is all the less surprising when you consider that they've been plucked from their roots and are in the process of dying. No wonder they're finicky! You'd be finicky, too.

The DIY rules for florals are pretty much the same whether you're dealing with fresh flowers or faux, with the exception of the intense level of care that you must exercise when manipulating organic matter. You can yank on artificial petals and stick fake stems with pins all you like, but you'd better have a very firm idea of what you're doing when arranging fresh blooms. This is where trial runs come into play. If you're planning on making your own fresh flower arrangements, do a few trial runs with the cheap stuff most supermarkets sell in big green buckets somewhere near the produce section. You'll feel way more confident when you're racing against the clock to assemble your florals in the hours before your nuptials.

Silks and flower alternatives are a different story altogether. You can leave them scattered around your living room for as long as you like before sitting down to figure out just how they ought to go together, and you can put them together and pick them apart without doing significant damage. When something falls off, it can be glued or pinned back on mercilessly. And once you've settled on an arrangement you like, your bouquet can sit around for ages without wilting, browning, or kicking the bucket. Just be sure you cover your creation loosely to protect it from dust, the blanching effects of sunlight, and the sharp teeth of mouthy pets.

Bouquet tutorials abound, though the process is fairly simple when you have the right tools at your disposal. You're going to want to buy a bunch of florist's wire and florist's tape from somewhere like Save-on-crafts.com—a site that incidentally has a crapload of DIY floral tutorials. Pick up a wire cutter if you don't already have one, because they're good for cutting florist's wire and for trimming back overly bushy faux blossoms. Bigger is better, because some silks have really thick stems. There are special rose dethorners you can buy, though sharp knives can work just as well. Ribbons are pretty integral, and you might want to grab some pins as well. Before you do anything, find a nice flat workspace you can take over for as long as you need to—if this is something you've never attempted before, distractions will kill your concentration.

The simplest bouquets are hand-tieds, which are basically nothing more than a bunch of gathered stems wired together. If you've been bookmarking pictures of your favorite bouquets, have your computer handy or print them out so you can have a crib sheet of sorts. You can even sketch out an overhead view of the bouquet you envision so you know what to put where. Here's the shortest possible tutorial: Gather together your flowers in a configuration you find aesthetically pleasing, wiring them together as you go. Once you've got a really sweet-looking bouquet going on, wire in some greenery in such a way as to make it frame the flowers. When everything has been wired tightly, wrap the part of the stem you plan to hold in florist's tape until it's smooth. Then cover that with ribbon using the braiding trick at Eleganceinbloom.com/englishgarden.html and pin it. *Bam!* You have achieved a bouquet.

That is, of course, not all you can do. There is lots more floral crafty goodness at Save-on-crafts.com/weddingcrafts2.html, and you can find instructionals for just about every kind of bouquet by searching for "make a ???? bouquet," where "????" is the type of bouquet. Get creative! Why not make a candy bouquet like the one at Visionsofsilk.com/How_to_make_a_candy_bouquet.shtml? The same goes for centerpieces—you'll find exactly the sort of tutorials you need by searching for "create floral centerpieces," "make wedding centerpieces," and "DIY centerpieces." The simplest centerpieces are just glass bowls filled with fresh flowers, some water, and something like pebbles to stabilize and weigh down the whole works. This usually looks far more elegant than complicated centerpieces made up of multiple components. Give yourself enough time and you can deconstruct any floral decoration in your mind; then all you need to do is figure out how to rebuild it yourself.

You can still be a DIY diva even if flowers just aren't your bag. Making paper flowers is easy as pie if you're good at following directions. Look at Opane.com/rose.html for roses, Origami -instructions.com/origami-lily.html for lilies, and Origami.island -three.net/tulip.html for tulips. If those seem too complicated, scour the net for easier paper-folding instructionals, because there are definitely more than a few good ones out there. Whatever it is you want to do, there is a set of directions somewhere online that is going to help you do it. Want to make a crystal bouquet? Do it: Geocities.com/ chris_breecher/beadbouquets.html. A floral headpiece? Do it: Save -on-crafts.com/makflorheadg.html. Centerpieces and boutonnieres? Do it: Jrroses.com/weddingflower3.1.html. You get the picture.

In the end, don't let the complexity of floral (or nonfloral) DIY scare you into hiring a florist when that's not what you really want to do. Learning a new skill is sometimes difficult, but that's no reason to give up without even trying. Devote just a little time to your craft of choice, and you'll inevitably surprise yourself. For all you know, you're destined to be the next DIY goddess!

Browse Blooms

- Bellarugosa.com
- Bloomeryweddings.com/blog
- Brides.com/weddingstyle/decorations
- Creativegardensnh.com/gallery.html
- Kellysweddingflowers.com/gallery/main.php
- Kremp.com/g-Clutch-Bouquets-269
- Marthastewart.com/wedding-bouquets-and-flowers
- Myweddingflowerideas.co.uk
- Theflowercompanies.com/weddinggallery.asp
- Wedding-flowers-and-reception-ideas.com

Find Fresh Flowers

- 1800flowers.com
- Americanfloraldistributors.com
- Bigrose.com
- Bridesnblooms.com
- Californiaorganicflowers.com
- Farmstogo.com
- Fiftyflowers.com
- Flowerbud.com

- Flowersandfreshness.com

- Freshrosepetals.com

- Growersbox.com

- Organicbouquet.com

- Proflowersweddings.com

- Theflowerexchange.com

Carry Silks Instead

- Afloral.com

- Amazonfoliages.com

- Bouquetgarden.com

- Fastsilkflowers.com

- Globalsilks.com

- Pyob.com

- Silkgardens.com

- Silkspecialties.com

- Usifloral.com

- Weddingsandflowers.com

Pick Something Different

- Asian-inspiration.com/buy-origami-bouquets.html

- Austrian-crystal.net

- Bergodesigns.com

- Enduringrose.com/rose-bouquets

- Flowersofwood.com

- Flyboynaturals.com/flowers-foliage.html

- Greatflowerz.com

- Mommymakesroses.com

- Porcelainroses.com

- Rosecityfreezedry.com

- Sparklingsweetorigami.com/bridesdreampaperrose.html

- Weddingbouquets.net

- Weddingflowersforyou.net

- Weddingshowergifts.com/crystal_bouquets/index.shtml

- Woodyaflowers.com

DIY

- Applebride.com/pages/Make_your_own_bouquet

- Bloom4ever.com/howto/howto01.htm

- Expertvillage.com/videos/boutonniere-instructions-floral.htm

- Gardenandhearth.com/weddingonabudget/round bouquet.htm

- Interiordec.about.com/od/weddingflowers/Wedding_Flowers.htm

- Paperblooms.com/web-content/howtofoldroses.html

- Save-on-crafts.com

- Video.about.com/weddings/Make-a-Wedding-Bouquet.htm

- Videojug.com/film/how-to-make-a-wedding-bouquet

- Visionsofsilk.com/wb.shtml

- Weddingdayoriginals.com/crystalbouquetsandacc.asp

Preserve Your Bouquet

- Allseasonspressed.com

- Curbly.com/jcarracher/posts/898-Preserving-flowers-with-Borax

- Everlastingsflowers.com

- Florage.com

- Floralartist.com

- Keepsakefloral.com

- Lonestarfreezedry.com

- Thefloralportrait.com

- Timelessblooms.com

Chapter 16
Putting It in Writing

Where weddings and wastefulness intersect, you'll find paper sitting smugly. There's just no getting around it—even if you're careful to choose only recycled paper and paperless "paper," it's highly likely that your custom hand-painted announcements and invitations are eventually going to end up in someone's recycling bin. Electronic invites are great for your everyday get-togethers, but sites like Inviteforgood.com just don't seem to be catching on with brides-to-be. You could call all of your future invitees to let them know they need to save the date, call them again to ask them to show up when you say your vows, put up a sign at the ceremony explaining who's who, and then glue your phone to your ear so you can call everyone who sent you a gift to say thanks. You'll want to subscribe to some kind of unlimited calling plan.

Yes, you could reach out and touch someone and stay on the right side of etiquette . . . but you won't. It's just not convenient, and besides, people love getting something in the mail that isn't another stupid bill. For once, the WIC is not jerking you around—you can certainly get by without buying STDs, invitations, and thank-you cards, but why would you want to complicate your life like that?

Since the first European monk was commissioned to whip up

some illuminated invitations in the Middle Ages, trees have been giving their lives so brides- and grooms-to-be can be sure that their loved ones will show up on the right date, at the right time, in the right place. Generally, town criers were the de facto invitation givers of their day. The invention of the printing press could have revolutionized the wedding stationery business as it existed way back in the 1500s, but it didn't. No one wants a smeared, hard-to-read invitation, which is exactly what the heavy lead type tended to produce. It wasn't until the invention of mezzotint printmaking (i.e., metal-plate engraving) that wedding invitations became accessible to a wider audience. When lithography took off in the 1800s, it suddenly became easier than ever to get people to come to your party. The upper echelons of society favored invitations dripping with calligraphy, of course, and they still do.

The range of options open to brides- and grooms-to-be has grown. Engraving remains one of the most expensive and elegant forms of printing—soft paper is placed on an etched copper plate with ink-infused depressions, and high-pressure stamping causes the paper to pick up the ink in the indentations. Picking an engraved invitation out of a lineup is easy because the paper is indented on the flipside. Letterpress printing uses raised inked letters to impress text onto paper, leaving behind a vibrant image. It's an old-fashioned process that enjoyed a resurgence in popularity when hobbyists started flocking to small print shops for lessons in letterpress. A third process, thermography, mimics the dimensionality of engraved printing by heating inks and powdered resin to create raised images.

Knowledge is power, even when you're buying wedding stationery. Educate yourself so you're not stymied by the terminology associated with papercraft and printmaking. There is a wedding-specific glossary at Beau-coup.com/wedding-invitations-etiquette-invitation-glossary.htm that defines all of the terms you'll come across, but a search for "printmaking glossary" can help you delve into an in-depth exploration of the topic if you're so inclined. Paper isn't just paper when you're talking about pricey invites—there's linen, vellum, jacquard, parchment, and more, in addition to card stock. Learn more about the standard paper options at Beau-coup.com/wedding-invitations-etiquette-invitation-paper .htm, but don't forget to check out wedding stationery made from recycled paper, handmade paper infused with flower petals or seeds, and treeless options like hemp, kenaf, bamboo, and even elephant-dung paper.

Of course, if you're having a smaller wedding, handwritten invitations can be a nice touch—provided you have the penmanship for it. Not up for laboriously writing out two hundred individualized invitations? You could leave the invitations to the pros, buy some really fantastic notecards from Paper-source.com or Thestationerystudio.com, and ask your mom and/or your FMIL to send handwritten engagement announcements. Correspondence informing family and friends that you're scheduled to get hitched is, however, one of those optional expenses that you can cut out of your budget without offending anyone. Do everyone a favor and send formal announcements to only those people who will be invited to your wedding to avoid confusion and hurt feelings. Engagement announcements can even stand in for STDs if you and your SO have already chosen a wedding date.

Paper takes on many forms in its role as an accessory to matrimony. There are the aforementioned announcements as well as custom-printed engagement party invitations that are nearly as expensive as actual wedding invites. They seem less expensive until you realize that they're sold only in packets of twenty-five or so, meaning that the per-item price is about the same. Then you have your bridal shower, bridal tea, bridesmaid luncheon, and bachelorette party invitations, which tend to be pink and girly. Bachelors either don't need or don't particularly want invitations—stag party invites are out there on sites like Announcingit.com, but good luck finding cards emblazoned with anything other than boobs, golf, cigars, or snifters. Brides- and grooms-to-be can also invite their peeps to be maids and men via "Be my bridesmaid" and "Be my groomsman" greeting cards like those found at Advantagebridal.com/wiyoubemy brc3.html.

That's a whole lot of paper, and you haven't even sent out your STDs yet! Naturally, there's no shortage of printed rehearsal dinner invitations on the web, but let whomever is planning this particular event know that verbal invitations are a-okay. After you've got the wedding invitations squared away, you may consider printing up ceremony programs so your guests know who's who. If you're putting matching tags on your favors or having place cards printed, now's the time to get that done. Search for—you guessed it—"favor tags" or "place cards" to find the retailers you need. Favors like those found at Americanbridal.com/plachol.html are place card holders by default, eliminating the need for anything like a preprinted tag. And finally, when you think you're absolutely done with all things paper, there are still the thank-you cards to think about.

If at any point you find yourself at a loss for words, head over to Verseit.com or Mygatsby.com's Word Wizard at Mygatsby.com/wording_for_invitations.jsp. There you'll find sample text for engagement announcements, bachelor and bachelorette party invites, shower invites, STDs, rehearsal dinner invitations, reception cards and response cards, and the pièce de résistance, your wedding invitation.

Making the guest list and obtaining the necessary addresses is one of the most difficult parts of the entire wedding planning process. Chapters 6 and 7 referenced a hypothetical guest list created in either Excel or the spreadsheet program that comes bundled in Openoffice, but consider using Docs.google.com so you can share your list with your intended, your parents, and anyone else who might be able to provide you with the addresses that are still missing. Start compiling your guest list as early as possible, because getting all of the info you need will probably be a lot like pulling teeth. Your initial spreadsheet should have the following column headers: Invitee, Accompanied By, Relationship, Address, Phone Number, and Number Attending. Once you've got most of the necessary fields filled in, you can add column headers like Table Number, Gift, and Thank You.

Your spreadsheet will prove helpful more than once over the course of your engagement. The RSVP feature on your personal wedding website may be tied to the name and address spreadsheet you create. If you decide to use the seating software mentioned in chapter 7, you can upload your guest list into most of the available programs. When you send your STDs through a company that does the mailing for you, having a premade spreadsheet can save you the trouble of having to retype the names and addresses of all your invitees. Are you planning to hire a calligrapher? E-mailing your calligrapher a modified copy of the guest list you already have on hand is a lot easier than creating an entirely new list.

The list of names and addresses you and your loved ones draw up should include invitees and invitees only. Some people, in a misguided attempt to keep their head counts low without leaving anyone out, create an A list and a B list. The A list invitations go out first, somewhat earlier than usual. The B list invitations are sent only once enough negative RSVPs from A-listers roll in, ensuring that the guest list never grows too large. Maybe this sort of thing worked as planned back in the days before instant communication methods hit the scene, but it just won't fly in this day and age. You'll be the one who gets bitten in the ass when Aunt Millie receives her invitation a month after hearing her A list relations chatter away about your upcoming wedding.

If you'll be addressing your own nuptial correspondence, know that traditional etiquette rules demand that you abbreviate nothing. While addresses written in this manner look rather striking—Mister Clarence Montgomery Daniels, Twenty-six Beauregard Street North

> ## A. J.'s "Eh" Experience
>
> "I checked out a few online print shops and the prices were only slightly cheaper than real-life stores. We had some samples sent to us for a slight charge, then I ordered the official invites and everything turned out fine. In the end, we had just enough invitations, but lots of extra thank-you cards. The company we used mailed extras of everything we ordered, just in case. It was an okay experience—the quality was good, they got to us pretty quickly, but there was nothing overtly exceptional about it."

West, White River Junction, Vermont 05009—the US Postal Service *hates* them. The machines that read addresses are programmed to look for cues in the form of abbreviations, and your announcements, invitations, and letters of gratitude will take longer to reach their intended recipients when a real live human being has to sort them by hand. It's no longer considered heinously offensive to flub on someone's title or honorific, but the rules aren't tremendously complicated. Go to Emilypost.com/everyday/forms_of_address.htm for the skinny on address etiquette.

And speaking of mail, trial postage runs are a must. The stuff you're sending may be no heavier than your average dispatch, but size comes into play when postage is being calculated. Oversized and undersized envelopes require extra stamps because they can't just be shot through the automated postage readers. When you're ready to do some mass mailing, take one self-addressed copy of your announcement, invitation, or card and bring it to the nearest post office. Tell the counter jockey that you're planning to mail a whole lot of whatever it is you have and you'd really like to make sure you know how much postage will be necessary. When your communiqué arrives back at your own address in time and intact, you can be reasonably sure that you can mail the rest without worry.

When you're buying matrimonial stationery, order plenty of extras. Invitations and thank-you cards inevitably get lost in the mail. Scrapbookers may ask you for extra copies of your wedding announcements and STD cards. It would really suck to come to the end of your engagement period and discover that you don't have a single invite left over to put away in your keepsake box. Unmarried couples living together and families that include young children can receive shared correspondence, but unmarried couples living apart should receive any mailings separately. Be cool and include anyone above the age of thirteen as an individual entity when sending STDs and invitations.

Not That Kind of STD

STDs are no laughing matter! Unless you're getting married in your hometown and inviting only those people who can drive to and from your affair in a few hours or less, giving guests advance warning is a courtesy. These cards evolved alongside the destination wedding because brides- and grooms-to-be needed some way to inform potential guests that getting to the ceremony would involve booking rooms in Cozumel rather than filling up the tank in the Buick. STDs are basically a no-fuss way of giving people enough time to make whatever travel arrangements are necessary—you might even save them a little money by giving them a chance to book early.

Some invitees may balk at your decision to send a postal reminder four to six months in advance of your nuptials because they regard the whole practice as presumptuous. STDs are indeed just another product of WIC ingenuity, but they're not entirely useless. You can always limit your mailing list to only those people who will have to travel vast distances or make complicated arrangements because your fête falls on or close to a holiday. This way, you'll save money and avoid ticking off any oversensitive individuals on your guest list. On the other hand, there's no reason you absolutely need to shell out a bunch of cash to pass a simple message along. Once you know where and when your wedding will be, phone calls and e-mails can get the job done.

That said, there are all sorts of totally cool STDs out there. (Did you ever think you'd be reading that sentence?) A search for "photo greeting cards" reveals dozens of sites that specialize in creating greeting cards emblazoned with the snapshot of your choosing. Check out Thefavorshop.com for STDs that guests can stick directly onto their wall calendars. If you'd rather they stick your STDs to their refrigerators, sites like Magnetqueen.com and Savethedatemagnet.com will whip you up some personalized magnets. They may be somewhat pricier than other STDs, but they're the ones guests are least likely to misplace.

Postcards are a pretty obvious choice. If you have the wristular fortitude, you can buy stacks of imaginative postcards from Cafepress.com or Etsy.com sellers and write them up yourselves. Brides- and grooms-to-be who'd rather not deal with the hassle of schlepping a huge stack of postcards to the post office can just hit up Premiumpostcard.com or Shutterfly.com/learn/photo_save _the_date_cards.jsp. Visit either site to create a custom postcard that will be mailed to your designated recipients on whatever date you choose. It doesn't get much easier than that.

Charging admission to your matrimonial celebration is supertacky, but that doesn't mean you can't print up some tickets. Go to Says-it.com/concertticket to make a custom event ticket—download and print your stub or order it in magnet or sticker form. You can get something a bit more professional looking from Admitone products.com or Ticketprinting.com. For a casual wedding, you could even use tickets with tear-off stubs as invitations.

The STDs you send should include your full name and your intended's full name, some text that describes the purpose of the correspondence (e.g., "We're getting married, so save the date!"), the date and locale of your nuptials, and the URL of your wedding website. Some brides- and grooms-to-be find that adding "Invitations to follow" somewhere on the STD itself cuts down on the number of people who will assume that the STD is the invitation and get all flustered because they're not sure how to respond.

Because there are so many types of STDs, costs will vary significantly from supplier to supplier. Saving money means shopping around for the best prices on preprinted postcards, magnets, and whatever else. Even if you've never once seriously thought about printing your own invitations, don't automatically reject the notion of DIY STDs. The people who can benefit from an early reminder will be grateful that you took the time to send them a little something regardless of what that little something looks like.

Where the Heck Are We?

When weddings and receptions take place at the same site, and that site happens to be in the town where the families of both the bride and groom have lived for generations, *and* neither of the newlyweds-to-be went away to college, *and* no one involved in the proceedings has out-of-town friends, no one is going to need directions. Those attending the celebration know to make a left at the old oak tree even though the sign was knocked down in the summer of '01. They know that if there is even the slightest chance that the creek is flooded, they should plan on taking an alternate route. There is no question of your guests getting lost, as they are traversing streets and avenues they have known their entire lives. It's a pretty picture, right? Too bad it's so far removed from reality.

As was mentioned in the very first chapter, it's getting less and less common for people to live, much less get married, in their hometowns. Relatives and friends are separated by thousands of miles, and finding a wedding location that is accessible to everyone often means choosing a locale somewhere in the middle. Then, of course, there are the pals and girlfriends who live four states away and the aunts and uncles who never left the old country. The Inter-

Mapmaker, Mapmaker, Make A. J. a Map

"I found Studiowestdesigns.com via a Google search, then checked out the samples on the site. It was low-key and artsy, but still completely professional. I could tell he'd be able to get the job done, and I was right. We e-mailed back and forth to make sure the directions were exact—he even checked and rechecked the Mapquest.com directions himself—and the images appeared exactly the way I wanted them. I was so happy, I ended up hiring him to do our seating chart!"

net is partly to blame. We can bond and communicate with people from far away in real time, which means it's easy to feel close to someone who is really a half day's plane ride away. The good news is that you probably enjoy relationships with people from a variety of backgrounds and cultures.

The bad news? None of them is going to have any idea where they're going when your wedding day arrives. Luckily, you can save all your nail-biting anxiety for some other day, because you can almost guarantee that your loved ones will find their way to and from everywhere they need to be with custom wedding maps. Attractive, custom maps that help wedding guests navigate unfamiliar territory are something of an anomaly. Whereas adding the words "custom" and "wedding" to any product usually inflates the price to something akin to the GDP of a small country, printed wedding maps tend to be reasonably priced, because they're usually printed with a single ink color on simple card stock.

In your search for a mapmaker, look no further than your browser. For example, Weddingmaps.com designs individualized maps with cute graphics and fancy fonts. But while the site's maps are indeed attractive and do fit right into most standard invitations, not everyone has a couple of hundred dollars to devote to custom map production. While you could create your own using Maps.google.com and an image-editing program, maps are usually an afterthought that comes to mind once those guests who RSVP'd affirmatively start e-mailing everyone and their mother for directions. If you stuffed a map—custom or otherwise—into your invites, you can rest easy until people start losing them.

When the map insert you paid good money for ends up in the recycling bin, Weddingmapper.com steps up to the plate. The site uses Google Maps to create a custom map that includes those same cutesy graphics as well as links back to your website and to the websites of all of the locales featured on the map. The map itself has its own dedicated (and customizable) URL, so guests can return again and again to check and recheck the directions once you've shared the link via e-mail or posted it on your website. There are other free map creators, but Weddingmapper.com is by far the most useful and well-designed online map available to brides- and grooms-to-be.

What makes a good map? Be sure your guests understand the scale of your map, e.g., how far apart the hotels, airports, and wedding day destinations actually are. If your family and friends will be staying in the area for multiple days, consider creating a larger map that includes restaurants, local attractions, and other places of interest to out-of-towners. You'll be busy coordinating last-minute details, but your guests may find themselves with little or nothing to do if they're not given a recommendation or two. But don't go nuts—a map that's too busy may be hard to read when it comes time for guests to find their way to the ceremony and reception.

The Honour of Their Presence

Once upon a time, invitations included an outer envelope, an inner envelope, a folded invitation card, a response card with its own envelope, a reception card, and a bunch of little squares of tissue paper that kept runny ink from getting all over everything. Really elegant invitations were made of oversized, heavy ecru card stock engraved with richly colored inks. You can still get invites of this sort, but be prepared to pay a lot for them. There is an art to packing a multicomponent invitation, and the whole process is thoroughly outlined at Rexcraft.com/Custom/Rexcraft/Rexcraft_Etiquette.cfm. To make a long story short, response cards, RSVP envelopes, and reception cards take up different positions depending on how the invitation itself is folded and where the text appears. The thing is, it's unlikely that any of your invitees will be particularly familiar with this paper-folding etiquette, so don't sweat the small stuff.

The big players in the nuptial-paper world are the invitations, which come in hundreds of sizes, shapes, colors, and configurations. That said, be prepared to see the same paper and printing options again and again and again if you're planning on buying mass-produced invites. An affiliate program launched by Carlson Craft has, to some extent, dominated the online invitation world with their "CCeasy" program. You're going to see a lot of online invitation shops that look just like the sample site at Free.cceasy .com—the prices appear to be set by Carlson Craft, so you're not going to find a better deal unless you can find a store that isn't a part of the CCeasy program but carries the same merchandise. Good luck with that.

You can stick it to the mainstream by looking at the many, many alternative options out there. The plainest of modern invitations typically consist of one envelope, a single invitation card, a response card with an envelope, and a reception card, but there's no reason to settle for unadorned vellum. The inner envelopes and tissue squares of yesteryear have been replaced by ornate ribbons and charms, brightly colored wraps, and complicated systems of overlays. The more intricate invitations are usually the most visually interesting, but they can also leave recipients feeling a little confused. If you suspect your loved ones won't be able to navigate the complex scheme of knots and bows on highly embellished invites, opt for something simpler.

Some invitations will always be more impressive than others. Oslopress.com crafts dramatic invitations made of laser-engraved birch, cherry, oak, maple, and walnut woods. At Bluemagpie

Having a Design Background Helped Leah

"I did go to a stationery store to check out some invitations before I decided to make them myself, and I was disappointed with how generic the regularly priced invitations were. The nicer invitations were ridiculously overpriced, and you couldn't even customize the wording very much! The people at the store were very nice, but the stuff they were selling just wasn't what I wanted.

"When I was creating the invitation designs, I looked at a lot of different invitations to find the right wording. I even ran the wording I liked by both sets of parents to get their approval. I also watched a great DIY video at Paper-source.com about how to use pocket envelopes in different ways, which gave me the idea of screen-printing a design on the front of them.

"Paper-source.com was my, uh, paper source for invitations and envelopes. I printed and cut the invitations on regular white card stock, because I couldn't find anything that I was satisfied with online. Plus, when you're a designer, it makes sense to design your own wedding invitations. I really liked being able to personalize my design, because there were people who wouldn't make it to the wedding, which meant that the invitation would be the only keepsake they'd have.

"For our STD cards, I created a postcard with our picture and had it printed up online at PSprint.com. The site has a mailing service, but creating a postcard, typing in 150 addresses, and then never getting to see them just didn't seem as fun as writing out the addresses myself."

invitations.com, you can order custom-designed invites in beautiful fabric enclosures. Would you prefer that each of your invitations be hand-painted by an artist? Stop by Momentaldesigns.com to get a feel for the cost of originality. It's not at all difficult to find invitations in bottles, scrolled invitations, seeded invitations that can be planted, and cards that come wrapped in silk envelopes. Be aware, however, that impressiveness is almost always pricey.

When it comes time to order your invites—think four months before the wedding—make sure that you know what inserts you'll need and what you plan to say. Have a look at your printer's paper, type, and package options so you aren't thrown for a loop when you realize that RSVPs are not in fact included in the $205/75 invitation price. Invitation pricing varies by site, because some companies will nickel-and-dime you to death while others find it easier to charge one price for invitations with all of the related accessories. If you haven't come across anything you've really liked, narrow your search parameters. Searching for "unique wedding invitations" or "unusual wedding invitations" is a waste of time, because every company out there wants to think its wares are unique and unusual.

You'll retrieve a better selection of links by searching for things like "yellow wedding invitations," "fabric invitations," "pocket fold invitations," "seal-n-send invitations," and "eco-friendly wedding invitations." Never underestimate the power of Google's image search to expose you to stuff you might never have found otherwise. Browsing becomes a lot more fun when you can look at eighteen different invitations from eighteen different shops on a single page. You can also cull inspiration from blogs dedicated to the paper arts, like Papercrave.com and Bellainvites.blogspot.com, or search your favorite wedding blogs for posts about invites. If you don't find anything that you like, some small presses like Goosefishpress.com will create a custom invitation based on your specs.

Write out your text in any program with a spell-checker before you place your online order, because invite sellers are under no obligation to help you correct your typos. Conscientious companies will contact you before processing your order to make sure anything that looks like a typo was actually intentional, but don't bank on their proofreading skills. Check your text twice, and you'll only have to place your order once. Better yet, get someone you know to give your invite text a once-over. That person may catch errors that your brain misses. Wondering how exactly to word your invitations and invitational accessories? A search for "wedding invitation etiquette" will net you plenty of how-tos, but it's easy to master the basics.

Whoever pays for the wedding is technically the host, and it is that person who has the honor of issuing the invitation. It used to be that the bride's parents were automatically the hosts because that's just how things were done. Now that nuptial celebrations cost a small fortune, it's common for multiple family members to chip in and for the engaged couple to shoulder a good chunk of the financial burden themselves. Some brides- and grooms-to-be are uncomfortable being the hosts, even if they did foot the bill. You can pay tribute to your parental units by listing them as the hosts even if they haven't given you one red cent.

A standard but slightly informal invite will read something like this:

Stuart and Leslie Thompson
request the honour of your presence
at the marriage of
Kristina Deann Thompson
to
Teddy Edwin Forecastle
on Saturday, the Nineteenth of May
at twelve o'clock in the afternoon
The Banana River Country Club
Merritt Island, FL
Reception to follow

Let's say that Kristina's parents are divorced, but she's close to both parents:

Stuart Thompson and Leslie Thompson
request the honour of your presence
at the marriage of
Kristina Deann Thompson
to
Teddy Edwin Forecastle
on Saturday, the Nineteenth of May
at twelve o'clock in the afternoon
The Banana River Country Club
Merritt Island, FL
Reception to follow

But, hey, what about the beloved stepparents? They can get in on the action like so:

Stuart Thompson and Leslie Thompson
&
Zina Voinovich and Mary Lane
request the honour of your presence
at the marriage of
Kristina Deann Thompson
to
Teddy Edwin Forecastle
on Saturday, the Nineteenth of May
at twelve o'clock in the afternoon
The Banana River Country Club
Merritt Island, FL
Reception to follow

If the groom's parents have gotten involved, you get this:

Stuart Thompson and Leslie Thompson
&
Zina Voinovich and Mary Lane
request the honour of your presence
at the marriage of
Kristina Deann Thompson
to
Teddy Edwin Forecastle
son of Jack and Lynn Forecastle
on Saturday, the Nineteenth of May
at twelve o'clock in the afternoon
The Banana River Country Club
Merritt Island, FL
Reception to follow

You can even use this as an opportunity to pay tribute to the deceased:

Stuart Thompson and Leslie Thompson
&
Zina Voinovich and Mary Lane
request the honour of your presence
at the marriage of
Kristina Deann Thompson
to
Teddy Edwin Forecastle
son of Lynn Forecastle and the late Jack Forecastle
on Saturday, the Nineteenth of May
at twelve o'clock in the afternoon
The Banana River Country Club
Merritt Island, FL
Reception to follow

When no parents at all are involved, invitations generally look like this:

The pleasure of your company
is requested at the marriage of
Kristina Deann Thompson
to
Teddy Edwin Forecastle
on Saturday, the Nineteenth of May
at twelve o'clock in the afternoon
The Banana River Country Club
Merritt Island, FL
Reception to follow

Spelling "honor" like the Brits do is supposed to add a little class to the invitation, in case you were wondering about that. It's a pretty standard practice, as silly as it is. The reason the wording above is less than perfectly formal is because it includes the parents' whole names instead of calling them Mr. and Mrs. Thompson, Ms. Voinovich, and so on. You can play with the format quite a bit without offending anyone. There are all sorts of places to put quotes, verses, and bits of wordplay in wedding invites. Brides and grooms who are forming blended families sometimes list their children as the hosts. You'll find all the wording you need—from season-specific text to second-wedding text—at Invitationconsultants.com/sw-wedding.aspx.

Response cards can be worded any which way. Know that if you include "Number of persons attending: _____" on the card, you're opening up a can of worms that involves droves of uninvited guests. Lines like "Will ____ Attend" confuse people, so keep your RSVPs as simple and as straightforward as possible. Have a look at the example cards at Frugalbride.com/replycards.html to see what some of your wording options are. Just make sure that you include an "RSVP by" date somewhere on the card—ask that they be sent back no later than three weeks before the wedding. There will still be those people who never bother to reply to your invitation, but if you're on the ball about entering responses into your spreadsheet, you'll know who they are.

As soon as you place your invitation order, ask to have proofs sent to you via e-mail so you can check for typos and errors a third time. Not every online printer will grant this request, but if you've budgeted quite a bit for your invites you'll generally receive proofs as a matter of course.

Ideally, wedding invitations should be sent out two months before the event so people have plenty of time to send their response cards back to you. You need to either address your own envelopes or hire someone to snazz them up with some fancy calligraphy. There are people out there who have made envelope calligraphy their business, and the smarter ones advertise their penmanship skillz online. You send your invitee address list to the people behind Calligraphylady.com and Greatbird.com/cia/callig.php, and they'll shoot you back beautiful addressed envelopes. As you search for the individuals who provide this service, be sure to read the (ahem) fine print. Some outfits advertising calligraphy actually offer computer calligraphy.

At some point, you may encounter the suggestion that you bring your invitations to the post office counter to be hand-canceled by employees. If your invites are particularly large or particularly small, they'll do this automatically and charge you nonmachinable postage rates when you go in for your trial run. You'll have to pay a similar surcharge when you've opted to use sealing wax to class up your envelopes. You can ask that your invitations be hand-stamped even if you're using conventionally sized envelopes, but there's no way to guarantee that your invites won't be tossed into the general mail pile as soon as you walk out the door. Some brides- and grooms-to-be ship their invitations to post offices in towns with romantic names like Romance, AR, or Valentine, VA, so they can be hand-canceled there. Reach out to the relevant postmaster before shipping your precious invitations off to be stamped so they don't get lost forever in the corner of some small-town mail depot.

Get with the Program

To answer your question, no, you do not need wedding programs. If your attendees are wondering just who so-and-so is or what the whole thing with the sand was all about, they can ask you when you make your rounds at the reception. Programs are only truly useful when your wedding ceremony involves a lot of audience participation. Certain religious rites require guests to stand, kneel, and sit, or to offer up specific verbal responses during the service. When your loved ones come from numerous spiritual and cultural backgrounds, a program that outlines what is expected of them can be a welcome relief.

What else are programs good for? Some people get nervous when reading verses or poems in front of a ceremony's worth of wedding guests and talk at inaudible volumes as a result. Brides and grooms who aren't used to projecting (i.e., they've never done theater) can suffer from the same affliction. Printing readings and/or vows in your program can help attendees understand your whispers. Your programs should also serve as keepsakes listing the event, the date, the participants, an explanation of any rituals you've incorporated into the ceremony, and the order of events. Some couples include a short blurb about how they met and a photo. Programs can also offer you a little space in which to honor loved ones and relatives who were indirectly involved in the wedding planning process as well as those who are alive only in your heart.

Programs can be anything from a single letter-sized sheet to a professional-looking trifold pamphlet. Some have elaborate covers, but most don't. They can mirror your invitations or not. Honestly, there isn't all that much room for creativity here, though you can get programs printed on fans at sites like Lbnpc.com/fans.html and Bridalprograms.com. Do not underestimate how grateful your guests will be for those fans at a summertime outdoor wedding! There are hand-painted wedding programs and custom programs made to match your wedding colors. All in all, your search for wedding programs will likely be one of the least visually interesting parts of your nuptial quest unless you want to drop a wad of dough on 'em.

If you're wavering on programs or don't really have the budget for them, you can include everything you might have put in a program on your wedding website. Guests can get a feel for what the ceremony will entail and "meet" the wedding party without your having to knock down a bunch of trees. On the other hand, if you have all the money in the world to spend on matrimonial stationery, why not skip the program and give your guests some heavy reading material? The people at Courtship-stories.com will make you a glossy full-color mini magazine-style booklet documenting your entire relationship. The best part is that you don't have to waste a lot of precious time composing an essay, because your courtship story is about you, not by you.

Gratitude Is Never Optional

Spend enough time on those wedding forums mentioned in chapter 2 and you're bound to come across nervous newlyweds desperate to know whether it's all right that they have not yet sent out their thank-you notes. Who can blame them? It's not always easy to know what to say when someone buys you a waffle iron. As much as you love waffles, you may feel slightly ridiculous waxing poetic about how much you love getting up on a Saturday morning to whip up a batch of breakfast with that iron. Yet that's exactly what you need to do! If you've always thought of thank-you cards as being forced formal greetings, think again. These tokens of gratitude can be as serious or as silly as you want them to be, as long as the message contained within comes from the heart.

A Google search for "thank-you card" will net you more than five million results. Unfortunately, you'll find Americangreetings .com among the first few. Don't let that fool you into thinking that you can get this chore out of the way quickly by sending e-cards appended with multiple addresses. You can send out boilerplate announcements, STDs, and invites, but it simply isn't nice to thank people for the gifts they've been gracious enough to give you using generic blocks of dull text. Your guests won't say anything if you don't send along a personalized thank-you, but they may remember your faux pas next time they're tempted to buy you a little something.

Perfection is not the goal here—your guests would much rather receive an awkward thank-you note than waste their time wondering whether or not you received their present. A lot of brides- and grooms-to-be find themselves riddled with anxiety because they do not have the first clue what to say—especially when writing thank-yous for gifts that kind of suck. But in a day and age where handwritten notes are a rarity rather than the norm, the sentiments you send will be appreciated even if your penmanship is atrocious, your words are stilted, and your gratitude is obviously a bit strained. The good news is that there is a basic formula you can follow:

- An acknowledgment of the giver, e.g., "Dear So-and-So"

- An acknowledgment of the gift itself, e.g., "Thank you so much for the wonderful set of nesting boxes."

- A description of how you will use said gift, e.g., "They will come in handy as we organize our lives together, and they blend in so wonderfully with our decor."

- A nod to the past and future, e.g., "We're so happy you made it to the wedding, and we hope to see you again very soon."

- Another expression of your gratitude, e.g., "Thanks again!"

- Your regards, e.g., "Love, So-and-So"

Specific thank-you card rules can be found all over the web, at sites like Ourmarriage.com/html/thank_you_cards.html and Entertaining.about.com/cs/etiquette/a/thankyou.htm, but the basic rules will almost always apply. Both you and your honeybunch need to sign the card and, no, you can't sign for each other unless you've perfected each other's signatures for business purposes. Common etiquette states that thank-you notes should be sent within three months of the receipt of a gift. That acceptable delay sounds great until you remember that your gift list is most likely going to grow and grow during those twelve weeks. Do yourself a favor and send out your thank-yous as presents roll in; be as strict with yourself as you need to be. Your loved ones will be delighted by your thoughtfulness, and you won't end up spending a dull Sunday afternoon writing out a stack of overdue notes.

If you receive a nice fat check or a big ol' wad of cash, you can write something along the lines of, "Thank you for your generous gift. It means so much to us right now because we're saving for our first home." You may very well intend to spend that money on a sweet muffler mod, a three-day drinking binge, or a full set of porcelain veneers, but don't let it slip your mind that you recently tied the knot. Your older, more conservative relatives likely want to imagine you slipping into the guise of the ultimate grown-up. Keep your thank-you cards clean and upright, and let them enjoy their fantasies while you enjoy your spankin' new muffler.

Buy more thank-you cards than you think you'll need, and buy them in a color scheme you won't be sick of after the wedding. You don't want to get stuck chucking seventy-five blue-and-white wedding-bell thank-you cards into your recycling bin because they've become obsolete. A large box of simple, elegantly designed blank thank-you cards like those sold by Crane.com or Finestationery .com will serve you well before *and* after you say "I do." Many people write thank-you cards for the first time ever in their lives when they get hitched. The smartest among them take all they've learned about the etiquette of gratitude and apply it in their lives forevermore. After all, appreciation is one of those things that will never go out of style, and people who send well-worded thank-yous tend to get more gifts than those who don't.

First Impressions

Everyone's got a printer, which means that everyone should be able to bust out their own wedding stationery at the drop of a hat, right? Hardly. Creating your own wedding stationery requires a lot of paper, a lot of ink, and a lot of futzing with everything to turn out a product that doesn't look like crap. The most precious tool you have at your disposal is patience, and you're going to need it in spades. Somehow, the text never lines up quite right the first time, and printer ink has a tendency to smear on card stock if you aren't careful. But if you're ready to delve into the world of DIY paper, don't let the challenges stop you. It's just that you need to know what you're up against before you commit yourself.

Before you can make anything, you need the right supplies. If you want to save money but fear your printer, you can order preprinted stationery kits that require assembly. Kits like those on offer at Invitationkitsdirect.com and DIYhangtags.com come complete with paper, embellishments, and easy-to-follow printing directions. The worst thing you can do is mistake blank stationery for print-it-yourself stationery—some paper products are designed for home printers while others aren't. The easiest way to find what you're looking for is to search for "printable wedding invitations," "printable favor tags," or "printable save-the-dates." "Printable" is obviously the key word here. Suspect your particular printer is going to chew up and spit out your blank invites? That's why you should always order sample stationery before placing a bulk order.

Tutorials and templates abound, and it's a good thing, too. The guide at Myexpression.com/ArticlesWedding/DoItYourselfWedding Invitations.cfm (and the links in the main article) will introduce you to some invite types, the supplies you'll need, and some creative DIY ideas. Do-it-yourself-invitations.com/wedding-invitations

.html looks like a clever ad for website-building software, but that doesn't change the fact that the step-by-step directions are thorough and easy to follow. The lesson you can learn from that site is look everywhere, because you never know where you're going to find easy instructionals. For example, search for "wedding" at Office .microsoft.com/en-us/templates and eighty-one free downloadable template results come up. Thanks, Microsoft!

Having the right software definitely helps. At Lcipaper.com/ accessories/software.shtml you can buy packages of fonts and graphics that will spiff up your nuptial correspondence above and beyond what Word can do. But opt for Crane's wedding stationery, and you can simply plug your product number into the box at Crane .com/social/imprintables to grab the coordinating templates. When it comes time to make your program, check out the fold templates at Weddingboutique.us/templates.html. Just download the DOC file you want, open it in Word, replace all of the relevant text, and print out your personalized wedding program. If you want to delve deeper into design, the tutorial at Pegaweb.com/tutorials/wedding -invitation/wedding-invitation.htm demonstrates how to create parchment-paper-style wedding invitations in Photoshop, though the instructions work fairly well with a little tweaking in the Gimp (the free image-editing program mentioned in chapter 13).

Finding the instructions you need can be as easy as searching for things like "DIY wedding invitations," "wedding invitation tutorials," "wedding invitations Photoshop," and other similar search parameters. The more varied your searches, the more likely it is that you'll find a product and tutorial that makes your wedding stationery dreams come true.

In the event you decide to print your own invites and the paper you purchase does not come complete with a printing guide, all is not lost. Fire up the nearest word processing program, create a text box that is the same size as your invitation, and adjust your text so it looks nice. If you have a lot of extra stationery, run a test sheet

Jeanette, the DIY Queen

"We found a lot of great info online when we were creating invitations because the templates that came with the package we bought were terrible. No big deal when you consider that I bought all of my stationery—including invitations, thank-yous, place cards, and everything else—for $50. It was nice to know that a lot of people had the same difficulties we did, and the advice offered up by former brides and grooms helped a lot. In the end, we did successfully print our own invites, though we really ought to have given ourselves an extra two hours of print time.

"We thought about buying preprinted magnets for our STDs, but then we tracked down some printable magnet paper at Staples.com. Printing them ourselves was a lot more fun than placing an order with someone else. I think our willingness to do a lot of this stuff ourselves made our whole wedding feel a lot more personalized."

through your printer to see if your text is printing where it ought to. Alternately, you can cut a piece of cheap white paper down to the size of your invitation and shoot that through. It's highly unlikely that your text will be prettily situated on your very first try. Now you'll have to mess around with the text and print more test sheets until the text is sitting right. Before you start sending actual invites through, make sure you know whether to put them into the printer faceup or facedown by sending through one last sample sheet with a mark on one side.

Voila! You just mastered the art of DIY wedding stationery!

Save the Date

- 321forkeeps.com/video-story-cards-for-weddings.aspx
- Freshimpressions.us/MagnetShapes.cfm?
- Postcards.com/Save-The-Date-Postcards.html
- Premiumpostcard.com
- Save-the-date-cards.com
- Save-the-date-wedding-magnet.com

- Savethedatemagnet.com

- Says-it.com/concertticket

- Shutterfly.com/learn/photo_save_the_date_cards.jsp

- Snailers.com/create/choose.php?id=4

- Specialeventpostcards.com

- Vistaprint.com

Steer Guests in the Right Direction

- Aardvarkmap.net

- Idomaps.com

- Idoweddingmaps.com

- Maps.google.com

- Propertyapex.com/map

- Snappymap.com

- Studiowestdesigns.com/maps.html

- Weddingmap.com

- Weddingmapper.com

- Zeesource.net/maps/home.do

Invite Your Invitees

- Blissfuldetails.com

- Bluemagpieinvitations.com

- Custompaper.com

- Goosefishpress.com

- Hellolucky.com

- Invitationconsultants.com

- Invitationinabottle.com

- Loveyourinvite.com

- Majesticinvites.com

- Momentaldesigns.com

- Mrboddington.com

- Mulberryinvitations.com

- Mypersonalartist.com

- Outvite.com

- Papelvivo.com

- Stylartwedding.com

- Thepetalpress.com

- Twistedlimbpaper.com

- Weddingpaperdivas.com

- Writestyleinvites.com

Get with the Program

- Bridalprograms.com

- Courtship-stories.com

- Lbnpc.com/fans.html

- Wedding-programs.invitesite.com

Print Your Own

- Crane.com/social/imprintables/DIY_programkit.aspx

- Diyhangtags.com

- Gartnerstudios.com

- Invitationkitsdirect.com

- Invitedesigner.com/ecatalog

- Lcipaper.com

- Mountaincow.com

- Myexpression.com/weddinginvitations.cfm

- Mygatsby.com/wedding_invitations/do_it_yourself.jsp

- Paper-source.com

- Paperandmore.com/articles/makeinvitations.html

- Papermojo.com

- Rexcraft.com/Custom/Rexcraft/Rexcraft_DoItYourself
.cfm

- Weddingboutique.us/templates.html

Chapter 17
The Ride
of Your Life

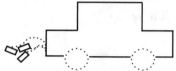

Walking on your wedding day? It's a thought. Green brides- and grooms-to-be may plan from the get-go to hoof it from their ceremony space to the reception site. The problem is that road grime doesn't exactly look good on a clean, bright hemline or an immaculate dress shoe. There's always the possibility of changing into your finery once you've reached your destination, but that means either carrying a fifteen-pound gown or sending your nuptial garb on ahead in someone else's car. You could take public transport, but subways serviced by the city won't always be as clean as you'd like them to be.

If you're dead-set on walking, do yourself a favor and get married on the beach. Or have your ceremony and reception in the same beautiful spot—you can always take a few leisurely turns around the grounds of the country club or state park. A tea-length dress can protect you from some of the omnipresent grunge you'll encounter outdoors, but why take chances? The popularity of Trashthedress .com (a photo blog dedicated to destructive wedding photography) proves that getting dresses dirty makes for fun photographic opportunities, but brides usually wait until after they've said "I do" to go wearing their gowns out all over creation.

Let's say, for argument's sake, that you're actually planning on arriving at your ceremony in some kind of vehicle. You may even be taking that same vehicle to your reception. What's it gonna be? There's nothing wrong with taking your own car and asking your attendants to chauffeur themselves. You're all adults capable of navigating the average American highway. Heck, some of your friends and relatives may even have mad backroad skills that help them evade traffic in all its forms. These are the people you'll want to follow to the reception, obviously.

There are downsides to doing your own driving on the day of your matrimonial celebration. A well-kept hired car will be as close to spotless as it's possible to get. If you can't say the same thing about the interior of your own automobile, it's time to make a side trip to the car wash. Schmutz under the seat can smear itself on clean, polished surfaces in the blink of an eye, but at least it's something over which you have a modicum of control. What about weather systems, traffic jams, and breakdowns? Can you see yourself changing a tire in a tux or getting out to ask for directions in a gown?

As cheesy as limos can be, there are a couple of compelling reasons to hire one. A good chauffeur will provide you with the smoothest possible ride in rain, sleet, or snow, ensuring that you don't inadvertently show up at your ceremony space smelling like

Leah Rode Shotgun

"We didn't use a limo or a car service, mainly because the whole wedding took place at a venue only three miles away from the hotel we were staying at. As a result, we could be as flexible as we wanted to be at the reception. There was no driver on the clock waiting for us, which meant we could stay and party or not. Knowing that I could leave when I wanted or send someone to pick up something in an emergency made me feel better."

spilled champagne. A great chauffeur will know almost every alternate route and shortcut, almost guaranteeing that the meticulous schedule you've drawn up isn't unduly influenced by unexpected traffic. A truly amazing chauffeur will competently handle car troubles on the fly without ever getting even a smudge of motor oil on his immaculately pressed uniform.

You can rent your transportation without dropping a wad on a stretch Hummer, though truth be told, that is one option among many. Ask yourself what you're looking for. Do you want a reliable ride to your ceremony, to your reception, and then home? Perhaps you're looking for something with fiber-optic mood lighting, a fully stocked bar, and a bitchin' sound system. The best time to start looking for wedding day transport is about six months before the wedding. While limo companies don't usually get booked super-early like some other nuptial service providers, there's no reason to drag your feet. This is particularly true if you're looking for something out of the ordinary, like a super-stretch limo or a classic Rolls Royce, because specialty cars can book up fast.

Presumably you've set some sort of transportation budget. The prices car services will quote you will be based on different factors. Limo rentals tend to be cheaper between November first and the end of March. Hiring a car on Saturday is more expensive than hiring a car on Friday or Sunday. Take a larger vehicle on a longer trip and you'll pay more, naturally. White cars tend to be more expensive than black or silver cars. Prices soar during prom season. Surprisingly, hiring a car for a short period of time isn't always the most wallet-friendly option. Car companies don't want to have to drive for an hour to cart you around for an hour, so most prefer to schedule their services in three-hour blocks.

A luxury sedan will cost you about $55 per hour with a three-hour commitment. A limo will run you something like $100 per hour, and a stretch SUV can cost as much as $300 per hour. Expect to pay more for less common cars. Some limo outfits will automatically charge you a 20 percent gratuity on top of whatever you pay for your rental, while others have already factored gratuities into their prices. Be sure to ask what the deal with gratuities is when you're researching car services so you don't end up inadvertently tipping your driver twice. Remember that you're paying for blocks of time, not road time. The clock is still ticking even when your butt isn't actually planted in a seat.

Finding the chauffeured car companies in your area is insanely easy. There's the old standby Maps.google.com—search for "limousine near" and your zip code. A good number of the results you get will be taxi and shuttle services, but the relevant listings won't be hard to pick out. When you see company names like Bert's VIP Limo and Party Fun 411, you can be pretty sure you'll find what you're after. There are also scads of sites that exist for no other reason than to connect limo companies with potential clients. Plug your dates, times, and needs into Limo.com's car search and you'll receive listings of the limo companies in your area, descriptions of their fleet cars, the capacity of each vehicle, and, in most cases, close-up shots of the interiors and exteriors of each type of car on offer.

You can even find reviews at Limos.com/content/search_post_limo_reviews.aspx, though the site only accepts critiques of their affiliate members. If you aren't searching for a particular company because you're still looking for the right car service, you can enter "limo" into the search box in place of an actual company name to see results for fifty car service companies in your state. Most of the reviews do all but gush, but you can be reasonably sure that someone is doing something right when a company has earned itself fifty positive reviews.

When it comes time to hire a car, you can't just call up the company you like best expecting that it provide certain amenities. Some companies will go out of their way to provide you with a tuxedoed chauffer, complimentary champagne, an honest-to-goodness red carpet, a sign proclaiming your newly married status, and more.

Plenty of limos come stocked with glasses, napkins, and ice, but if you want anything other than soda, you'll have to bring it along yourself. If you want to ride around in a vehicle with mirrored ceilings, a flat-screen TV and DVD player, a chandelier, and a hot tub, there is a company out there that will be able to make your dreams of excess come true. It's just going to take you a little longer to find them.

Who's riding in your hired car, anyway? Having the entire wedding party shuttled to and fro can get a little complicated if you're using one larger car. Groomsmen who are also playing the role of usher need to be at the ceremony location forty minutes before the event begins to seat guests, and bridesmaids and the bride herself may still be getting ready at that point. Do you want to be ferried from the ceremony to the reception? Your transportation requirements are going to be very different if all you want is a car to shuttle you and your new spouse away from the reception in style. Ultimately, your needs will depend on your situation, so don't assume you have to spring for multiple cars or luxury amenities because you've come across other brides- and grooms-to-be who are going all-out on transportation.

Traditionally, the bride and her attendants arrive at the ceremony location in specialty transportation, like a limo or party bus. If that vehicle is large enough, the entire wedding party will then take it to the reception. If not, the bride and groom can snag a little alone time before their party by asking their maids and men to make other arrangements. Alternately, you can arrange to have a second vehicle arrive at the ceremony site so everyone can enjoy some vehicular luxury. Some brides- and grooms-to-be ask parents and grandparents to ride along, though this is by no means common.

Choose a company with a reputation for outstanding customer service and the manager of that company will be able to help you choose the car configuration that's right for you. Just be sure you know exactly how many people you want to transport *and* how they'll be dressed. Eight gals in poufy petticoats may not fit comfortably in a ten-person limo. No matter what you plan to rent—limo, party bus, or classic car—go and have an in-person look at the company's fleet. Look at cars that are in your price range and cars that you can't afford. A car service that takes good care of its entire fleet probably isn't going to send a jalopy to your door on your wedding day. Don't make the mistake of thinking that you'll just happen to get one of the few really nice cars when there are rusted-out old-model vehicles all over the lot.

Visiting the fleet is especially important when you're interested in hiring something fancy, like a Rolls Excalibur or Silver Cloud. Some car companies advertise these cars even though they don't actually own them, and when a bride- and groom-to-be want one, they contract out the hire. If something goes wrong, your chances of getting the refund you deserve will go way down when the car company you're dealing with is nothing but a middleman.

Before you make a verbal commitment or sign any kind of contract, e-mail your contact to ask about the specifics of your rental. There are fewer car company checklists out there than there are florist checklists or catering checklists, so you'll have to dig a little if you're looking for a lengthy list of questions. One of the most comprehensive lists can be found at Limopages.net/Resources2 .asp?show=wedding, but you can jump-start the rental process with the following questions:

- How long have you been in business? How large is your fleet?

- Do you own all of the vehicles you offer? How old are your cars?

- Can you give us a copy of your pricing breakdown in writing? Are your overtime charges included in that list?

- Do you offer multivehicle or extended-hours discounts? How about wedding packages with upgraded amenities?

- Will we automatically be charged a gratuity?

- Can our wedding party drink alcohol in the automobile? Will glasses and napkins be provided?

- Can we meet with our chauffeur prior to the wedding? What will they wear on our wedding day?

- If there is an emergency on your end, will you provide a backup car?

- Do you have a list of references we can contact?

- Are you licensed and insured? Can we see your certificate of coverage?

Ideally, your contract should include your name and the date of your wedding; the name of your driver; the pickup time and location; drop-off locations; the duration of your reservation; the make, model, model year, and color of your hired car; the number of people riding in the vehicle; the amenities included in your chosen package; the total package price, including any gratuities; the amount of your deposit; potential damage fees; and the company's overtime, refund, and cancellation policies. Too bad contracts are seldom ideal! You can see a sample contract at Absolutlimousine .com/Absolut_contract.pdf—notice that it's missing a lot of the aforementioned points. You can request that your chosen car service company add to its standard contract, but there's no guarantee the company will say yes.

Seeing as you're already thinking about cars, this might also be a good time to consider parking. When you were interviewing the manager or owner of your reception venue using the questions in chapter 7, the topic of valets may have come up. You won't need a parking attendant or a team of valets if the venue is laid out in such a way that guests can park their own cars and then stroll comfortably to the main doors. Remember that there may be ladies in heels! If the building is not within stomping distance of the parking lot—or if your venue, like many in crowded urban areas, doesn't have parking—you should consider hiring two or three valets per one hundred guests. The only dedicated valet search site is Bestvaletparking.com, but you'll have to slog through nationwide listings for health care valets and corporate valets. Go straight to Maps.google.com to look for valet companies in your area.

Stretching Out

Say the word "limousine" to yourself and the first image that comes to mind may be a long and shiny black car with darkly tinted windows. You are indeed envisioning a limo, but that's only one kind of limo. The word "limousine" is adapted from "Limousin," the name of a French region. The region's innovative shepherds invented the original limousine, which was a hooded cloak, not a car. In an interesting twist, the name of the cloak was coopted by coach makers who specialized in covered carriages. When cars hit the scene, you could call any hired car and driver that sat passengers in the back of a limousine. Some limos had bloated rear seating, but you definitely weren't going to cram twelve people into one unless you were trying for some sort of record.

A company called Armbruster built the first stretch limo in 1928, before realizing that it was a hell of a lot easier to convert existing cars into limousines. How exactly does one convert a car into a limo? If you guessed they split a car in two and reunite the split ends with a long frame, you're right. You can see pics of the process at Limo.net/conversion.html, though clicking through the photos adds a whole new dimension to riding in a lengthy limousine. You'll see lots and lots of Lincoln limos when browsing for the right car service because Lincoln Town Cars are built on an isolated frame that lends itself to safe and simple conversions.

In a standard stretch, you and your carmates sit side by side on benches installed on one or both sides of the limousine. You may also come across the less popular stage limos, which have multiple doors and the same kind of row-style forward-facing seating you'll see in larger station wagons. If you're eyeing one of those stretch Hummers, know that some of them have the same kind of forward-facing seats. Super-stretch limos are just somewhat longer than your usual stretch, and SUV limousines are exactly what you think they are. Your options will be somewhat limited by the number of people who have called dibs on seats. For comfort, subtract two from the max passenger capacity of whatever sort of limo you rent. In other words, a fourteen-person limousine will comfortably seat twelve.

You can book a limo on the Internet if you're willing to use a company that contracts out its business. For example, ABCtrans .com/abctrans is affiliated with limo outfits all over the world, and it offers online booking at Limomagic.net, though the site's functionality is spotty at best. You run the risk of not getting quite what you paid for, since it's not like ABC is doing spot checks of all of its affiliates. If you really want to make a reservation over the web, get your quotes online from Limos.com and then negotiate via e-mail. Don't forget to check out the interior and exterior shots of the cars;

it's the best way to learn the differences between the many kinds of limousines out there.

White weddings require white limos, right? Not necessarily. A white stretch does complement both the bride and the event, but it'll cost you more. White limos look great in photos when they're clean, but if it's even slightly muddy on the road, that picture-perfect shot is going to need some serious editing. Black limousines look sophisticated and elegant, though caravans of them are sometimes associated with funerals. Overall, they're less expensive and easier to reserve on short notice because there are lots of them on the road. Then again, the salt cities lay down in icy weather can rob a black limo of its shine in no time flat. Before you opt for a white limo because it will look better in your photos, consider that a white dress can really pop against a stark black background.

Saving a little dough can be as easy as downsizing. A six-seater limo can transport you, your intended, and your honor attendants. Bars in cars are cool, but they cost extra and you can't possibly drink enough to recoup that cost. Lose the booze, the DVD player, the custom sound system, and the other extras when you're cutting costs. You may be able to arrange for a less expensive ceremony-to-reception pickup/drop-off service that won't require you to shell out for a three-hour block. Just make sure you have some way to get home (or wherever) once the party's over.

On the other hand, if you're ready to go all-out on your

wedding day transportation, consider springing for a sexy exotic car or a pimped-out luxury limo. There are the aforementioned Rolls Royces, Bentleys, and beautiful classic cars from as early as the 1930s. There are restored hot-rod limos, converted 727 limos, Ferrari limos, and limos with sunken dance floors. Like vintage? Scope out limos from every conceivable era at My.net-link .net/~dcline/limocls1.htm. The fact is that there's no way you can look bad when you're posing in your wedding day finery in front of a shiny, mint-condition 1927 Packard Senior. As corny as it sounds, a hot car really can make your outdoor wedding photos look awesome.

Limos? Yawn.

Big groups mean big cars. Party buses make the upgrade easy because they're usually cheaper than the monolithic stretch SUV limos. Banish thoughts of dorky yellow buses—party buses do indeed look kind of uncool on the outside, but they are totally sweet on the inside. A list of party bus amenities will read just like a list of limo amenities, with the usual leather seats, crazy lighting, entertainment systems, and built-in bars. The smaller, more common buses carry twenty or so passengers, while the deluxe charter buses can transport up to forty rowdy partygoers. Hit up AAgetawaycoaches.com to scope out the interiors of some of these crazy buses and grab a quote.

If that's not flashy enough for you, there are exotic car rental outfits in almost every major city. Find Lamborghinis, Ferraris, Maseratis, and more at Exoticcarrentals.biz/exotic-reservation .html, a company that will either find you the car you want in your locale or ship you the car you want. For local listings, try doing a Google search for "exotic cars" and the name of the nearest city. Be aware, however, that many companies that claim to rent out exotic cars have fleets full of Mini Coopers, Porsches, and Scions. Including the car you're looking for in your search parameters will help you eliminate useless results.

Do you have a loved one who eats, sleeps, and breathes cars? That friend of yours who has the mint Jaguar Mark II might be willing to lend it to you on your wedding day as long as you promise to wipe off the fingerprints before returning it. Consider arriving in a pristine muscle car, a vintage VW van, or something equally funky. A freshly washed and waxed black Mercedes can easily take the place of a limo, and you may even be able to convince someone close to you to be your chauffeur for the day. Just get a red carpet from Partycheap.com and you'll be all set.

Finding the really interesting transportation options in your area will take a little creative investigating, because there are no dedicated search portals for things like checker cabs and horse-drawn carriages. Locate any old school cabbies in your area by Googling "checker cab rental" and the name of the urban center closest to your wedding locale, but be prepared to slog through results that include conventional taxi companies that are checkered in name only. For equine transportation options, hit up Maps.google.com and look for "stables near ?????," where "?????" is the zip code. Nearby stables may not actually rent out horses and carriages, but they'll probably know someone who does. Use the same search techniques to find restored trolley cars, dog sleds and sleighs (where climatically appropriate), matching Vespas, or a tandem bicycle. As long as you remember that every form of alternative transportation will bring with it unique logistical challenges, you'll be all right.

There's no reason to limit yourself to land transportation. If your ceremony and reception sites are on the water, you can pull up to the nearest dock in a rented boat. Search for "boat rental" and your zip code, or find the nearest marina at Marinamate.com. You can charter a helicopter at Helicopterrides.thrillplanet.com—wedding party transfers are one of the services the company offers. Getting from place to place in a hot-air balloon isn't practical, but that doesn't mean you can't enjoy an open-air interlude between your ceremony and your reception. Find a willing balloonist at Hotair balloon.thrillplanet.com or 1800skyride.com/BalloonRides. When your guests want to know why you were late to your own reception, just tell them you were off getting high and enjoy the looks you get for the rest of the night.

Find Your Ride

- Allweddingcompanies.com/transportation
- Busrates.com
- Limodeals.com
- Limos.com
- Limousine.cometo.us
- Limousinesofamerica.com
- Nlaride.com/t_home.cfm

Book It Online

- AAgetawaycoaches.com
- ABCtrans.com/abctrans
- Exoticarexpress.com
- Exoticcarrentals.biz
- Findexotic.com
- Uscoachwayslimousine.com

Chapter 18

Lawfully Wedded Bliss

You may have realized by now that you're not the only one with a vested interest in your upcoming nuptials. Your mom wants to impress the gals from her bridge club, so they were all invited without your knowledge. The manager from the reception venue has been leaving you messages informing you that the table settings you liked best carry a $3-per-plate surcharge. And vendors you aren't even sure you actually hired are trying to hit you with the up-sell by reminding you over and over again that you should get whatever you want because this is your big day. As you do your best to deal with the wants, whims, and demands of these people, don't forget that there is yet another body that wants in on the action. The governemnt wants to know who you're going to marry and when you plan to tie the knot, and it wants you to pay it for the privilege.

If you have no interest in formally legalizing your union, feel free to skip ahead to the bit about finding an officiant or changing your name. In fact, if you're skipping the legalese altogether, your options are wide open, because you don't have to worry about officiant requirements or specific vows. Some people go this route because they don't want to get the government involved in something as personal as marriage, while others face legal challenges that stand in the way of their being able to marry. Still others simply feel no need to have their emotional connections laid out in contractual form. If this sounds like you, anyone under the sun can perform your ceremony, and you can get married to whomever you like whenever you please.

Chances are, however, that you're planning on standing before some sort of registered officiant and you'll be filling out some paperwork before you can consider yourself hitched. It's not the only way to get married or the best way to get married, but it's still the way most people go about it—just like more women change their last names than men, though that, too, is optional for both parties. A name change requires even more paperwork and, in many states, one or more trips to the local courthouse for people of the male persuasion. New brides have it relatively easy in this area because it's still common for women to take their new husbands' names and still rather uncommon for men to take on their wives' names. But the times, they are a-changing!

Avoid surprises and look up the legal requirements for marriages and civil unions in the state where you plan to wed a few months before the wedding is scheduled to take place. Because nothing is ever simple, residents and nonresidents abide by a different set of rules in some states. But in all cases, marriage licenses are obtained in the office of the county or city clerk. The people who hand out the licenses? They're either unfailingly cheerful because they love seeing people in love make a commitment or unfailingly grouchy because they've had to deal with way too many starry-eyed lovebirds.

After you file your application, your friendly (or not so friendly) clerk may tell you that you'll have to come back in one day, two days, or if you're in Wisconsin, five whole days. Whether this applies to locals, people from elsewhere, or both is up to the state. Residents may be able to take a marriage preparation course that eliminates the waiting period, and both groups may be eligible to pay a lower licensing fee after sitting through secular or religious prep courses. Age limits and ID requirements vary by state. That blood test nonsense you hear about in old movies? The practice has been abolished in all but a handful of states. Find out if yours is among them at Marriage.about.com/cs/marriagelicenses/a/bloodtest.htm. Then visit USmarriagelaws.com to find out what you'll need to bring to the county clerk's office.

But watch out—marriage laws can change and may differ slightly by county. When in doubt, give the clerk a call (many of the city and county office numbers are listed at the previous URL—a quick Google search for "marriage" and the county you're marrying in should net you the rest) and find out how it prefers weddings in that locality to be kicked off. In most states, you can get married immediately after receiving the license, and there may even be qualified officiants on site so you don't have to wait for more than a few quick breaths to be joined in matrimony.

If you think the regular marriage contract isn't strict enough and you happen to reside in Arkansas, Arizona, or Louisiana, you can arrange to have a covenant marriage. Covenantmarriage.com offers an in-depth look at this practice, which limits the grounds for no-fault divorce in a marriage. And if you'd rather forgo the pressures of a wedding altogether—wait, why are you reading this book?—go to En.wikipedia.org/wiki/Common-law_marriage to find out if your state supports common-law marriage. You may already be married in the eyes of the law!

Grab your license a month, two weeks, or a few days prior to your wedding. Most licenses are valid thirty or more days (though South Dakota requires that brides- and grooms-to-be use theirs within twenty days), and in some states there are no laws dictating when a license will expire. Getting it ahead of time means that forgetting a document or two won't be the end of the world because you can just turn the car around and try again tomorrow. Plus, you can panic to your heart's content when the clerk asks if either of you has been married before and your future spouse grins sheepishly.

Giving yourself plenty of time is especially important when marrying in another country, as you may have to translate many documents as well as submit a Single Status Affidavit (also known as a Certificate of No Record, available at Apostille.us/Documents/single_status_affidavit.shtml) to prove that you're unencumbered. There are useful resources online for people who are planning to get hitched in a land far away, like Travel.state.gov/law/family _issues/marriage/marriage_589.html and Flyawayweddings.com/legal/make-it-legal.php. Be ready to face off against a whole roll of red tape, depending on your country of choice.

Involving the state in your nuptials means that you can't immediately settle back into your old routine once you say "I do." After your witnesses sign on the dotted line, assuring the state that you really did promise to love, honor, and whatever, your marriage license gets sent back to the clerk's office, where it magically becomes a marriage certificate. If you filled out your mailing information correctly, you will receive a certified copy of this document a week or so later. Feel free to file or frame your gratis copy, then do whatever is necessary to order ten or so more. They're generally inexpensive, and you may find you need the extras when all of the companies who want proof of your marriage fail to make good on their promise to return the copy you sent. Order certified copies of your marriage certificate through Vitalrec.com/marriagelicenses or write to the clerk in the county where you wed.

An Official to Officiate

Officiants come in many flavors. There are priests and rabbis, ordained individuals from a wide variety of religions, justices of the peace, pagan priestesses, judges, cantors, and notaries public, and sometimes any old warm body will do. Because states still have the final say over all things marriage, the flavors you can choose from will vary depending on your locale. Northernway.org/marriagelaws .html breaks it down by state, but being that most of the text is pulled straight from the pages of dusty law books, it can be confusing. In some counties, anyone from your best friend to your plumber can get the necessary authorization to perform a legal marriage for one day by paying a fee. Typically, five people are required to ensure a wedding ceremony is legal: the bride, the groom, the officiant, and two witnesses.

Finding an officiant is easy when you've been a part of a religious institution for your entire conscious existence. In fact, the choice is basically a no-brainer—who else but the person who's been guiding your spiritual growth for years upon years will do? If you're not a member of a church, synagogue, temple, or coven (or whatever), the question of who will officiate your wedding can be a thought-provoking one. Picking a justice of the peace or judge at random after browsing Yellowpages.superpages.com can seem a tad impersonal when you're planning one of the landmark days of your life.

You can always church-shop using the directory at Worship quest.org, unless you're not even remotely Christian or remotely comfortable doing something like that. If you're in the market for a rabbi, you may be surprised to discover that many rabbis won't marry couples who come from outside of their congregations. That's not to say that there is no point in even looking—a Google search can help you find liberal or unaffiliated rabbis in your area.

If you're Muslim, any fellow Muslim who knows the ins and outs of Islamic tradition can officiate, though many mosques (find one at Islamicity.com/orgs or Islamicfinder.org) have marriage officers well versed in local legal requirements. Interfaith couples can also run into roadblocks, so if that describes you and you're shopping around, try Rcrconline.org/rabbi.htm or Interfaithfamily.com for rabbis and Weddingministers.com for just about everything else.

For those brides- and grooms-to-be who are spiritual but not religious, a Unitarian Universalist minister can provide a welcome middle ground. Finding a congregation is as easy as visiting UUA .org/aboutus/findcongregation. Atheists, humanists, and otherwise secular folks don't need to put on a mask of religiosity to avoid a city hall ceremony. Though meddling relatives may try to convince you that marrying in a house of worship is the way to go, there are plenty of nonaffiliated, nonreligious celebrants out there. Humanist -society.org/celebrants/celebrant.html can help you find a legal officiant who will leave deism at the door when they guide you through your vows.

Some of the most personal and intimate weddings are those officiated by relatives or friends of the bride and groom, but not everyone is blessed with an ordained aunt or pal who's a priest. This problem is no problem at all, however, because nowadays it's easy to get ordained. The Universal Life Church (a nondenominational faith founded in 1959 and located in Modesto, CA) will ordain anyone with an Internet connection for free at ULC.net. Credential certificates, religious literature, and wedding ministry packages cost extra, but are generally reasonably priced. Or have your favorite friend or family member become a part of the Spiritual Humanist clergy at Spiritualhumanism.org, which also provides free ordination services.

Be aware, however, that some of the stodgier states and counties have decided that members of the Internet ministry are less qualified than their seminary-school-graduate peers. Because there are usually no specific written guidelines that determine who can and who cannot be called a licensed minister, a nameless, faceless bureaucrat may decide your marriage is null and void. Have your newly ordained loved one check with the local clerk to see how your state feels about the Universal Life Church and other online ordination clearinghouses. Newly ordained clergy may have to register with the state and pay a fee before becoming an official celebrant.

If your nuptials are taking place in California, Massachusetts, Alaska, Virginia, or Michigan, anyone can apply for permission to perform marriage rites. The permit is valid for only one day, so be sure the individual you've chosen to officiate knows what day you plan to get hitched.

There are at least two notable exceptions to the standard five-person rule previously mentioned. In Colorado (see Colorado .gov/colorado-how-do-i/get-married.html), there's no need to go hunting for the perfect officiant because you (i.e., the plural you, the bride and groom) can perform your own wedding ceremony. The same is true in certain Pennsylvanian counties, where the process is known as self-uniting. Imagine standing before your loved ones and reciting your wedding vows without any interference from a third party—and without spending a few hundred bucks on the usual officiant's fee.

In Montana, five people still need to participate in the wedding, but they're not who you'd guess. The state's double-proxy law allows

Jeanette Looked for Churches with an Online Presence

"We were so tempted to have a friend officiate. Our original intention was actually to have a friend we'd met online perform our ceremony—he's ordained and has performed plenty of weddings. When that plan backfired because of his own issues, we started scrambling to find someone else.

"As it happened, my MOH offered the services of her mother, who is an ordained Episcopal minister. I was pleased as punch with the idea, being that her mother has meant a lot to me over the years. She was equally pleased when I asked her to officiate, which was great—except that she was five states away. Her church required six hours of premarital counseling prior to any weddings, and Chris's school didn't offer couples counseling in its counseling center, so there went that idea.

"It was back to the Internet for us. I looked at local Episcopal churches using the Yahoo! Yellow Pages until I found some with websites. Only then did I start calling around to find someone willing to work with us."

the bride and groom to be absent at their own nuptials—provided at least one of them is a Montana resident or a military (wo)man. Attorneys typically stand in for the absent newlyweds.

Legal issues aside, make sure the officiant you're leaning toward is right for you before you take the plunge and book them for the day. Most officiants have their hearts in the right place, but don't expect every one you meet to gel with your idea of what an officiant should be. Yours should be someone you feel comfortable around and someone you know will perform the ceremony you want. If you feel pressured to incorporate vows or rituals you don't like into your ceremony, move on, because there are plenty of officiants out there who will work with you to make your vision a reality.

As you interview your chosen flavor of officiant, make sure that they are qualified to solemnize marriages in your state. It may seem like a scenario straight out of a sitcom, but there really have been husbands and wives who found out years later that their supposedly legal marriage really wasn't. Find out about fees or donations and any premarital counseling requirements they may have. Feel free to request references and make sure they have a backup officiant they turn to in the event of emergencies. Ask to see each officiant's standard vows and find out whether they are willing to deviate from those vows to accommodate your wishes or traditions. Ultimately, you want to be sure that your officiant isn't going to have any problems giving you creative control of part or all of your wedding ceremony. Your faith or state may require you and your intended to utter certain words before you can call yourself husband and wife, but there's always going to be room for improvisation if you choose your officiant wisely.

Vows are vows in most states. But in some states, brides and grooms must orally consent to marry each other, declaring that they take each other as husband or wife. The specific words may differ, but the sentiment remains the same, and you'll find statements that fulfill the requirements in almost all of the vows you come across. Any officiant worth their salt will know what the requirements are for your state and will include them in their ceremonies.

A Rose by Any Other Name

The majority of people a new bride encounters will assume she has changed her name or is planning to do so in the near future. Whether you decide to change your name is entirely up to you, and you shouldn't give in to the pressure to rush down to the nearest Social Security office with marriage license in hand if that's not who you are. Traditionally, a woman would not *legally* change her name after marriage. This did not present much of a logistical problem, as wives did not have a great deal of legal clout outside of their ability to influence their husbands' decisions. Upon marrying, only a woman's social title changed.

In casual situations where her husband was not present, she would likely be referred to as Miss Maidenname, which is also the name that would appear at the top of her personal stationery. In a formal setting, she would be called Mrs. Husbandname. If she happened to have earned a professional title, she might be Dr. Maidenname. A fictional bride might be Miss Jane Doe, Mrs. John Smith, or Dr. Jane Doe, but never Mrs. Jane Smith. Mrs. John Smith was in its entirety a title rather than a name.

Nowadays, everyone is too busy to give much thought to the connotations of the name of the person standing in front of them at the checkout counter, so society as a whole tends to accept whatever is printed on a credit card or driver's license at face value. It's a good thing, too, because there are no longer any hard and fast etiquette rules surrounding postmarital name changes. Women who do decide to change their last name have it easy, because almost all of the forms they'll encounter will be tailored toward individuals with two

X chromosomes. In a way, this is your chance to get creative; changing your name will never be this easy again. Hate your last name? Ditch it! Want to make up some funky combination of both of your names? Do it!

Here are some of the more popular options:

- Mrs. Husbandsname

- Ms. Husbandsname

- Mrs. Husbandsname-Wifesname

- Mrs. Wifesname-Husbandsname

- Ms. Wifesname

- Mrs. Wifesname

- Mr. Wifesname

You can also become Mr. and Mrs. Nameyoumadeuptogether, though you and your spouse may end up spending a lot more time filling out petitions and affidavits than you ever thought possible. Being that some states still reject the idea that any man would want to change his name to his partner's, new husbands looking to update their identities frequently find themselves the victims of wrist cramps. Find out more about how to change your name the old fashioned way at Wikihow.com/Change-Your-Name, but keep in mind that the requirements you'll run up against in the process will differ by state. If you're so inclined, you can even change the name that appears on your birth certificate—find out how at Drbecky .com/birthcert.html.

Changing your name can be a minor annoyance or a huge pain in the rear. How frustrating the process is depends on whether you live near a city center and have reliable transportation. Let's say you decide to go the old-fashioned route by taking your lucky groom's

𝓜𝓻𝓼. 𝓙𝓮𝓪𝓷𝓮𝓽𝓽𝓮 𝓢𝓸-𝓪𝓷𝓭-𝓢𝓸

"The name-change kits and guidelines were terrible, and New Jersey's version of online help is to say 'call and we might get back to you within a month.' Chris found out absolutely everything we needed to know online—but the websites he used were about as user-friendly as being a passenger on a constipated horse."

name. Your first stop is going to be your local Social Security Administration office, where you will hand in form SS-5 (Social security.gov/online/ss-5.pdf) and a copy of your marriage license. You may have to sit in a crowded waiting room for any number of hours to do this. Pass the time by practicing your new signature. The IRS should at some point just grab your new name from the giant Social Security database, but you can always send them a notice of your new name along with a copy of your marriage certificate, just to be sure.

Your next stop will be the closest department (or registry) of motor vehicles. Find out what the office is going to want from you by searching for "name change" at DMV.org. In Massachusetts, for example, your updated Social Security card, current driver's license, and a copy of your certified marriage certificate are required, but some other states allow you to get a brand-spankin'-new license without getting a Social Security card first. And, yes, there will be a form. Bring your car's registration with you if you want to see your new name on that, too. Then, if you're not traveling anytime soon, hit up the post office and send off form DS-82 (Travel.state.gov/passport/forms/ds82/ds82_843.html) with your marriage certificate and some headshots to get your new passport. Leave all the name changing until after you're back from your honeymoon if you're traveling out of the country; even the slightest differences on pieces of identification can spell hassle.

Once you do officially become Mr. or Mrs. So-and-So, you need to tell the world that you've changed your name so your records don't get lost in the transition. While you're figuring out who

Leah Decided to Wait

"I traveled abroad more than once after the wedding. After thinking about it, I decided that jumping through hoops to get a new passport with a new name in the time frame open to me would be a hassle I didn't want to deal with. When I'm ready, I know I'm not going to have any trouble finding the information I need online."

you need to get in touch with to do this and what they're going to want to see from you, you're going to come across sites like Bridekit .com and Missnowmrs.com, which sell bundles of forms and claim to make changing your name a hassle-free experience. Don't waste your money. As tempting as it is to believe you can pawn off the hard work on someone else for twenty or so bucks, the kits usually contain nothing more than official forms you can download for free elsewhere and a business letter template with blanks for your name.

There are some good free instructions online that will ensure you don't forget to tell some important person or organization that you've changed your name. Bridelaw.com is one of the best, and it was compiled by the law office of Douglas N. Smith, so you know it's not going to steer you wrong. It may take a few weeks before you realize how many companies, agencies, and groups use your name for billing and filing purposes, so don't worry if the whole convoluted procedure takes a while.

And don't forget to have your mail forwarded, if necessary. Fill out the form at Moversguide.usps.com to save yourself a trip to the post office.

However you handle the name-change question, the one constant you'll come up against is that someone at some point is going to think you made the wrong decision. Change your name, and you'll be accused of bowing to an antiquated tradition. Keep your name, and you're suddenly too progressive. If you get criticized because you've chosen to retain your identity, point your detractors toward Lucystoneleague.org to help them understand your choice.

Your spouse's parents may feel cheated out of a namesake. Your grandmother may accuse you of betraying your family. Whatever. Feel free to tell those people who make the mistake of voicing their empty criticisms that it's none of their beeswax.

Learn About License and Officiant Requirements

- Aweddingministers.com/requirements.htm
- Ehow.com/articles_5217-marriage-license.html
- Marriage.about.com/cs/marriagelicenses/a/officiants.htm
- Marriage.about.com/cs/marriagelicenses/a/usmarlaws.htm
- Secular-celebrations.com/weddings/staterules.htm
- Usmarriagelaws.com
- Usmarriagelaws.com/search/united_states/officiants_requirements/index.shtml
- Weddingdetails.com/questions/license.cfm

Find Your Officiant (or Designate One)

- Canalopeweddings.com
- Clergy.mind-n-magick.com
- Ehow.com/articles_5232-wedding-officiants.html
- Gatheringguide.com/event_categories/wedding_officiants.html
- Goddessmoon.org/Clergy/crisis/clergy_listings.shtml

- Humanist-society.org/celebrants/celebrant.html

- Interfaithofficiants.com

- Localweddingofficiants.com

- Rabbirentals.com

- Theclergynetwork.com

- Weddingministers.com

Make Your Officiant Official

- Beordained.com

- Dudeism.com/ordination.html

- Ficotw.org

- Firstnationministry.com

- Ordination.com

- Ordination4all.com

- Pulc.com

- Roseministries.org

- Spiritualhumanism.org

- Thelovechurch.org

- ULC.net

Change Your Name (or Address)

- Findlegalforms.com/xcart/customer/home.php?cat=782
- Kitbiz.com
- Moversguide.usps.com
- Thenamechangekit.com
- Ultimatekits.com
- Weddinghelpers.com/kit.html

Chapter 19
Get Married, Not Harried

Let's face it: It's easy to succumb to stress when you're planning what may very well prove to be the largest party you host in your lifetime. Many brides- and grooms-to-be feel pressured by their loved ones and each other to make the day of their nuptials utterly, completely, and flawlessly perfect. Add to that the fact that there is just so much that can go wrong, and you have a never-fail recipe for prewedding stress. It may seem as if tension is an unavoidable part of the planning process, but that's just not true. If it was, hardened criminals would be forced into the event planning business as punishment for their crimes. Instead, enterprising and creative people craft whole careers out of their penchant for choosing colors and table settings.

There are a lot of steps you can take to make the whole complicated and overblown business of getting married less traumatic and more enjoyable, but the very best one involves concentrating on your strengths. At the heart of every nuptial celebration, there is at least one individual who browsed, bargained, compared, shopped, sampled, crafted, critiqued, and complemented to make it all happen. There is a good chance that you are both talented and imaginative, though it's equally likely that your particular aptitudes don't extend outward in all directions. You can greatly improve your chances of looking back on your engagement with a smile instead of a grimace by focusing the majority of your energy on those details that excite and inspire you.

Maybe you're a serious budget diva, and you get a total kick out of making the most of your money at sites like Cheap-chic-weddings.com. Or you may be one of those unique people who salivate when thinking about putting together twenty multipart centerpiece kits from Surroundings.com while on a super-tight deadline. Once you have a clear idea of what you like doing, think about what gets your intended's motor running. If your future spouse has a music collection that rivals that of the largest nearby library, they may very well get a kick out of choosing the reception music. Heck, if they're handy with all things electronic, they may even be able to rig up a makeshift sound system that really rocks. The more you enjoy all of the little tasks you have to undertake during the planning process, the happier you (not to mention all of the people in your general vicinity) are going to be.

You can also take this line of thinking in the opposite direction when considering what duties you might like to delegate. Hate the whole concept of DIY? Then for the love of all things matrimonial, do not assume you and your bridesmaids are going to have a jolly

What Mattered Most to Leah

"Being able to do things online really made a difference—I don't think I could have planned my wedding at all without the Internet. Coordinating bridesmaids from two countries and three states and keeping in touch with two families in different parts of the country while planning an event taking place three hours away from my house could have been monumentally stressful. If I'd been organizing it the old-fashioned way, it would have cost three times as much and taken twice as long to plan. I might have eloped!"

old time sitting on your living room floor folding paper roses until the wee hours of the morning. Don't ask your SO to handle the budget if he or she routinely overdraws the checking account. As the days and weeks fly by, you may be tempted to do all sorts of things it would never occur to you to do in any other circumstances. In the name of staying true to your budget or saving time, baking a wedding cake, sewing a gown, and putting together fifty floral arrangements can suddenly seem like no trouble at all. If you're a whiz with a stand mixer, a crack hand with a needle, or generally dexterous, fantastic! But realize that this may not be the best time to discover you're not the next Martha Stewart.

Whatever your preferences, latch on to them as you think about themes, colors, and everything else. Keep your limits in mind when you're writing out your weekly agenda. While you won't be able to avoid every tedious job that raises your hackles, there's no reason to sacrifice your sanity in the name of perfection. Once you have a good idea of what you absolutely don't want to do—learn calligraphy, interview wedding bands, visit bridal salons with your FMIL—forget everything you've ever learned about what a wedding reception should look like or the details it simply has to include.

From the moment you find yourself affianced, you're going to be faced with people telling you that your wedding experience will be incomplete if you don't do X, Y, and Z. The truth is that the only way your experience will prove incomplete is if your intended decides to ditch the day altogether. People will still find spots to sit if there are no ushers or place cards. A shortage of fanciful sweets won't make or break the reception. There is no one item or ritual that is so integral to the matrimonial spirit that altering it or leaving it out will negatively impact your wedding for years to come. And while there are indeed many things that can go wrong at a wedding, these tend to go unnoticed by all but the bride and, in some cases, the groom.

So don't feel anxious if your wedding vision goes against the grain; just roll with it. Limit your options as you realize what those

Jeanette Knew Where to Draw the Line

"I cannot stand shopping, and since I'm not five foot nine and a size four, looking for ideas in your standard bridal magazines and websites was not an option. You wouldn't think that looking at flowers would make me feel fat, but damn if it didn't sometimes. Being able to look at things in a neutral context on my own time was really important to me. It was more comfortable for me to browse away from the influences of the WIC. That made a world of difference."

options are, and stick to the budget you and your intended composed even when you're tempted to go a little crazy because, hey, you're only going to get married once. If you come up absolutely empty in your searches for the perfect stuff, do some soul-searching and some Google searching. Think about your lifestyle, your personality, and your expectations for the day, then take a second look at some of those checklists. It may be that the perfect place cards and cake topper are out there waiting for you on sites and in online shops that have nothing at all to do with weddings. Who cares if less-than-hip relatives look askance at the action figures perched on top of your three-tiered Hostess cake?

Just remember that your ability to get what you want may be dependent on your willingness to cooperate with others, make certain concessions, and negotiate. Planning a wedding won't automatically cause gray hairs to sprout from your scalp, but it can (and probably will) test your patience.

Why Worry?

Keep in mind that there is a lot of hype perpetuated by the WIC. In the grand scheme of things, your wedding day is one day out of thousands and may not, in fact, turn out to be the happiest day of your life. Sure, it's the day you and your intended will make the ultimate commitment, but the entire rest of your lives will be the expression of that commitment. It will be a joyous, rapturous, wonderful, beautiful day, no matter what goes wrong. Really. You may not believe that on the days where nothing seems to be going your way, but that doesn't make it any less true. When you're handling a list of responsibilities that spans eight whole months, you can't bank on every single detail unfolding precisely how you want it to. Be flexible, and repeat this mantra as often as necessary: "It's just one day."

Here's the basic stress-reduction short list:

- Eat well and exercise (Holisticonline.com/stress/stress _exercise.htm)

- Do a good turn (Helpothers.org)

- Delegate, delegate, delegate

- Get some sleep (Medicinenet.com/sleep/article.htm)

- Stick to your budget (refer back to chapter 6 as necessary)

- Communicate your feelings (Drnadig.com/feelings.htm)

- Go out with the girls or the guys (Citysearch.com)

- Learn to say *no* (To-done.com/2005/06/how-to-say-no)

There are other ways you can beat tension, but the tips above represent the simplest and most practical measures. If you're feeling anxious about hypothetical calamities that seem wholly unavoidable, positive visualization can help you distance yourself from thoughts of imminent disaster. Whatever it is that is haunting you—be it flubbed vows, stained gowns, or goofy DJs—picture the opposite happening. Your mental movie should be detailed so you can immerse yourself in it fully and fool your brain into believing that a positive outcome is inevitable. Yes, it sounds goofy and kind of out-there, but upbeat visualizations can have a hugely uplifting impact on your state of mind. Successconsciousness.com can help you get started, but there are literally thousands of websites that can show you how to think positively, get happy, and attain peace of mind during the most stressful situations. Want a daily dose of bliss? Try Dailyom.com, Pathwaytohappiness.com, or one of the many other sites that will send you inspiration via e-mail.

The only problem with the more ethereal sorts of solutions is that they aren't very constructive. Getting over stress is only the first step; then you have to get things done. It's easy to affirm that you're no longer bummed out by some looming problem, but that doesn't absolve you of having to fix said problem. When the problem is that you're trying to please everyone all the time, you have to acknowledge that and then learn to stop nodding quietly when people ask if they can bring an uninvited date or your grandfather asks you to include meat in the vegetarian buffet you've been dreaming of for months. Don't forget that you have plenty of choices. Compromise if you want to, but feel free to say no. People will cut you some slack if you don't give them what they want.

And do not be afraid to ask people for help. If you feel you're not getting much support from friends, relatives, or your intended, don't waste a lot of time wondering why. Don't make assumptions about their motives, because the conclusions you come to on your own will likely be way off base. Remember, the event you and your SO are putting together on your computer was designed by you. The people who care about you most in this world may be desperate to help you but have no idea where to start. Every time they feel inspired to do something for you, they draw a blank as to what you need from them. It doesn't help any that you're spending so much time online, as convenient as that is for you. As crazy as it sounds, they may think you have everything under control.

When the pressure is mounting, get philosophical. If people in your life make outrageous demands or subvert your wishes, remind yourself that all of the wedding 'zillas are just people who are feeling a little overwhelmed. Weddings tend to bring out the 'zilla in everyone, but that doesn't mean they're monsters. You shouldn't take every disappointment on the chin and then turn the other cheek with a smile. But if you're stressing over stuff you can't change, like people's attitudes, your bank balance, or your spouse-to-be's involvement in the planning process, you're better off doing your best to be content with those blessings you can be grateful for. Read up on gratitude at Abundance-and-happiness.com/gratitude.html. Let everything else go. Get over it. Don't waste a single second giving in to the blues. Once you accept that there is no such thing as a perfect wedding (or a perfect person), you can move past the need to retain complete control and refocus your energy putting together a seriously fantastic celebration.

Be careful, though. Get too blasé about the entire affair and you're liable to find that all of the vendors you really hoped to book have been reserved by other couples and you have to place a rush order to get everything you need in time. Procrastination is definitely not the answer. In fact, the more you put wedding-related responsibilities off, the more they are going to freak you out. But don't bang your head against the wall when the idea of calling yet another photographer has you foaming at the mouth. Switch gears, and work on something you enjoy for a while. Three weeks' worth of procrastination is problematic, but there's almost nothing that can't be safely put off for a day or two.

Strive for balance. Planning a wedding while also working, attending to the needs of your loved ones, *and* satisfying your own needs can be a real pain. Even when you're successfully researching, buying, and making reservations online every time you get a few minutes to yourself, there are some things you just have to do offline. Maybe your mom wants to go shopping at a moment's notice or the baker called to ask if she could move your appointment forward by an hour. It's the unexpected things that will really drive you crazy if you're not prepared to make changes to your schedule on the fly. Learn to manage your time more efficiently at Stayhitched.com/time.htm and then keep tabs on each and every pending duty using the task manager apps at Tadalist.com or Todoist.com.

As a last resort, when feelings of prenuptial worry just will not go away no matter how hard you try to ease them, look into insurance for your wedding. Commonly called event insurance, it protects your investment in case of postponements due to inclement weather, military deployment, or even terrorism; cancellations caused by illness or injury; or financial losses caused by AWOL vendors or officiants. It can also cover damage to the ceremony or reception site, the cost of missing gowns and tuxes, and gifts that get grabbed by nefarious individuals with sticky fingers. Wedsafe.com offers coverage of up to $50,000 for cancellation or postponement for a one-time premium of $405. Depending on your policy, you may be able to recoup costs for just about any catastrophe other than cold feet.

Pushy Parents? No Prob.

Maybe you've been dreaming of your wedding for two decades now. Or maybe you were absolutely convinced that you'd be single all your life until the very second you got engaged. Doesn't matter. When the deal was sealed, you and your future spouse both started thinking about what weddings mean to you, both as individuals and as a couple. You may not yet know or much less care what kind of food will sate your guests at your reception, but you're going to have a chocolate fountain, come hell or high water. The mere mention of weddings may evoke thoughts of gloriously sunny seaside ceremonies in your mind's eye. But if you haven't already reserved your gurgling mass of sticky and sweet or obtained a permit to stand on the strand (read up on beach usage laws at Beachweddingsbytheknot

.com), you may find yourself battling with insidious outside influences attempting to steer you toward options they think are better, more appropriate, or perhaps even tastier.

Collectively, these influences are known as parents. As they frequently reminded you during your childhood years, they brought you into this world and they can take you out of it. You may now find yourself listening to a similar yet subtly different declaration: "I brought you into this world . . . Wouldn't it be nicer to have the cold poached salmon instead of those miniburgers you like so much?" Sure, it's veiled in a subtext of guilt that involves thirty-three excruciating hours of labor, braces, college tuition, and years of emotional support, but it's still there.

If your parents or your future in-laws are donating a big chunk of change to make your big day special, they're going to have some leverage, most notably where invitees and locale are concerned. That doesn't mean, however, that you should play the part of the martyr, sacrificing nuptial delight in the name of peace and harmony.

Conflicting expectations cause confusion and hurt feelings, which in turn cause stress. It's stress, of course, that leads brides- and grooms-to-be to cackle madly while perusing sites like Etiquettehell.com. The simplest thing you can do to limit stress caused by a glut of moms and dads who just want to have their say is to communicate what *you* want out of your wedding. This is easier than it sounds and easiest when you outline your likes and dislikes before the collective parental body ever has a chance to start making demands. That way, your desires will already be right there on the table. It's a lot more difficult to contradict someone's demands than it is to make your preferences known. Your parents and FILs may not even bother piping up about less important matters if you've already made clear your expectations. Differences in faith, generational customs, and personal style may still arise, but you'll have already defined your position.

Of course, there's still the matter of moolah. As it says in chapter 6, you're going to need to know where the money to pay for your wedding is coming from. Savings accounts and suppositions do not mix, so try not to get too attached to the idea of a $30,000 wedding when you and your honey have a couple thou in the bank and your parents don't have a lot of extra green lying around. Sure, they may have been socking away money for your marriage for years, but until you know that, don't go booking the fanciest florist in town. Remember that more money flowing into your hands in the form of parental gifts can mean giving up that much more control.

When your relationship gets a little strained, don't hesitate to sit down with your elders to discuss the pressure you're under. Let them know that you care about their opinions and will do everything you can to meet their needs, then remind them that there are some specific elements of your wedding that you're just not willing to toss out so you can cater to other people's whims. Hopefully, they'll understand right away how important it is to you that your wedding be a reflection of your personality. If not, they'll just have to get used to the idea—and they will when they see that you're willing to compromise in other areas. Refer to How-to-negotiate.com as necessary, and try to fight the temptation to post your craziest in-law stories to Ihatemyinlaws.com. Use Truebrideconfessions.com; it's anonymous.

If your folks aren't pushy parents, you have dodged a bullet that ends up lodged in the gut of many a harried spouse-to-be. Consider yourself lucky. But stay on the lookout for people who are just as opinionated and domineering. People do so love to chime in uninvited when weddings are the topic of discussion. The period of engagement leading up to and culminating in a wedding is usually emotionally charged, and if you aren't careful, your need to ensure everyone else's happiness can cause you to neglect the feelings of one of the most important players in this matrimonial drama: you.

Remember Personhood? How About Coupledom?

That said, don't spend the months and weeks preceding your nuptials with your nose to the keyboard twenty-four hours a day, seven days a week. There is a wonderful individual (i.e., your future spouse) waiting just outside the limits of your monitor's glare, and there is a good chance that they are trying diligently to capture your attention. However invested they are in your upcoming wedding, they probably wouldn't mind doing something other than completing seating charts. And right about now they're probably thinking how nice it would be to spend some time with you without having to explain why they haven't gotten those last few family addresses from "their side."

When there is a wedding that needs planning, one of the first things many couples sacrifice is quality time together. But even though the limited span of hours not filled by sleeping, working, cooking, eating, cleaning, and everything else you do to maintain your standard of living seems like the best time to get some heavy planning done, why not gag your inner wedding coordinator for the day? You could even devote an entire weekend to utterly wedding-free prewedding fun. Remember all of those things you two used to do together before you even considered marrying each other? It's time to revisit some of those things before you forget about them entirely. You'll be glad you did when your nuptials are days away, pressure is being heaped upon you from all sides, and you're still on cordial speaking terms with the person you'll be spending the rest of your life with!

Have some fun, for goodness' sake. Visit Localhikes.com or Trails.com and go for a hike. Find a new favorite restaurant at Zagat .com. Browse Bedandbreakfast.com or BBexplorer.com and get away from it all for a nice long weekend. For every activity you can think of, there's probably a website or a search engine dedicated to it.

At some point during your engagement period—especially if it's a long, busy, or tedious one—you may give real thought to eloping. Most couples that don't plan to run off into the sunset together won't end up going that route, no matter how many times it's brought up in the heat of the moment. But there's no denying that it's sometimes fun to think about blowing all of the deposits and leaving for some faraway destination well in advance of your wedding day.

Your elopement fantasy might even involve skipping town on the night before you're slated to tie the knot, just to stick it in the eye of everyone who harassed you while you tried to juggle your job, your wedding, and your sanity. Before you get lost in Letsrunoff.com or find an officiant willing to marry you on the fly on Canalope weddings.com, think it through. If you're seriously considering eloping, sit on the idea for a few days. A lot of couples start off their married lives in secret, resulting in a lot of disappointed moms, dads, grandparents, aunties, and uncles. In the end, it's your choice (and there is nothing wrong with elopements) but keep in mind that your choices will have an impact on others.

As your wedding day draws ever closer, remember that a little stress is nothing to be worried about. The butterflies doing backflips in your belly are not a sign that you're having second thoughts. Real second thoughts tend to appear fully formed in the forefront of the mind, and they don't just cause a little tension to settle in the shoulders; they scream out an easy-to-understand warning. Get a deep-tissue massage, talk to a friend about anything but weddings, or put some high-energy music on your MP3 player and go for a long jog. Find a nearby spa using Spafinder.com and get your girl on. Do whatever it is you really loved to do before you ever even considered flipping through a bridal rag. Even if it's just for a few minutes at a time, try to remember what it felt like to be a human being instead of a bride- or groom-to-be. Never, ever, ever underestimate the power of a few hours of purely selfish, luxuriant, hedonistic "me time."

Beat Stress

- Coping.org/growth/stress.htm
- Stayhitched.com/stress.htm
- Stevegjones.com/weddingstresshypnotherapycdmp3.htm
- Stress-relieving.com
- Thefirstdance.com
- Weddingstresscoaching.com

Have a Laugh

- Etiquettehell.com
- Goingbridal.com
- Ihatemyinlaws.com
- Inlawssuck2.wordpress.com
- Snopes.com/weddings/weddings.asp
- Truebrideconfessions.com
- Uglydress.com
- Visi.com/~dheaton/bride/the_bride_wore.html

Pamper Yourself

- Gildentree.com
- Homespagoddess.com

- Nationwidemassage.com
- Nevaehbyspagram.com
- Relaxdepot.com
- Spafinder.com
- Spaindex.com

Get Insured

- Agentprotectmywedding.com
- Insurancewide.com/lifestyle_insurance_wedding.html
- Onedayevent.com
- Wedsafe.com

Chapter 20
The Final Countdown

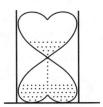

Picture this: It's a week before your wedding. The perfect dress—which was purchased online, of course—is hanging out of sight in an unbleached cotton garment bag. Intricate centerpieces for fifteen tables have been assembled and are waiting in boxes for their big-day debut. All of your vendors have been given the necessary final head counts. You and your intended have tried on your wedding bands more than once, as they arrived by mail a few weeks back. And, miraculously, you have received response cards from every single person who received one of your custom-made invitations.

All right, maybe that last bit isn't exactly probable. Brides- and grooms-to-be going back hundreds, if not thousands, of years have waited in vain for those last few responses, so don't take it too hard if the wedding is approaching fast and you're still missing twenty or so RSVPs. You can approach this all-too-common difficulty in a number of ways. Some people, especially those whose receptions include a large buffet, simply overestimate the head count. Others operate under the assumption that the missing responses all belong to individuals unable to attend and cross their fingers.

Ensuring peace of mind, however, is usually a matter of reaching out via e-mail or phone to the slackers on your guest list. Whether you meet with stories of replies lost in the postal system or tales of forgetfulness, grit your teeth and be nice. As easy as it is to check off "vegetarian meal" and pop a card in the mail, some folks just aren't detail oriented. If you forgive them their errors and move on, you'll have one less thing to worry about in the scant hours leading up to the main event.

What *should* you be thinking about? Well, there is the aforementioned head count, and it's always a good idea to confirm addresses, times, and services with your chosen vendors (or helpers). Be specific when discussing your expectations and outlining the rundown of events. Pay any outstanding balances if you feel comfortable doing so before services have been rendered. As previous communiqués have likely taken place over e-mail, there is no reason not to fire up your computer when confirmation time rolls around.

If you do decide to stay in touch using that old staple, the telephone, try this trick: Instead of listing your vendor contacts by company name or the names of the people you've talked to so far, program them into your cell under the service they provide. That way, when you need to reach your caterer in a hurry to up your count one last time, you can scroll right to "Caterer." Better yet, set all your vendor phone numbers to voice dial and scream *"bakery!"* at the top of your lungs when you get that e-mail that says that there is a pecan shortage and tortes are just not happening. That way on the day of your wedding, you can hand the phone to your stalwart MOH and ask her, "Deal with this, please?"

This is a good time to remind everyone who is playing a role in your wedding what they should be doing right about now. Your attendants should be picking up their dresses or suits in the very near future. The MOB and the MOG have hopefully chosen dresses and are in agreement where colors and cut are concerned.

If no one has planned a rehearsal dinner, now is the time to make that happen if you intend to hold a rehearsal. Some people

Jeanette Nixed the WIC

"Honestly, I tried to stay away from wedding retailers when it came to things like gifts—along with just about everything else—because I'd find something great on one of those sites and then find the same item for a third of the price on eBay. We spent a lot of time looking for the right groomsmen's gifts because Chris wanted to find something fitting and unique, and we didn't even bother looking at the usual groomsmen gift sites."

invite all out-of-town guests to what can easily become an event in and of itself, complete with invitations that match the predominant wedding colors and favors for attendees. However, if your rehearsal is taking place the evening before your wedding and you'd much rather have a quiet meal and turn in early, don't hesitate to voice that to your future in-laws. Traditionally, the parents of the groom choose a venue and foot the bill for the whole shebang, but the old who-pays-for-what guidelines don't always apply. There's no rule stating that those participating in the rehearsal must receive a fancy sit-down meal for their time and trouble, but someone does need to feed them, even if the festivities are limited to meeting up at your apartment for pizza and beer.

Gifts are probably starting to roll in, and it's time to start writing up those thank-you cards. Feel free to open gifts as you receive them—instant gratification, yay!—but remember that the best time to send thank-yous is whenever you and your intended receive a gift. If you let your collection of gifts pile up, you're going to wind up devoting an entire day to gratitude. Sure, it's a nice sentiment, but it's wrist-achingly tedious in practice.

And speaking of gifts, have you bought a little something for each of your attendants? How about your folks? You may even decide to give your honey a little prenuptial present. These gifts, like all gifts everywhere, are optional, but doing something nice for someone else can temporarily take your mind off of those last few missing response cards. Staying away from wedding retailers altogether can be a nice change of pace—and you'll be less likely to spend money on accessories you never before thought necessary. Yes, your groomsmen will forgive you if you don't spring for the novelty cufflinks from Wildties.com.

Like surprises? Most people do, but that's no reason to tempt the gods by ignoring the impact weather and traffic conditions will have on your wedding day. Weather.com has a wedding weather forecast that will help you decide whether the gals in your wedding party need to bring their matching pashminas. They also offer a rush-hour traffic forecast that details road conditions, so you're not stuck in a limo with hungry attendants, all of whom are drinking, while you wait for emergency personnel to clear the highway so you can make it to the reception in time for cake.

You're probably going to be plenty busy during this, the final week of your unmarried life, but if you find you have a few moments to spare, why not give some thought to your honeymoon? It may be that your postnuptial excursion is already in the bag, but plenty of newlyweds delay their honeymoons. Even the shortest so-called destination weddings require that all the participants take a few days off work, and your boss may be none too happy to hear you want a few more days off after that. Financial and logistical concerns can also influence your postwedding plans. If your day-to-day responsibilities get in the way of your being able to party hearty after the main matrimonial event, you can still plan the honeymoon of your dreams. You may not be going anywhere in the near future, but you can always browse Expedia.com and other travel sites to search for cool destinations at to-die-for prices.

When you do make travel plans, try searching for both honeymoon and nonhoneymoon packages. The former may net you plenty of cool extras, while the latter will likely be somewhat less expensive. You have proved to yourself and to the world that you can wrangle vendors, research like a pro, and make your matrimonial vision a reality; there's no reason you can't plan a simple vacation. There is a site for every type of traveler. All you need to do is decide whether you'd prefer to bask on the beach, book an alternative eco-adventure, see the sights, or make a difference in someone's world.

For the most part, your experiences in the days leading up to your nuptials will be similar to those of Luddite brides- and grooms-to-be who pounded the pavement instead of firing up their browsers. Sure, you and your attendants will be touching base in the pages of your group blog so everyone knows what needs to be done when, and your guests will be devouring the last-minute updates you posted on your website, but you're still going to have to go and grab your marriage license with your honey in tow (don't forget those IDs!), swing by the seamstress and the tux shop, pack and assemble whatever needs packing and assembling, and play the part of wedding coordinator for a few more days.

That Could Never Happen to Me

If you think your wedding plans are so airtight that nothing can possibly stand in the way of your matrimonial bliss, think again. Even if you spend your days managing multi-million-dollar accounts for clients who demand nothing less than perfection, the complexity of the average wedding makes it a chaos magnet. The hardest-working and most talented vendors are still subject to the vagaries of traffic and weather. Eagle-eyed relatives who want nothing more than to make it to the church on time may accidentally transpose a three with an eight while reading addresses. Your perfect outdoor ceremony can become a soggy mess when the rain begins to pour from the heavens. And then there are the little things. Your seamstress is a goddess with a needle, but threads can still break. Waterproof mascara seldom lives up to its name. That pepper-and-onion omelet that was the perfect foil for your morning jitters may leave you smelling less than rose-petal fresh.

Where the big catastrophes are concerned, your only real option will be to grin and bear the resultant delay. Don't worry about it—your guests may get a little fidgety when they have to wait for the buffet components to arrive or the rain to clear up, but only the most gauche will voice their discomfort. In return, you should forgive them their tardiness and their eccentric taste in kitchen gadgets. Your more experienced friends and family are not kidding when they tell you that there is no such thing as the perfect wedding. As you nurse your third mimosa in the confines of the bridal chamber while your already late officiant sits on a gridlocked road five miles away, just remember: No one ever tells the bride and groom that the wedding sucked.

However, the fact that mishaps will happen doesn't mean that you need to humbly bow to the inevitable without putting up a fight. Put aside all those things you can't change, and focus your attention on everything that you can. Emergency kits are a simple way to give the fickle finger of fate a run for its money. Yes, you may snap a strap or find yourself squaring off against a stain, but you'll be prepared to face these snags with the tools you need to overcome them—which in this case means things like safety pins, breath mints, feminine protection, stain eraser, and cotton swabs.

Depending on how busy you are as you enter the nuptial home stretch, you can make your own emergency kit or buy one of the many cute kits for brides and grooms. More common online (most can be found at Amazon.com) than in actual shops, these collections of useful items come packaged in miniature briefcases, chic makeup bags, and gift baskets. They do tend to be pricier than the sum of their parts because they are sold as novelty items marketed toward people buying gifts for brides, grooms, and bridesmaids. As great as they look on the outside, the kits are filled with sample-size toiletries that cost next to nothing at the drug store. What should you include? Every comprehensive wedding website will have, somewhere in its site map, a survival checklist you can consult, and every one of them is slightly different. The list at Bridesdiary.com.au/articles/articledetail.aspx?id=89 details just about everything a bride-to-be will ever need.

The core items in a kit for women are typically:

- Needles and thread in appropriate colors

- Small scissors

- Tweezers

- Safety pins

- Bobby pins

- Extra makeup

- Deodorant

- Lotion and sunscreen

- Tissues

- Medicines like pain relievers, antihistamines, and antacids

- Hairspray, gel, and a hairbrush

- Breath mints, tooth-whitening strips, and floss

- Eyedrops

- Tampons or pads

- Nail polish and a nail repair set

If you're a DIYer, you should probably fill a second kit with lightweight wire, beads, extra candles, and whatever else might come in handy while fixing a broken centerpiece or pew bow. Whether the kit you buy or create could double as a nursing station during a national emergency or is nothing more than the usual contents of your handbag, you're not going to end up using everything you pack, but you may end up being someone else's guardian angel. In fact, consider stocking venue bathrooms with baskets of cotton balls, tissues, tampons and pads, a nail file, medicines, hairspray, breath mints, and hand sanitizers. Stomach troubles, headaches, and stray hairs can appear without any prior warning, but if you've come prepared, there's less of a chance that the normal levels of matrimonial chaos will darken the mood of your day.

Give as You've Received

Human beings are not yet a self-sustaining element of Earth's ecosystem, but that doesn't mean you should use your nuptials as an excuse to forget about your commitment to recycling and reusability. At the end of the day, you can rely on guests to take the favors, centerpieces, and whatever other decorative items aren't clearly the property of your reception site, but you're still going to have a great many leftovers. With everything you'll have on your mind on the day of your wedding, you may be tempted to toss whatever possible so you can get down to the business of honeymooning. Before you do, consider that there are plenty of people out there who would be more than grateful to be on the receiving end of what for you is no longer useful.

For example, if your meal was served buffet style, you may find you have plenty of leftovers that haven't been touched. Finding a destination for perishable food items isn't always easy because many homeless shelters and soup kitchens won't accept them. But a quick visit to www.Sober.com/Directory/Halfway+Houses/default.html can help you find a halfway house or other institution in your area that may be capable of dealing with leftover banquet foodstuffs. If your search comes up blank and the idea of tossing out perfectly good

food ruins your appetite, churches (find one with Worshipquest
.org), synagogues (search at Uscj.org/Find_a_Synagogue_Sea5425
.html), and other charitable organizations might be able to help you
pair your leftovers with hungry folks.

Though many people dream of passing their wedding day duds
on to their offspring, the reality is that only a very small percentage of daughters wind up wearing their mother's gown. Truthfully,
storing something as fragile as a wedding gown can be a real trial.
Most of the storage boxes and bags you'll come across at dry cleaners
don't deliver on their promises, and you could end up with a gown
that is cracked at the creases, yellowish, and covered with tiny brown
spots that seem to appear out of nowhere but are actually caused
by all sorts of environmental factors. With proper care, a wedding
gown can last many decades, but it's easier and often more reward-
ing to give it away. Yes, give it away. The gown that clothed you as
you married the person of your dreams can go on to be the delight
of many a blushing bride.

While the same religious or charitable groups that accepted
your food may also be able to help you find a bride-to-be in need,
you can be sure your gown is making a difference by donating it to
projects such as Brides Against Breast Cancer at Makingmemories
.org or Bridalgarden.org, which benefits Sheltering Arms Children's Service. Your bridesmaids can join you in your philanthropy
by donating their dresses to organizations like Glassslipperproject.
org and Promshopproject.com, which pair girls unable to afford
prom wear with the dresses that will make their dreams come true.
Many of the charities that accept used wedding gowns are local,
but they usually have a web presence, and most are happy to accept
gowns via mail.

Fresh flowers, doomed from the start to a short life ending in
the mulching machine, can bring people joy for a few more days
when donated to hospitals, nursing homes, and anywhere else
people might want a little cheering up. Call ahead, though, as many

facilities can only accept fresh flowers during certain times of day. You can also give table arrangements to guests who live nearby so they can enjoy them or take all of your flowers home with you, hang them upside down until they're dry, and incorporate them into your decor.

Finally, you're going to discover you're inundated with stuff after your marriage is official if you went the DIY route. Extra silk flowers, ribbons, tea lights, votive holders, and so on most often end up relegated to the backs of drawers and closets, where they are forgotten. But most all of the crafty ingredients for your standard wedding ceremony and reception can be used in other ways, which means that there will always be someone who can benefit from your supply overflow. Try posting them on your local Craigslist.org board or join Freecycle.org to connect with people looking for precisely what you have. If nothing else, you can drop off all of your extras at the nearest Goodwill or Salvation Army, and it will make sure that your excess goods end up in the hands of someone who either wants or needs them.

The best part about donating unused wedding paraphernalia to people who will really appreciate it is that your nuptials will be all the more green for your having done so. You can minimize the ecological impact of your I dos without ever serving a sit-down tofu dinner or wearing an unbleached hemp dress by making sure that your wedding day waste is minimized. Dresses, centerpieces, and table settings can find new life in someone else's home or at someone else's wedding instead of ending up at the city dump months or years down the line.

Pat Yourself on the Back

Congratulations! You just planned a wedding! You. Planned. A. Whole. Wedding. From start to finish. And you did it without the

What Happens After "I Do"?

More than a year has gone by since A. J. said her vows, and she still daydreams wistfully about her hectic engagement.

"I miss the excitement of looking at everything and thinking about how people would respond or how all of my choices would fit together. I miss wondering if it would really feel different to be married, which it definitely does in so many small ways. I'm not usually the girly-girl type, but I definitely felt feminine while planning our wedding. Everything was so soft and pretty and romantic."

Jeanette occasionally misses the hustle and (ahem) bustle of planning a wedding—especially when she sees wedding dresses in store windows—but maintains that the pace of married life doesn't leave a lot of room for daydreaming.

"It's funny . . . I think I might have missed it if I hadn't been so busy after the wedding. We were saving up for a house, then buying the house, and then moving into the house. Then there were a hundred other projects I had to take care of. But every so often I'll get an idea for a great centerpiece, and it's been more than a year since the wedding."

As for Leah, she doesn't miss it at all.

"I was honestly completely relieved to be done with wedding planning. Once the wedding is over, there's still a lot of wedding-related stuff that you have to do— write the thank-you notes, make sure the pictures get distributed to whoever wants them, send final payments, and so on. It was an incredibly satisfying experience, by which I mean successfully planning a huge event. Still, I was really happy that it was over."

services of a wedding coordinator and without stepping away from your computer . . . er, much. There is nothing you can't do, because *you rock*. Hopefully you'll look back on this period of your life as the years pass and smile as you think about the time (and money and sanity) you saved by buying and booking online. If you've been lucky, people haven't pressured you to change your celebration to fit their ideas about what good and proper weddings look like. And if you've been thorough, you've probably picked up some serious researching and organizational skills that will serve you well for the rest of your life.

Now that you're at the end of your nuptial journey, don't be surprised if you miss the shopping and the planning. On the other hand, plenty of newlyweds feel a distinct sense of relief when the last party stragglers have gone home, they've changed out of their formal clothing, and they finally get a chance to breathe after spending hours looking their best and making small talk with people they haven't seen in decades.

Whatever you feel just before and just after your nuptials, own those feelings. Weddings are a big deal in the lives of those planning them, but it's not often that someone acknowledges the hard work brides and grooms put into arranging everything from the roof over their guests' heads to the food and cake those guests are shoveling into their mouths. You and your spouse are going to have to be your own cheering section, because it's the two of you who will be traversing the years together. And you deserve it—even if the wedding you have isn't precisely the wedding you envisioned, it's still your wedding. That alone makes it special. So have fun! Don't forget to eat! Know when to say when during seemingly endless snapshot sessions!

And one last thing: On the day you tie the knot, minutes will fly by faster than you're used to, and you'll probably forget as many details as you remember. The photographs you receive later will help you recapture some of those lost moments, and putting them up on Flickr will ensure that you can look at them no matter where you are in the world. As other people share their impressions of your wedding day, your remembrances will be even more complete. One way you can safeguard your most precious matrimonial memories for the rest of your life is to take a mental picture of the day that you can carry with you forever. Don't just glance around at the centerpieces, cake, guests, and your spouse-to-be. Stop, take a deep breath, and drink in the day you orchestrated. Commit the beauty, togetherness, and joy to memory in a complete and thorough mental picture.

(Of course, if you're still afraid you'll forget important details, you can always write your special memory down and send it to yourself in an e-mail that will arrive ten, twenty, or even thirty years from now using the mailer at Futureme.org.)

Congratulations, and best of luck!

Prepare for the Worst

- Abernook.com/prod/grooms-wedding-day-kit.asp

- Msandmrs.com/bridesmaid.php

- Shopintuition.com/product.asp?pid=9325

- Store.weddingish.com/bremkit.html

- Wishingfish.com/weddsurvkit.html

- Withyouinmindinc.com

Keep an Eye on Conditions

- Accuweather.com/fashion.asp

- Fly.faa.gov/flyfaa/usmap.jsp

- Traffic.com

- Weather.com/activities/driving/rushhour

- Weather.com/weddings

- www.Fhwa.dot.gov/trafficinfo/index.htm

Share the Love

- Bridalgarden.org/charity.html
- Glassslipperproject.org/yostate.htm
- Heavenlyangelsinneed.com/WeddingGowns.html
- Makingmemories.org
- Princessproject.org/princess
- Thebridesproject.com
- www.Idofoundation.org/resources/dresses

Plan Your Honeymoon

- Bedandbreakfast.com
- Camping.com
- Crossculturalsolutions.org
- Cruise.com
- Expedia.com
- Globeaware.org
- Gonomad.com
- Greentortoise.com
- Homeexchange.com
- Hotels.com
- Iexplore.com

- Oattravel.com

- Orbitz.com

- Transitionsabroad.com/listings/work/volunteer/index
  .shtml

- Travelocity.com

Index

Index

Index